AF697650

Studies in Qur'an and *Ḥadīth*

Studies in Qur'an and *Ḥadīth*:

The Formation of the Islamic Law of Inheritance

David S. Powers

UNIVERSITY OF CALIFORNIA PRESS
Berkeley · Los Angeles · London

University of California Press
Berkeley and Los Angeles, California

University of California Press, Ltd.
London, England

© 1986 by
The Regents of the University of California
Printed in the United States of America

1 2 3 4 5 6 7 8 9

Library of Congress Cataloging-in-Publication Data
Powers, David S.
Studies in Qur'an and Ḥadīth.
Revision of thesis (Ph.D.)—Princeton University, 1979.
Bibliography: p.
Includes index.
1. Inheritance and succession (Islamic law)
I. Title.
LAW 340.5'9 85-16819
ISBN 0-520-05558-6 (alk. paper)

In loving memory of my father,
Louis L. Powers (1921–1985)

Contents

Tables

Preface

This study grew out of a doctoral dissertation submitted to Princeton University in the summer of 1979. When I began my doctoral research I was interested, not in the Islamic law of inheritance itself, but in the intergenerational transmission of property in medieval Islamic Spain and North Africa, as reflected in the *fatwā* (*responsa*) literature. As my research progressed, however, I was attracted to a discrepancy between the prescriptions of Islamic law, which impose compulsory rules for the division of property, and the actual manner in which wealth and property were passed down from one generation to the next. Briefly, I found that property owners utilized a wide range of legal fictions to circumvent the potential effects of the law of inheritance in an effort to convey wealth and property to whomever they wanted and in whatever proportions they desired. Why is it, I began to ask myself, that people were bypassing the law of inheritance, which has such firm roots in the Qur'an, and which is generally held up as a model of legal sophistication and accomplishment? It was this question that sent me back to the text of the Qur'an and—although I did not know it at the time—to a totally different research question and methodology.

Influenced by revisionist scholarship on the subject of Muhammad and the Qur'an that had appeared recently, I began to entertain the possibility that what we know as the Islamic law of inheritance (in Arabic, the *ʿilm al-farā'iḍ*, or science of the shares) is not identical to the system of inheritance revealed to Muhammad. By means of a literary analysis of several Qur'anic inheritance verses and prophetic *ḥadīth*, I sought to demonstrate that the operation of the "science of the shares" is predicated upon a series of assumptions—about readings, syntax, the meaning of words, etc.—that represent a secondary stage of development. I endeavored to expose these assumptions and, on the strength of linguistic and lexicographic evidence, attempted to work backward from the accepted understanding of these texts to what I believe to have been their original significance; having accomplished this, I was able to reconstruct the system of inheritance which, I believe, was received by Muhammad. This system, referred to in this book as the proto-Islamic law of inheritance, differs from its Islamic counterpart in several important respects that will be spelled out in detail on the following pages.

After completing the dissertation, I set about looking for evidence in the historical sources that might support my hypothesis regarding the transformation of proto-Islamic into Islamic law during the course of the first century A.H. During this second stage of research, I turned to the rich resources of the Qur'an commentaries, the *ḥadīth* literature, and legal works, and found that my hypothesis led me directly to a series of controversies over the meaning and significance of the very Qur'anic verses and prophetic *ḥadīth* in which I was interested. I have used this material to turn the dissertation into a series of six independent but interrelated studies that focus on major structural elements of the phenomenon under investigation. In addition, I have sought to provide an historical explanation for the transformation from proto-Islamic to Islamic law, drawing on evidence in the sources that suggests a link between the postulated transformation and a number of issues in early Islamic history, especially the controversy over the office of the caliphate in the years following Muhammad's death.

The thesis to be advanced on the following pages challenges at least two generally accepted tenets. First, I argue that the Muslim community is not in possession of the original reading and understanding of several Qur'anic verses and prophetic *ḥadīth* or of the system of inheritance received by Muhammad. To put it differently, I maintain that, in the years following the Prophet's death, certain people manipulated the text of the Qur'an in an effort to alter the significance of the verses in question. Aware of the sensitivity of this assertion, I have endeavored to formulate my arguments throughout the book in such a manner as to disparage neither Muhammad nor the Qur'an. Secondly, I take issue with Schacht's contention that Islamic law did not begin to develop until approximately one hundred years after the Prophet's death. In making this argument, Schacht virtually ignored the Qur'anic legislation, to which he devoted only eight pages in his classic work, *The Origins of Muhammadan Jurisprudence*. It is my contention that any attempt to investigate the origins of Islamic law should take the Qur'an as its starting point; by studying the Qur'anic legislation on inheritance, I hope to qualify Schacht's skepticism by demonstrating that Islamic law did, in fact, begin to develop during the Prophet's lifetime, albeit not in the manner that Islamic tradition relates.

A few technical details should be mentioned here regarding the composition of the book. In the interests of economy, I have transliterated all Arabic citations, with the exception of one crucial passage that appears in chapter 1. The system of transliteration used here follows that suggested by the *International Journal of Middle East Studies*, except that I have written Muhammad for Muḥammad, and Qur'an for Qur'ān. Familiar geographical names such as Medina, Basra, and Kufa are given in their common spelling. I have followed the convention of using b. for ibn except at the beginning of names. Concerning the dates of the Muslim calendar, I have designated their Christian equivalent in the text by placing the Muslim year first and then the Christian year, as in 1/622; otherwise a date refers to the Christian calendar, except when designated as A.H.

A translation of Qur'anic verses that are cited frequently in the book will be found in appendix A.

Parts of chapters 1 and 5 of this book, in slightly revised form, have appeared in *Studia Islamica* and *Arabica* and are used here with the permission of the editors of those journals.

Publication of this book has been aided by a grant from the Hull Memorial Trust Fund at Cornell University.

There remains the pleasant duty of thanking those who in various ways have contributed to the making of this book. Many teachers, colleagues, and friends, too numerous to list, have read individual chapters, and I take great pleasure in thanking all of them here. Special thanks are due to Avram Udovitch, who supervised the dissertation and who, over the years, has been a ready source of good counsel and encouragement. I am grateful to the two readers for the University of California Press, Gautier Juynboll and the second, anonymous reader, who read the entire manuscript with great care and offered numerous suggestions that have improved both the style and the content of the book. I owe a special debt of gratitude to Patricia Crone and Michael Cook, who read and responded to several chapters with their usual thoroughness, and who offered many useful comments and criticisms. My friend, Penny Beebe, read an early draft of the manuscript and offered many suggestions on grammar, syntax, and style; if the book reads smoothly, this is in large part due to her efforts. I also wish to thank Barbara Metcalf, Phyllis Killen, and Richard Adloff of the University of California Press for their guidance, support, and meticulous editorial assistance. I am grateful to Helen Van Arsdale and Dede Sorensen for their assistance in typing portions of the manuscript. Finally, I wish to thank my wife Jane, who has kept me in the twentieth century while I have been writing about the seventh, and without whose support and encouragement this book could not have been written.

Introduction

The Schacht Thesis

The writings of the late Joseph Schacht, in which he sketches the broad outlines of the history and development of Islamic law, constitute the benchmark of all modern studies on this subject. The Schacht thesis, as elaborated in his *The Origins of Muhammadan Jurisprudence* and reiterated in *An Introduction to Islamic Law*, may be summarized as follows: Islamic law, as we know it, did not exist during the lifetime of Muhammad or for the greater part of the first century A.H. Although the Qur'an laid down certain rules in the areas of family law, inheritance, and ritual, the first generation of Muslims, Schacht contends, paid only perfunctory attention to these rules and drew only the most elementary conclusions from them; indeed, in several instances early legal practice diverged from the explicit wording of the Qur'an. As for the *ḥadīth*, "reports" conveying alleged acts and sayings of the Prophet, these, Schacht argues, came into existence only at the end of the first century A.H. The actual foundations of Islamic law were established not by Muhammad and his Followers, but by the early *qāḍī*s, legal specialists appointed by the Umayyad governors, who transformed the popular and administrative practices of the Umayyads into the religious law of Islam. As the groups of legal specialists grew in numbers and cohesion during the first decades of the second/eighth century, they developed into the "ancient schools of law" located in Kufa, Basra, Medina, Mecca, and Syria. At this time, scholars began to pay serious attention to the Qur'anic norms and to draw formal conclusions from them, a process that resulted in the emergence of a "living tradition," i.e., the anonymous consensus of a given generation of scholars. In order to justify their reliance on majority opinion, the jurists projected the living tradition backwards, ascribing it, first, to some of the great figures of the past who had died around the turn of the first century A.H., then to prominent early Companions of the Prophet, and finally to Muhammad himself. During the lifetime of Shāfiʿī (d. 204/820), and as a result of his efforts, the value of formal traditions about the Prophet began to supersede the living tradition of the schools; this led, in turn, to the wide-scale fabrication of *ḥadīth* which claimed to be the reports of ear- or eye-witnesses to the words or acts of the Prophet, handed down orally by an uninterrupted chain of authorities.[1]

The initial reaction to the Schacht thesis was one of unqualified praise and acclaim,[2] and only a handful of writers expressed any criticisms or qualifications.[3] Subsequently, there emerged a substantial literature devoted to criticism of Schacht that either refined some of the details of his assertions or disputed his basic position.

The former group includes several historians who criticized

1. J. Schacht, *An Introduction to Islamic Law*, pp. 10–49; idem, "Law and Justice," pp. 539–55.

2. See the following reviews: H. Ritter, *Oriens* 4 (1951): 308–12 ("a thorough, methodical and highly original book"); A. Jeffrey, *Middle East Journal* 5 (1951): 392–94 ("meticulous in detail, sober in judgement, and clear in exposition. It becomes perfectly clear from this analysis that the origins of the juristic system of Islam are in the practice of the Umayyad period"); W. M. Watt, *Journal of the Royal Asiatic Society* (1952): 91 (a "landmark . . . study . . . likely to be accepted by Western scholars and to be the basis of all future work on the subject"); J. N. D. Anderson, *Welt des Islams* 2 (1952): 136 ("a new landmark . . . The validity of his main contentions appear inescapable"); J. Robson, *The Muslim World* 42 (1952): 61–63 ("one can only admire the critical insight which has enabled the author to come to his conclusion and support it so convincingly"); S. D. Goitein, *Hamizrach Hehadash* 3 (1952): 412–14; G. Ryckmans, *Muséon* 65 (1952): 314–15.

3. E.g., J. W. Fück, *Bibliotheca Orientalis* 10 (1953): 196–99; and A. Guillaume, *Bulletin of the School of Oriental and African Studies* 16 (1954): 176–77 (the assumption of wholesale fabrication of legal traditions from the Prophet "seems somewhat too drastic . . . It seems to be going beyond the range of probability to deny that the life and example of the Prophet carried any weight in his community after his death"). See also *Mohammedanism* (Oxford: Oxford University Press, 1953), p. 56, where H. A. R. Gibb labels as excessive the "radical rejection of the whole system as an artificial creation of later Muslim scholasticism."

certain aspects of Schacht's thesis while accepting the validity of its general framework. S. Vesey-Fitzgerald, conceding that *ḥadīth* had been forged on a large scale, suggested that the legal rules mentioned in these "false stories" may nonetheless reflect the views of Muhammad.[4] The British legal historian, N. J. Coulson, also acknowledged the validity of the broad outlines of Schacht's thesis and conceded that "the vast majority of the legal dicta attributed to the Prophet are apocryphal and the result of the process of 'back-projection' of legal doctrine."[5] But Coulson was troubled by the apparent break or discontinuity that the Schacht thesis created between the Qur'an and the formation of Islamic law, and he argued that the Qur'anic legislation, and especially the detailed rules relating to family law, would have given rise to an immediate and continuous development of the law:

> The Qur'an itself posed problems which must have been of immediate concern to the Muslim community, and with which the Prophet himself, in his role of supreme political and legal authority in Medina, must have been forced to deal. When, therefore, the thesis of Schacht is systematically developed to the extent of holding that "the evidence of legal traditions carries us back to about the year A.H. 100 (sc. A.D. 719) only," and when the authenticity of practically every alleged ruling of the Prophet is denied, a void is assumed, or rather created, in the picture of the development of law in early Muslim society. From a practical standpoint, and taking the attendant historical circumstances into account, the notion of such a vacuum is difficult to accept. This is not to suggest that the chain of transmission, or the *isnād*, of this Tradition or that is authentic, for this is, in the great majority of cases, demonstrably not so; but it is suggested that the substance of many Traditions, particularly those which deal with the obvious day-to-day problems arising from the Qur'anic laws, may well represent at least an approximation to a decision of the Prophet which had been preserved initially by general oral tradition. If this practical premise is accepted then it is a reasonable principle of historical enquiry that an alleged ruling of the Prophet should be tentatively accepted as such unless some reason can be adduced as to why it should be regarded as fictitious.[6]

4. S. Vesey-Fitzgerald, "Nature and Sources of the Shari'a," pp. 93–94.

5. N. J. Coulson, *A History of Islamic Law*, p. 64.

6. Ibid., pp. 64–65. For a discussion of the ensuing "debate" between Schacht and Coulson on the origins of Islamic law, see David S. Powers, "The Will of Saʿd b. Abī Waqqaṣ: A Re-assessment."

Others were content to qualify the Schacht thesis by pushing the origins of Islamic law back farther than Schacht had suggested, albeit not so far as Coulson would have it. G. H. A. Juynboll challenged Schacht's assertion, which had been based upon a statement attributed to Ibn Sīrīn, that the use of the *isnād* (chain of transmission) began only in the second quarter of the second/eighth century. This assertion followed from Schacht's taking the word *fitna* in the aforementioned statement as referring to the events following the death of the Umayyad Caliph, Walīd b. Yazīd, in 126/744.[7] But Juynboll, after an extensive examination of the use of this word in the early sources, concluded that Ibn Sīrīn "was most probably speaking about Ibn al-Zubayr's revolt" (64–71/683–90).[8] Similarly, H. Djaït sought to qualify Schacht's assertion that "the real development of law and tradition was accomplished by the generation that was active between A.H. 100 and 125, i.e., that of Ḥammād and Aᶜmash," by arguing that the basis for the formation of Islamic law had been laid by the preceding generation, that of Shaᶜbī, Saᶜīd b. Jubayr, and Ibrāhīm al-Nakhaᶜī (A.H. 75–100).[9]

It took more than fifteen years for a systematic and sustained critique of Schacht's thesis to develop. In 1967, Nabia Abbott published the second volume of her *Studies in Arabic Literary Papyri*, devoted to Qur'anic commentary and tradition. A painstaking examination of early papyri, supplemented by an extensive study of the Islamic science of tradition, led her to the following conclusions: (1) *Ḥadīth* were transmitted, both orally and in writing, from the very beginnings of Islamic history; (2) reports about Muhammad, as transmitted by his followers, were subjected to a rigorous scrutiny at each stage of transmission; (3) the phenomenal growth of the *ḥadīth* literature in the second and third centuries A.H. was the result of the progressive increase of parallel and multiple chains of transmission, not of the fabrication of content.[10]

7. Schacht, *The Origins of Muhammadan Jurisprudence*, pp. 36–37. G. H. A. Juynboll, "The Date of the Great *Fitna*," p. 143.

8. Juynboll, "Date," p. 158.

9. H. Djaït, "Les Yamanites à Kufa au Ier Siècle de l'Hégire," pp. 180–81.

10. N. Abbott, *Studies in Arabic Literary Papyri* (hereafter "*SALP*"), 2:2. See the favorable remarks of J. Robson in *Journal of Near Eastern Studies* 27 (1968): 143–44, and the sometimes critical remarks of J. Wansbrough ("*zaᶜm* not *burhān*") in *Bulletin of the School of Oriental and African Studies* 31 (1968):

The year 1967 also witnessed the publication of volume 1 of Fuat Sezgin's *Geschichte des arabischen Schrifttums*, a large reference work designed to correct, update, and expand upon Brockelmann's earlier study of the history of Islamic literature.[11] Sezgin, in a lengthy analysis of the *ḥadīth* literature, comes to virtually the same conclusion as Abbott. On the basis of an examination of extant manuscripts, together with an analysis of the formulas used by the transmitters of *ḥadīth*, he argues that the process of recording *ḥadīth* began during the lifetime of Muhammad and continued in an uninterrupted fashion until the emergence of the great *ḥadīth* collections of the third/ninth century.[12]

In his *Studies in Early Hadith Literature* (1978), M. M. Azami concludes, like Abbott and Sezgin, that the process of recording *ḥadīth* had begun during the lifetime of Muhammad. Azami identifies numerous flaws and weaknesses in Schacht's argument. Like Coulson, he criticizes Schacht for his failure to pay serious attention to the Qur'anic legislation, and, like Juynboll, he challenges Schacht's identification of the *fitna* as the civil war following the death of Walīd b. Yazīd.[13] Further, he contends that Schacht fails to understand the meaning of certain Arabic texts, quotes statements out of context, argues from exceptions, and makes broad generalizations on the basis of a limited number of examples.[14] Azami raises a number of interesting questions in the course of an occasionally discursive analysis: How is it, for example, that, according to Schacht, the scholars of the first century A.H. were able to confine themselves exclusively to the discussion of ritual matters? Why would students project doctrine

613–16. Juynboll (*Muslim Tradition*, pp. 5–6) criticizes Abbott for her uncritical reliance on the information contained in *isnād*s and on the figures indicating the number of reports transmitted by individual transmitters. See also C. J. Adams, "Islamic Religious Tradition," p. 66.

11. Carl Brockelmann, *Geschichte der arabischen Litteratur* 2 vols.; *Supplement*, 3 vols. Leiden: E. J. Brill, 1937–43.

12. See the following reviews: F. Rosenthal, *Journal of the American Oriental Society* 89 (1969): 293–95; J. W. Fück, *Orientalistische Literaturzeitung* 68 (1973): 150–51; B. Spuler, *Der Islam* 46 (1970): 124–26; N. Abbott, *Journal of Near Eastern Studies* 29 (1970): 57. See also Adams, "Islamic Religious Tradition," pp. 66–67, and A. Rippin, "The Present Status of *Tafsīr* Studies," pp. 228–29.

13. M. M. Azami, *Studies in Early Hadith Literature*, pp. 215–17, 251–52.

14. Ibid., pp. 233–35, 237, 254–55.

back to weak authorities, rather than to highly respected ones? How is it, if the bulk of the *ḥadīth* were fabricated in the second and third centuries A.H., that we find traditions common in form and sense among the Sunnīs, Zaydīs, and Khārijīs? And why would the Kufans ascribe certain practices which they reject to prominent early Kufan authorities such as Ibrāhīm al-Nakhaʿī and Ibn Masʿūd? [15]

A "middle position," halfway between that of believers and skeptics, has recently been put forward in a monograph by G. H. A. Juynboll entitled *Muslim Tradition: Studies in Chronology, Provenance, and Authorship of Early Hadith*. Although he admits that at least some of the reports attributed to the Prophet approximate what he actually said or did, Juynboll maintains that, with only a few exceptions, it is unlikely that scholars will ever develop a method that will make it possible to demonstrate positively the historicity of these ascriptions. To state it differently, Juynboll does not deny that the Prophet's followers talked about him during the first forty or fifty years after his death, but he argues that the formal, standardized transmission of information about the Prophet began to develop only at some point in the period between A.D. 670 and 700. As the title of his book indicates, Juynboll has attempted to develop a method to identify when, where, and by whom these reports were first put into circulation.[16]

Schacht's thesis, despite these negative considerations, has stood the test of time. As Forte notes in a survey of Schacht's impact upon contemporary scholarship, "Nearly all Western Islamic scholars agree that Schacht's evidence against the authenticity of the traditions is virtually unassailable."[17] To my mind, however, Schacht's reasoning suffers from two fundamental weaknesses, the first having to do with his treatment of the Qur'an, the second with his blurring of the distinction between jurisprudence and positive law. Schacht concedes that "it is indeed obvious that many rules of Islamic law, particularly in the

15. Ibid., pp. 242–43, 252, 257.

16. The present study was completed before Juynboll's book became available in this country, and I have therefore made no attempt to apply his method to any of the *ḥadīth* discussed in subsequent chapters. It is my intention, however, to undertake such an anlysis in the near future.

17. D. Forte, "Islamic Law: The Impact of Joseph Schacht," p. 15. See also Adams, "Islamic Religious Tradition," p. 90.

law of family and the law of inheritance, not to mention worship and ritual, were based on the Koran from the beginning,"[18] but, at the same time, he argues that Islamic law did not begin to develop until ca. A.D. 725, approximately a century after Muhammad's death. He circumvents the contradiction by using a handful of examples to argue that early legal practice diverged from "the intentions and even the explicit wording of the Qur'an,"[19] and that "norms derived from the Qur'an were introduced into legal doctrine at a secondary stage."[20] (It should be noted that Schacht's study contains no more than four pages on "The Koranic Element in Early Muhammadan Law."[21])

As for the second weakness, Schacht indicated in the title of his major work that he was exploring the origins of Islamic jurisprudence, not positive law. Unfortunately, he was not always careful to keep this distinction in mind. Although Schacht suggested in the epilogue to *Origins* that the methods he had developed to trace the formation of Islamic jurisprudence might be applied to the development of positive law, to the best of my knowledge no such study has ever been undertaken. Yet Schacht and his followers write as if it had been convincingly demonstrated that both Islamic jurisprudence and positive law came into existence only ca. A.D. 725.

It follows from the preceding remarks that anyone who wants to shed light on the origins of Islamic positive law ought to begin with the Qur'anic legislation in the field of family law, inheritance, or ritual. Muslims living in the generations following Muhammad's death prayed on a daily basis, divorced, and divided up property, and it stands to reason, on *a priori* grounds, that the Qur'anic legislation on these matters would have provided them with guidance. I propose to trace the formation of the Islamic law of inheritance, known in Arabic as the *ʿilm al-farāʾiḍ* (science of the shares), in an effort to determine whether Schacht's conclusions in the sphere of jurisprudence properly apply to the field of positive law.

The thesis to be presented here is doubly revisionist. On the

18. Schacht, *Introduction*, p. 18; see also idem, *Origins*, p. 224, and idem, "Law and Justice," p. 545.

19. Schacht, *Origins*, p. 224.

20. Ibid., p. 226.

21. Ibid., pp. 224–27.

one hand I shall argue that the law of inheritance developed in a continuous manner, albeit with several early shifts of direction, from the time of the Prophet onwards. In this respect, my conclusions corroborate those of Coulson, Abbot, Sezgin, and Azami. At the same time I shall argue that the "science of the shares" developed in a manner quite different from that suggested by Islamic tradition. Specifically, I shall attempt to demonstrate that, in the years following the death of Muhammad, the Muslim community manipulated the reading and interpretation of the Qur'an in such a manner as to undermine the system of inheritance introduced by Muhammad (which I refer to as the "proto-Islamic law of inheritance"). First, however, it will perhaps be useful to outline the manner in which Muslim and western scholars have explained the formation of the *ʿilm al-farāʾiḍ*.

The *ʿIlm al-Farāʾiḍ*

"Learn the laws of inheritance (*farāʾiḍ*)," Muhammad is reported to have said, "and teach them to the people; for they are one-half of useful knowledge." In another version of this report, Muhammad states, "The laws of inheritance constitute one-half of all knowledge and are the first [discipline] to be forgotten."[22] These statements, whether or not they were spoken by Muhammad, reflect the great complexity of the *ʿilm al-farāʾiḍ*, which requires a knowledge of square roots and algebra in order to be fully understood. This is not the place to discuss the mathematical intricacies of the "science of the shares," which have been competently dealt with elsewhere.[23] Although it will be necessary to outline the system's mode of operation, my primary aim in this book is to explain, in historical terms, how the "science of the shares" came to assume its classical form.

22. A. A. A. Fyzee, *Outlines of Muhammadan Law*, p. 387. See Bayhaqī, *al-Sunan al-kubrā*, 6:208–09. But Ibn Khaldun (*The Muqaddimah*, trans. F. Rosenthal, 3:22) argues that "*Farāʾiḍ* here is intended to mean 'obligations' (*furūḍ*) imposed upon Muslims in connection with religious worship, customs, matters of inheritance, and other things. If understood in this sense, it is correct to say that [the *farāʾiḍ*] constitute one-half or one-third of scholarship. The inheritance laws [by themselves] constitute a much lesser portion of religious scholarship as a whole."

23. See, for example, Fyzee, *Outlines*, pp. 387–441; N. J. Coulson, *Succession in the Muslim Family*, pp. 29–101; and S. Gandz, "The Algebra of Inheritance: A Rehabilitation of al-Khuwārizmī," pp. 319–91.

The heirs of Islamic law fall into two broad categories, the *ʿaṣaba* (pl. of *ʿāṣib*) or "male agnates," and the *ahl al-farāʾiḍ* or "sharers." The first category includes all those males who are related to the deceased exclusively through male links: (1) the son and his descendants, (2) the father and his ascendants, (3) the descendants of the father, (4) the descendants of the paternal grandfather, and (5) the descendants of the paternal great-grandfather and higher grandfathers in ascending order. These five classes of heirs are related to one another in a hierarchical manner, and a member of a higher class totally excludes any and all members of a lower class from entering the inheritance. Within each class, a person nearer in degree of relationship to the deceased excludes all others in a more remote degree, e.g., a son excludes a grandson.

The second category of heirs, the *ahl al-farāʾiḍ*, includes those persons for whom a fractional share of the estate is mentioned in Q. 4:11, 12 or 176, i.e., the daughter(s), father, mother, husband, wife, uterine brother and sister, and consanguine and/or germane sister(s).[24]

The "science of the shares" imposes compulsory rules for the division of a minimum of two-thirds of any estate; bequests may not exceed one-third of the estate and may not be made in favor of any person who will inherit a fractional share of the estate, either as one of the *ahl al-farāʾiḍ* or as the closest surviving *ʿāṣib*.[25] Thus a Muslim does not exercise any significant control—in theory, at any rate—over the manner in which his property will devolve after his death; he/she may not institute one or more persons of his/her choice as a testamentary heir or heirs. The division of an estate typically proceeds in the following manner: (1) debts are paid off and bequests, if any, are distributed to the legatees; (2) whatever remains constitutes the "estate," which is divided up as follows: (a) the qualifying *ahl al-farāʾiḍ* take their shares "off the top"; (b) the residue, if any, is taken by the closest surviving *ʿāṣib*. Suppose, for example, that a man dies leaving his father, mother, wife, son, and brother. (Let us assume, for the sake of simplicity, that there are no debts or be-

24. Concerning the distinction between uterine and consanguine/germane siblings, see chap. 1. Note that the granddaughter, grandfather, and grandmother were added to the list of *ahl al-farāʾiḍ* by analogy to the daughter, father, and mother.

25. Except in the event that the other heirs agree to the bequest.

quests.) The father, mother, and wife, in their capacities as *ahl al-farā'iḍ*, inherit one-sixth, one-sixth, and one-eighth of the estate, respectively. The son, as the closest surviving *ʿāṣib*, inherits the remaining 13/24 of the estate, totally excluding the brother and all other male agnates from the inheritance.[26]

The Classical Islamic Representation

Detailed pronouncements on the subject of inheritance, whether in the form of Divine revelation or Prophetic *sunna* (precedent) were issued regularly during the twenty-two-year period between the beginning of Muhammad's mission in 610 and his death in 632. By examining these pronouncements in their reputed chronological order we can discern three distinct stages in the development of the law of inheritance. During the Meccan period (610–22), at least six verses regulating various aspects of testamentary succession were revealed to Muhammad. Then, shortly after the emigration to Medina in 622, Muhammad received a second series of revelations establishing compulsory rules for the division of property. Finally, after the conquest of Mecca in 630, Muhammad clarified the relationship between the first and second series of revelations by issuing two statements limiting the scope of testamentary dispositions.

Stage One (610–22): The Bequest Verses

The Qur'an commentators indicate that prior to the rise of Islam and at least until the beginning of the Medinan period, it was customary for the Arabs of the Hijaz to transmit property from one generation to the next by means of a last will and testament, an assertion that finds ample support in specific cases mentioned in the sources.[27] For example, when Badīl b. Abī Maryam, a Qurashī merchant belonging to the tribe of Banū Sahm, sud-

26. For further details on the "science of the shares," see Coulson, *Succession*, pp. 29–101; Fyzee, *Outlines*, pp. 387–441.

27. Ṭabarī, *Jāmiʿ al-bayān ʿan ta'wīl āy al-qur'ān*, 7:106: "*kāna al-nās yatawārathūna bi'l-waṣiyya.*" See idem, *Jāmiʿ*, 2:119.

denly found himself on the point of death while on a trading expedition to Syria, he designated his two traveling companions as the coexecutors of his estate and ordered them to convey his property to his family in Mecca.[28] Similarly, before Aws b. Thābit al-Anṣārī was killed at the battle of Uḥud in 3/625, he had apparently appointed two of his paternal cousins as the co-executors of his estate.[29] When these two, acting perhaps in accordance with the terms of Aws's last will and testament, refused to give any of the deceased's property to his wife, Umm Kuḥḥa, and daughters, the former complained to the Prophet that she and her daughters had been unjustly deprived of their inheritance.[30] These two examples suggest that the intergenerational transmission of property by means of a last will and testament was a normal and accepted procedure during the earliest years of Islam.

Indeed, it is against a background of testamentary succession that the first series of Qur'anic inheritance verses is best understood. Six verses (Q. 2:180–82, 2:240 and 5:105–6) regulating various aspects of testamentary succession were revealed to Muhammad "at the beginning of Islam":[31] Q. 2:180 enjoins a person contemplating death to leave a bequest for parents and relatives; Q. 2:181 holds accountable to God anyone who alters a last will and testament; Q. 2:182 encourages the reconciliation of parties who disagree about the provisions of a will; Q. 2:240 permits a testator to stipulate that his widow is entitled to a maximum of one year's maintenance, provided that she remains in her deceased husband's house; and finally, Q. 5:105–6 establish that a last will and testament, to be valid, must be drawn up or dictated in the presence of two trustworthy witnesses. These six verses reflect a system of inheritance that leaves the individual relatively free to determine whom his heirs will be and how much they will inherit.

28. Wāḥidī, *Asbāb nuzūl al-qur'ān*, pp. 206–07: *"fa-awṣā ilayhimā bi-tarikatihi"*; see also Suyūṭī, *Lubāb al-nuqūl fī asbāb al-nuzūl*, p. 136.

29. Wāḥidī, pp. 137–38 (no. 7).

30. Ṭabarī, *Jāmiʿ*, 4:262.

31. Zamakhsharī, *al-Kashshāf ʿan ḥaqā'iq ghawāmiḍ al-tanzīl*, 1:289; Bayḍāwī, *Anwār al-tanzīl wa-asrār al-ta'wīl*, 1:100–1; Nasafī, *Tafsīr*, 1:88; Alūsī, *Rūḥ al-maʿānī fī tafsīr al-qur'ān*, 2:75. I take the phrase "at the beginning of Islam" as referring to the beginning of Muhammad's mission, in Mecca, ca. A.D. 610.

Stage Two (622–30): The Inheritance Verses

The *asbāb al-nuzūl* (occasions of the revelation) teach that the permissive and discretionary system characteristic of the Meccan period came to an abrupt end in A.D. 625, as a result of the above-mentioned incident involving Umm Kuḥḥa, who allegedly complained to the Prophet that she and her daughters had been unjustly deprived of their inheritance from her husband by the deceased's paternal cousins. After listening to her complaint, Muhammad dismissed the woman "so that he might see what God would introduce."[32] The Divinity delivered his response to Muhammad in two stages, beginning with Q. 4:8, which affirms the right of women to inherit, and followed by Q. 4:11–12, which specify the exact fractional shares to which women are entitled. The latter two verses, together with Q. 4:176, which awards fractional shares of the estate to consanguine and/or germane siblings (hereafter these three verses will be referred to collectively as "the inheritance verses"), form the core of what would become the "science of the shares."[33]

Q. 4:11–12 and 4:176 reflect a conception of the nature of inheritance very different from that embodied in Q. 2:180 and 2:240 (hereafter, "the bequest verses"). In the bequest verses, the testator himself determines the type and quantity of the provisions to be made for parents, kindred, and wives, making the entitlement of the legatees dependent on the will of man, not God. In the inheritance verses, on the other hand, it is God himself who determines whom the rightful heirs are and how much they will receive ("God commands you concerning your children"). The last line of Q. 4:11 ("Your fathers and your sons, you know not which of them is closer to you in usefulness") contrasts the infallible wisdom of the Divinity with the fallible knowledge of man.[34]

32. Zamakhsharī, 1:476–77: "*Ḥattā yanẓur mā yuḥdith allāh.*" See also Bayḍāwī, 1:196; Rāzī, *al-Tafsīr al-kabīr*, 9:194; Wāḥidī, pp. 137–38 (no. 7).

33. For an English translation of these verses, see appendix A.

34. The transfer of control over the law of inheritance from man to God is rationalized by the nineteenth-century commentator, Alūsī, in the following terms: "Since the testator might not manage to estimate correctly the amount that he should bequeath to each one of them and he might possibly intend them harm, [God] took upon himself to clarify that right in such a manner that it would be certain to be correct . . . . He restricted [inheritance] to obligatory limits, i.e., one-sixth, one-third, one-half, and one-eighth, which could not be changed, so

The notion that the fractional shares specified in Q. 4:11–12 were established by God himself and are part of His plan for mankind is reinforced by the two verses that follow next in the Qur'an:

> These are the limits of God. Whoever obeys God and His Messenger, He will cause him to enter gardens under which flow rivers, to dwell there in eternity. That is the great triumph. (4:13)
>
> But whoever disobeys God and His Messenger and transgresses His limits, He will cause him to enter a fire, to dwell there in eternity. And he will be sorely punished. (4:14)

Stage Three (630–32): The Sunna of the Prophet

Islamic tradition presents the formation of the *ʿilm al-farāʾiḍ* in terms of a progression from the voluntary system reflected in the bequest verses to the compulsory rules found in the inheritance verses. This conception, however, calls for further explanation because Q. 4:11–12 themselves award shares of the estate to the heirs "after any bequest he bequeaths," thereby indicating that the power of testation had not been eliminated entirely. The question of the extent to which testamentary dispositions remained operative is answered by the *sunna* of the Prophet, which imposes two major restrictions upon the power of testation.

The first restriction was reportedly introduced shortly after the conquest of Mecca, in 630, during an encounter between Muhammad and Saʿd b. Abī Waqqāṣ. When Saʿd, who believed that he was about to die, asked the Prophet if he might bequeath his entire estate, Muhammad responded, "a bequest may not exceed one-third of the estate."[35] This restriction is generally understood as an attempt to strike a balance between the compulsory and voluntary aspects of the law of inheritance: a minimum of two-thirds is distributed among the heirs in accordance with the compulsory rules established in the inheritance verses,

---

that it was moved [from the realm of testate succession] to that of inheritance. And He said, 'God commands you', i.e., He took it upon Himself, since you were unable to estimate, on account of your ignorance." (*Rūḥ*, 2:76; see also idem, 4:336).

35. Bukhārī, *Ṣaḥīḥ*, 2:186. See also Muslim, *Ṣaḥīḥ*, 3:1250–53 (nos. 5–10).

and a maximum of one-third may be used to make discretionary bequests.

The second restriction had as its object the elimination of an apparent overlap between the voluntary and compulsory aspects of the law of inheritance. Q. 2:180 and 2:240 indicate that a person anticipating death should leave a bequest for parents and wives, while Q. 4:11–12 award these same persons a fractional share of the estate. Is it possible, then, for a parent or wife to receive a bequest of up to one-third of the estate in addition to the fractional share specified in Q. 4:11–12? Apparently not, for Muhammad is reported to have declared, on the occasion of his Farewell Pilgrimage (A.D. 632), "No bequest to an heir."[36] Muslim scholars take this statement to mean that a bequest may not be made in favor of any person who qualifies as an heir, i.e., any person who is awarded a fractional share of the estate. Furthermore, they maintain that the fractional shares awarded to parents in Q. 4:11 and to wives in Q. 4:12 superseded or abrogated (*nasakha*) the obligation to leave bequests for those same persons, as stated in Q. 2:180 and 2:240. Together, then, these two Prophetic dicta, "a bequest may not exceed one-third" and "no bequest to an heir," define the relationship between the voluntary and compulsory aspects of the law of inheritance.

Thus, Islamic tradition teaches that at the time of his death, Muhammad had laid the foundation for what would become the "science of the shares." This foundation was completed over the course of the next thirty years by Companions such as ᶜUmar, ᶜAlī, Zayd b. Thābit (to whom the first treatise on the *ᶜilm al-farā'iḍ* is attributed),[37] Ibn Masᶜūd, and Abū Mūsā.

The Superimposition Theory

The formation of the Islamic law of inheritance has been the subject of a number of studies by western scholars during the course of the past century. W. Robertson Smith, the nineteenth-century Orientalist, was perhaps the first scholar to trace certain basic elements of the Islamic law of inheritance back to the

36. Ibn Hishām, *Kitāb sīrat rasūl allāh*, p. 970: "*lā waṣiyya li-wārith*."

37. F. Sezgin, *Geschichte des arabischen Schrifttums* (hereafter "*GAS*"), 1: 395–96, 402. Portions of this treatise may be preserved in Bayhaqī, 6:208–63.

tribal customary law of pre-Islamic Arabia. In his *Kinship and Marriage in Early Arabia*, Smith suggested that the "fixed shares" (*farāʾiḍ*) of Islamic law are derived from pre-Islamic inheritance practices:

> [I]t is Mohammedan law and was doubtless ancient practice—for there is no express revelation on the point—that the blood-wit is distributed to the kin of the slain within the limits of inheritance. Under Mohammedan law the details of inheritance depend on degrees of kinship, near relations receiving certain fixed shares (*farāʾiḍ*); and very probably certain provisions of this sort, though in less fixed shape, existed before Islam, as regarded both inheritance and the division of the blood-wit.[38]

Smith identified the *ʿaṣaba* as another element of the tribal customary law of pre-Islamic Arabia that was carried over into Islamic law.[39] His discussion of the Islamic law of inheritance, with its emphasis on tribal, nomadic origins, set the tone for subsequent studies.[40]

Thirteen years after the publication of *Kinship and Marriage*, the French Orientalist, W. Marçais, developed a thesis which will hereafter be referred to as the "superimposition theory."[41] Unlike Smith, who focused exclusively on the nomadic aspects of Arabian society, Marçais recognized the presence and importance of settled forms of social organization in the Hijaz. Although he strangely insisted that the Medinese were at the same level of social organization as their *congénères*, the desert nomads, he noted that the Meccans enjoyed a much different level of social organization. Marçais sought the origins of the Islamic law of inheritance in an alleged disparity in the level of social organization characteristic of Mecca and Medina. He argued, largely on the basis of Khadīja's activities as a successful

38. W. R. Smith, *Kinship and Marriage in Early Arabia*, p. 65.

39. Ibid., pp. 65–66.

40. E.g., ibid., pp. 66–67: "That the law of inheritance should follow the law of booty is easily intelligible, for among the nomads waters and pastures were and still are common tribal property, and moveable estate was being constantly captured and recaptured. Plainly the original theory was that it also, since no man was strong enough to keep his own without help, was really tribal property of which the individual had only a usufruct, and which fell to be divided after his death like the spoils of war. Thus the whole law of the old Arabs really resolves itself into a law of war—blood-feud, blood-wit, and booty are the points on which everything turns."

41. W. Marçais, "*Des parents et alliés successibles en droit musulman.*"

merchant, that women in Mecca could own and inherit property.[42] In Medina, on the other hand, the right to inherit was supposedly restricted to males.[43] But by positing a higher level of social organization in Mecca than in Medina, Marçais painted himself into an intellectual corner, for Islamic tradition teaches that the Qur'anic inheritance verses (which, according to Marçais, reflect the level of social organization characteristic of the more advanced Meccans) were revealed to Muhammad in Medina. Marçais resolved this problem by suggesting that Muhammad, after arriving in Medina, decided to reform the male-oriented inheritance practices of the Medinese so as to bring them into line with the more advanced inheritance practices of his native Mecca. Marçais argued that Muhammad superimposed a successoral regime favorable to women upon the male-oriented inheritance practices of the Medinese—hence, the "superimposition theory."

Marçais subsequently disavowed his theory in a letter to another French Orientalist, G.-H. Bousquet:

> I now consider my hypothesis [concerning] a law of Mecca and a law of Medina to have been arbitrary and adventurous. We know nothing for certain about pre-Islamic Arabia. Little more was known when people in the Arab world began to take up these matters. It was the philologists and jurists of the towns, especially Basra and Kufa, who occupied themselves with these matters. Now, in these towns social conditions had been radically transformed during the 150 years [since the death of Muhammad].[44]

Marçais's renunciation of his thesis did not put an end to the superimposition theory. Bousquet, who rejected the idea of a duality of successoral regimes in Mecca and Medina as "*condamné*,"[45] argued that the adoption of a different methodology might facilitate the reconstruction of the tribal customary law of pre-Islamic Arabia:

> Is it necessary to despair of arriving at any conclusions regarding the successoral regime of pre-Islamic Arabia? I think not, at least not entirely. The thesis defended by Mr. Marçais is perhaps not so very unreasonable. A defense from a new and different per-

42. Ibid., p. 40.
43. Ibid., p. 35.
44. The letter is cited in G.-H. Bousquet and F. Peltier, *Les successions agnatiques mitigées*, pp. 97–98.
45. Ibid., p. 98.

> spective might succeed in reviving it. Instead of taking as our point of departure the information regarding pre-Islamic Arabia, which is so poorly known to us, one might take as the point of departure the Islamic law of inheritance and, in particular, the verses of the Qur'an which are easily accessible to us. We can then see if that which is known derives from that which is unknown. In this regard, we possess both the doctrinal lawbooks and the verses of the Qur'an, the authenticity of which have never been questioned. As for information regarding pre-Islamic Arabia, only the most prudent borrowings will be made from it.[46]

By means of this alternative method, which involved a close—but superficial—analysis of the Qur'anic inheritance verses, Bousquet came to the same conclusion that Marçais had reached earlier, to wit, that Muhammad superimposed a system of inheritance favorable to women upon the tribal customary law of pre-Islamic Arabia.[47]

The superimposition theory, which has subsequently been accepted by most legal historians,[48] may be restated as follows: The Qur'an establishes rights of inheritance between spouses and in favor of certain close female relatives by awarding these persons fractional shares of the deceased's estate. These rules do not, in themselves, constitute a complete system of inheritance, but merely modify the tribal customary law of pre-Islamic Arabia by superimposing upon it a new class of legal heirs. The *ʿaṣaba*, the heirs of pre-Islamic Arabia, still inherit, but now only after the claims of the Qur'anic heirs, the *ahl al-farāʾiḍ*, have been satisfied. These two heterogeneous elements, the tribal customary law of pre-Islamic Arabia and the Qur'anic legislation, were fused together to form the "science of the shares." The dual basis of the system accounts for much of its mathematical complexity.

Proto-Islamic Law

It is my contention that neither the classical Islamic representation nor the superimposition theory adequately accounts for the

46. Ibid., p. 98.

47. Ibid., pp. 117–18.

48. The most recent and most eloquent formulation of the superimposition theory can be found in Coulson, *Succession*, pp. 29–30. But the usefulness of this study is limited by its minimal critical apparatus and the absence of a bibliography. The lack of documentation is especially unfortunate in those sections of the book in which the author advances explanations of an historical nature.

formation of the Islamic law of inheritance. Both theories start from the assumption that the traditional understanding of the Qur'anic and prophetic pronouncements on inheritance is identical to the understanding of Muhammad and the early community. But this may not be the case. In part one of this study I shall demonstrate that it is possible to work backward from the traditional understanding of certain key Qur'anic verses and prophetic *ḥadīth* to what I believe to have been their original significance. I shall then attempt to reconstruct the system of inheritance introduced by Muhammad ("the proto-Islamic law of inheritance"), a system that not only allows for full testate succession, including the designation of a testamentary heir, but also is free of most of the mathematical complications of the "science of the shares." In part two I shall trace the process whereby the proto-Islamic law of inheritance was transformed, as a result of political, social, and religious conflicts that marked the generations following the death of Muhammad, into the *ʿilm al-farāʾiḍ*.

Part One

THE PROTO-ISLAMIC LAW OF INHERITANCE

1

Testate Succession

The Islamic law of inheritance places severe restrictions upon testate succession. A person anticipating death may dispose of no more than one-third of the estate in the form of bequests ("a bequest may not exceed one-third"), and he/she may not favor in this manner any person who stands to inherit one of the compulsory shares, e.g., a parent or spouse ("no bequest to an heir"). It is my contention, however, that the Islamic law of inheritance developed at a relatively late date and bears little or no relation to the system of inheritance introduced by Muhammad (proto-Islamic law). I shall attempt to substantiate this claim by reconstructing the proto-Islamic law of testate succession, according to which (a) a person anticipating death could, in fact, leave the bulk of the estate for a single testamentary heir of his/her choice; (b) a maximum of one-third of the estate was reserved for bequests to persons other than the testamentary heir, including (c) a parent or spouse.

The Designation of an Heir: A New Reading of Q. 4:12b

It is generally accepted among Muslim and non-Muslim scholars alike that the Qur'an contains no explicit reference to the designation of an heir in a technical, legal sense. The Islamic law of inheritance (*ʿilm al-farāʾiḍ*) imposes compulsory rules for the division of a minimum of two-thirds of any estate.[1] But I shall

1. For a concise summary of the operation of the Islamic law of inheritance, see J. Schacht, *An Introduction to Islamic Law*, pp. 169–74. A more detailed treat-

attempt to demonstrate here that at least one Qur'anic verse, Q. 4:12b,[2] can be viewed in such a manner that it explicitly refers to a man's right to designate a female in-law as his sole heir. This manner of viewing the verse, which has been overlooked by Muslim scholars for over thirteen hundred years, is supported by linguistic, grammatical, and historical considerations.

The Traditional Understanding

Q. 4:12b is traditionally read as follows:

> Wa-in kāna rajulun yūrathu kalālatan aw imra'atun wa-lahu akhun aw ukhtun fa-li-kulli wāḥidin minhumā al-sudusu. Fa-in kānū akthara min dhālika fa-hum shurakā' fi'l-thuluthi min baʿdi waṣiyyatin yūṣā bihā aw daynin ghayra muḍārrin waṣiyyatan min allāhi. Wallāhu ʿalīmun ḥalīmun.

These words, which occupy no more than four lines in the Arabic text of the Qur'an, have been a source of considerable controversy among the commentators. Ṭabarī (d. A.D. 923), for example, devotes no less than seven pages to these four lines.[3] Almost every word in the opening line of the verse is subject to dispute, and there may be as many as four or five different opinions, espoused by an even greater number of authorities, for every point in question. Yet, in the midst of all this confusion, one thing remains certain. No matter how much the authorities differ over details, there is universal agreement on the general meaning of the verse, namely, that it awards a fractional share of the estate to uterine siblings.[4]

A comprehensive analysis of Ṭabarī's treatment of Q. 4:12b is

---

ment of the subject will be found in Coulson, *Succession in the Muslim Family.* On the historical development of the *ʿilm al-farā'iḍ*, see W. Marçais, *Des parents et alliés successibles en droit musulman,* and G. H. Bousquet and F. Peltier, *Les successions agnatiques mitigées.*

2. All verse numbers quoted in this book correspond to the versification of the standard Egyptian edition of the Qur'an. Q. 4:12 is a long verse composed of two distinct sections, the first dealing with husbands and wives, the second, beginning with the words "*Wa-in kāna rajulun yūrathu,*" dealing with siblings. We are concerned here only with the second half of the verse. For a discussion of Q. 4:12a, see chap. 2.

3. Ṭabarī, *Jāmiʿ al-bayān ʿan ta'wīl āy al-qur'ān,* 4:283–89.

4. I shall return to this point on p. 29.

beyond the scope of the present inquiry. It will be sufficient for our purposes merely to outline the major semantic and syntactic issues, which are: the meaning of the word *kalāla*; the grammatical function of that word; the splitting of the compound subject "*rajulun . . . aw imra'atun*"; the inappropriateness of the pronominal suffix in the prepositional phrase *wa-lahu*; and finally, a single variant reading considered by Ṭabarī.

The meaning of "kalāla." The precise meaning of the word *kalāla* was the subject of an extensive debate among early authorities on the Qur'an. In his discussion of Q. 4:12b, Ṭabarī provides exhaustive documentation of this controversy, citing no less than twenty-seven separate *shawāhid*, or authoritative statements, in support of one definition or another. Actually, the debate ranged within rather narrow limits. The central issue was whether the word *kalāla* refers to the deceased himself (*al-mawrūth*) or to the heirs of the deceased (*al-waratha*). Support for either position was almost evenly divided. According to fourteen *shawāhid*, the word signifies "one who leaves neither parent nor child," so that it refers to the deceased. According to twelve *shawāhid*, the word signifies "all those except the parent and child," so that it refers to the heirs. Finally, one statement indicates that both definitions are possible.[5]

The controversy was resolved by Ṭabarī himself. After placing all the evidence in front of the reader, he delivers his own opinion and the reasoning behind it:

> Abū Jaʿfar [al-Ṭabarī] said: According to me the correct opinion in this matter is what these hold, namely that *al-kalāla* refers to those who inherit from the deceased, with the exception of parent and child. This is because of the correctness of the report adduced by us on the authority of Jābir b. ʿAbd Allāh who said: I said: "O Messenger of God, none but *kalāla* will inherit from me. So what about the estate?"[6]

Ṭabarī seems to resolve the issue by the process of elimination. He settles upon the "correct" definition of the word because, in the report attributed to Jābir, the word *kalāla* cannot possibly refer to Jābir himself, and must therefore refer to his heir or heirs.

The function of "kalālatan". The grammatical function of the word *kalāla* in Q. 4:12b is as difficult as its meaning. There is a

5. Ṭabarī, *Jāmiʿ*, 4:283–86.

6. Ibid., 4:286.

wide range of opinions as to the reason why the word occurs in the accusative case. Early grammarians proposed no fewer than three different explanations of the syntax of the phrase *wa-in kāna rajulun yūrathu kalālatan*, which opens the verse.[7] These three explanations, the last one being that of Ṭabarī himself, may be summarized as follows: (1) Some of the Basran grammarians view the passive verb *yūrathu* as an attribute (*ṣifa*) of the preceding noun *rajulun*, so that the phrase *rajulun yūrathu* is seen as a kind of noun-adjective phrase, with the sense of *rajulun mawrūthun minhu* (a man whom others inherit from). The noun *kalāla* is then seen as the predicate (*khabar*) of the verb *kāna*; the phrase *kāna . . . kalālatan* would mean "is one who leaves neither parent nor child." According to this explanation, the opening line of the verse means: "If a man whom others inherit from is one who leaves neither parent nor child." (2) Another Basran grammarian regards the phrase *yūrathu kalālatan* as a circumstantial clause, so that the opening line of the verse would mean "If a man is inherited from while leaving neither parent nor child." (3) Finally, Ṭabarī suggests that the opening line of the verse is actually a syncopated form of a longer phrase which he reconstructs as follows: *Wa-in kāna rajulun yūrithu* [*mutakalillahu al-nasbi*] *kalālatan* (emendation indicated by brackets). According to this explanation, the active verb *yūrithu* of the "complete" phrase was converted into the passive verb *yūrathu* of Q. 4:12b, thereby absorbing the two words within parentheses and leaving the word *kalāla* in the accusative case.[8]

Bifurcated subject: rajulun . . . aw imra'atun (*a man . . . or a woman*). According to the traditional reading of Q. 4:12b the verb *yūrathu* has not one but two subjects, both of which are read in the nominative case, *rajulun* and *imra'atun*. Normally, the two elements of a compound subject are linked directly by a conjunction such as *aw* (or). Indeed, in the continuation of Q. 4:12b itself the phrase *akhun aw ukhtun* (a brother or a sister) is encountered. Yet the compound subjects *rajulun* and *imra'atun* are separated from one another by two intervening words: *rajulun* (*yūrathu kalālatan*) *aw imra'atun* (intervening words set off by parentheses). Ṭabarī recognizes the awkwardness of the phrase and, so as to make the verse flow more smoothly, suggests a mental transposi-

7. The number of explanations increases with the passage of time. For a convenient summary, see Ibn Manẓūr, *Lisān al-ʿArab*, 1:593–94.

8. Ṭabarī, *Jāmiʿ*, 4:285–86.

tion of the order in which the words occur in the Qur'an. That is to say, although he does not dare change the text of the Qur'an itself, he proposes that the reader consider the opening line of the verse as if it read: *Wa-in kāna rajulun* (*aw imra'atun*) *yūrathu kalālatan* (transposition indicated by parentheses). This proposed emendation of the text is the very first issue raised by Ṭabarī in his analysis of Q. 4:12b.[9]

The inappropriateness of the pronominal phrase "wa-lahu." The opening line of Q. 4:12b contains yet a fourth problem to which Ṭabarī addresses himself. The "man . . . or woman" mentioned at the outset of the verse are later referred to by a third-person masculine singular pronoun, *wa-lahu*. Normally, one would expect the dual pronominal phrase *wa-lahumā*. Indeed, in the continuation of the verse we encounter just such a phrase, *minhumā*, referring back to the compound subject "brother or sister." Ṭabarī, conscious of the discrepancy, poses the following hypothetical question: "And if someone should say: 'Why is it said *wa-laHU akhun aw ukhtun* instead of *wa-laHUMĀ akhun aw ukhutun*?'", i.e., why the third-person masculine singular pronoun instead of the dual-pronoun suffix? In response to this question, Ṭabarī notes that a pronoun suffix referring back to a compound subject may be linked to both nouns, or to only one. In the latter case, it makes no difference to which noun it is linked. In support of this assertion, Ṭabarī quotes the following sentence: *Man kāna ʿindahu ghulāmun aw jāriyatun fa'l-yuḥsin ilayhi* (literally: Let him who has a slave-boy or slave-girl treat *him* well). Ṭabarī correctly points out that the phrase clearly means "let him treat *both of them* well."[10] Thus, the phrase *wa-lahu* in Q. 4:12b, although difficult, is not impossible; similar constructions are found elsewhere in Arabic.

Variant readings. Ṭabarī notes a single variant reading of Q. 4:12b. Although the majority of the Qur'an reciters read *y–w–r–th* as a passive verb, *yūrathu*, some read the same word as an active verb, *yūrithu*. Ṭabarī clearly indicates that no matter what the reading, the meaning of the verse remains the same. In both cases the verse awards a fractional share of the estate to one or more uterine siblings.[11]

Considering the extreme difficulty of Q. 4:12b, one might

9. Ibid., 4:283 (ll. 20–21).
10. Ibid., 4:287–88.
11. Ibid., 4:283 (ll. 22–25).

have expected to find several variant readings. Indeed, other sources indicate at least one more variant that Ṭabarī curiously failed to mention. Ibn Mujāhid, for example, notes a variant reading of a word that occurs towards the end of Q. 4:12b:

> There is a disagreement with regard to the reading of the letter *ṣād* in the phrase *yūṣ? bihā* in Q. 4:11 and 4:12: (1) Ibn Kathīr and ʿĀṣim, in accordance with the transmission of Abū Bakr, read *yūṣā bihā* in both verses. (2) Nāfiʿ, Abū ʿAmr, Ḥamza, and al-Kisāʾī read *yūṣī bihā* in both verses. Ḥafṣ said, on the authority of ʿĀṣim: The first one is [read] with a *kasra*, i.e., *yūṣī bihā*, and the second with a *fatḥa* over the *ṣād*.[12]

Why did Ṭabarī fail to mention this variant reading, which must have been known to him? He may have disregarded it on the ground that it has no effect whatsoever on the meaning of the verse. Certainly, it makes no difference whether one says "after a bequest that is bequeathed" or "after a bequest that he bequeaths." This consideration must be rejected, for it has already been shown that Ṭabarī was concerned with variant readings even if they have no effect whatsoever on the meaning of the verse. It is therefore possible that the omission reflects an attempt by Ṭabarī to avoid still another grammatical problem. Like the pronominal phrase *wa-lahu*, the active verb *yūṣī* would also be governed by the compound subject "a man ... or a woman." Therefore, one would expect to find the dual form of the active verb rather than an impersonal passive. The significance of the reading "*yūṣī*" is explained below.

Ṭabarī, in his analysis of Q. 4:12b, treats all of the abovementioned problems in isolation from one another, seeing no connection between any of them and the reading of the verse. Rather than give serious consideration to an alternative reading of Q. 4:12b, he is more inclined to transpose the actual word order, or to suggest that several words had dropped out. It will be argued below that a simple change in the reading of three words in Q. 4:12b eliminates at once all of the difficulties discussed above. These three words are *yūrathu*, *imraʾatun*, and *yūṣā*; henceforth, it will be convenient to refer to the traditional reading of Q. 4:12b as the "*yūrathu/imraʾatun/yūṣā* complex." Each one of these three words, and not just the first and/or the last, is given to an alternative reading. It is only when all three alter-

12. Ibn Mujāhid, *Kitāb al-sabʿa fiʾl-qirāʾāt*, p. 228.

native readings are taken into account that the alternative explanation of Q. 4:12b becomes evident.

Having examined the semantic and syntactic problems connected with the opening line of Q. 4:12b, we may now attempt to translate that verse into English. It should be evident that any translation of the verse will depend heavily upon the explanations of the commentators. Before proceeding on our own, let us consider how four western scholars have rendered this verse:

(1) "And if the man's or the woman's (property) is inherited by a kinsman who is neither parent nor child, and he have a brother or a sister . . ."[13]
(2) "And if a man or woman have a distant heir (having left neither parent nor child), and he (or she) . . ."[14]
(3) "If a man or a woman leave neither children nor parents and have a brother or a sister . . ."[15]
(4) "If a man or a woman have no heir direct, but have a brother or a sister . . ."[16]

In each case, faithfulness to the Arabic text has been sacrificed for the sake of fluidity in English: Each translator has changed the word order to read "man or woman" instead of "man . . . or woman"; the phrase *yūrathu kalālatan* has given rise to four different approximations in English; and finally, the inappropriateness of the pronominal phrase *wa-lahu* has been cleverly disguised by the last three translators.

The extent of the variation among these four translations reflects the difficulty of the opening line of Q. 4:12b. Indeed, because of this difficulty, there can be no entirely accurate translation into English of the opening line of the verse. This is no fault of either the English language or the translators themselves. As we have just seen, Ṭabarī himself could not make sense of the opening line of the verse without rearranging words here and adding words there. In the following translation, which is my own, an attempt is made to adhere to the Arabic text as closely as possible:

> If a man is inherited from while leaving neither parent nor child—or a woman—and he [*sic*] has a brother or a sister, each

13. *The Koran*, tr. by E. H. Palmer (London, 1928), p. 73.
14. *The Meaning of the Glorious Koran*, tr. by M. Pickthall (London, 1930), p. 80.
15. *The Koran*, tr. by N. J. Dawood (Middlesex, 1956), p. 367.
16. *The Koran Interpreted*, tr. by A. J. Arberry (London, 1955), p. 102.

> one of them is entitled to one-sixth. If they are more than that, then they are partners with respect to one-third, after any legacy that is bequeathed, or debt, without injury. A commandment from God. God is knowing, forbearing.

The general sense of the verse is clear, despite the awkwardness of the opening line. Q. 4:12b refers to a person who dies leaving neither parent nor child. It treats the case in which the closest surviving blood relatives of the deceased are one or more siblings who are awarded fractional shares of the estate, the sum total of which must not exceed one-third of its total value. The fate of the remaining two-thirds of the estate is not specified. Bearing in mind this, the traditional understanding of the verse, we may now proceed to a consideration of the relationship between Q. 4:12b and 4:176.

Q. 4:176, the very last verse of the fourth chapter of the Qur'an (*Sūrat al-Nisā'*), opens with an allusion to an unspecified question that was posed to Muhammad by several of his followers: *Yastaftūnaka* (When they ask you for a decision). The Divinity immediately instructs Muhammad on how to respond to the unspecified question: *Qul: Allāhu yuftīkum fi'l-kalālati* (Say: "God decrees for you regarding *al-kalāla*"). The reference to the word *kalāla* indicates a connection to Q. 4:12b, the only other verse in the Qur'an in which this word occurs.

Thus, we are once again compelled to consider the meaning of the difficult term *kalāla*. Ṭabarī, upon encountering this word for a second time, indicates that he has already explained its significance in the course of his discussion of Q. 4:12b. Lest there be any uncertainty, he reiterates his conclusion as to the meaning of the word, which he defines as "all those except parent and child."[17] From this point on, problems of grammar and syntax are subordinated to those of substance. Examination of Q. 4:12b and 4:176 (see appendix A) discloses a seeming contradiction. Both verses award fractional shares of the estate to siblings in what appear to be identical circumstances. In the former verse, brothers and sisters receive equal shares of the estate; in the latter, a brother receives twice the share of a sister! Furthermore, the two verses account for different amounts of the estate: Q. 4:12b awards a maximum of one-third of the estate, whereas Q. 4:176 distributes between one-half of the estate and its entirety. These discrepancies call for an explanation.

17. Ṭabarī, *Jāmiʿ*, 6:40.

The earliest authorities were unable to resolve the apparent contradiction without resorting to an interpolation of the text. The eventual solution to the problem was suggested by the fact that siblings may be of three types: uterine (same mother, different fathers); consanguine (same father, different mothers); and germane (same father and mother). The relative status of the three different types of sibling varies from one society to the next. Wherever kinship is reckoned through male links, consanguine and germane siblings enjoy a higher status than uterine siblings. These distinctions provide a reasonable solution to the problem. The exegetes suggest that the discrepancy in the *size* of the shares awarded in the two verses indicates that each verse treats a different *type* of sibling. Specifically, Q. 4:12b deals with uterine siblings, and Q. 4:176 deals with consanguine and/or germane siblings.

There is universal agreement among Muslim scholars as to the validity of this solution. Ṭabarī cites numerous early authorities who unequivocally state that the siblings in Q. 4:12b are in fact uterine siblings, whereas those in Q. 4:176 are actually consanguine and germane siblings. There even exists a variant reading of Q. 4:12b, attributed to Ubayy b. Kaᶜb and Saᶜd b. Abī Waqqāṣ, which adds the word *li-umm* to the consonantal text, so that the relevant section reads *akhun aw ukhtun li-umm* (uterine brother or sister). Many commentators point to this reading in support of the traditional interpretation of Q. 4:12b and 4:176.[18]

But the consensus of Muslim scholars with regard to the meaning of Q. 4:12b and 4:176 conceals a significant amount of early confusion and uncertainty among prominent Companions, including ᶜUmar himself, as to the meaning of those two verses. It is to this early confusion and uncertainty that we must now direct our attention.

Early Uncertainty

By the first quarter of the tenth century A.D., the framework of acceptable discourse regarding the significance of Q. 4:12b and 4:176 had been settled upon by Muslim scholars. Ṭabarī himself

18. Ibid., 4:287 and 6:40, 45, and 46; Zamakhsharī, *al-Kashshāf*, 1:486; Nīsābūrī, *Gharā'ib al-qur'ān*, 4:200.

simply fitted the historical material available to him into the mold that had already been established. Disagreement was permitted, but only within the boundaries of the accepted interpretation of the general significance of the two verses. Any statement or opinion that openly challenged the *status quo* had to be downplayed.

In the course of his discussion of Q. 4:12b and 4:176, Ṭabarī raises and responds to a number of problems. In my opinion, both the problems and the answers reflect nothing more than a fall-back position adopted by scholars after the *yūrathu/imra'atun/yūṣā* complex had been accepted as the preferred reading of Q. 4:12b. It is the reading of the verse that generates, not only the lexical and semantic difficulties discussed above, but also the apparent contradiction between Q. 4:12b and 4:176. The solutions proposed by Ṭabarī are actually presumed from the outset; they represent the consensus of the scholars as it had been hammered out by the beginning of the tenth century A.D., or earlier. Ṭabarī's support for this consensus is reflected in his arrangement of the material available to him so as to deflect the reader's attention from any statement that might constitute a potential challenge to the traditional understanding of the two verses.

Such statements were certainly in circulation during the first quarter of the tenth century A.D. This is especially clear with respect to statements concerning the meaning of the word *kalāla.* Reference has already been made to the twenty-seven *shawāhid* containing one or another definition of the word. In addition to this material, Ṭabarī had at his disposal at least thirteen other *shawāhid* which attest to a significant amount of confusion over the meaning of this word in the years immediately following the death of Muhammad. Although he does not omit this material, Ṭabarī arranges it in such a manner that the reader of his commentary is directed to the "correct" meaning of the word, without noticing the potential significance of these thirteen *shawāhid.*

The word *kalāla* occurs only twice in the Qur'an, once in Q. 4:12b and again in 4:176. In his analysis of the former verse, Ṭabarī cites only the twenty-seven *shawāhid* that support the traditional understanding of the meaning of that word, and he fails to refer to the existence of the thirteen *shawāhid* that present a potential challenge to that interpretation. In this manner, the definition of the word *kalāla* that Ṭabarī eventually settles upon becomes the operating assumption of his entire analysis of the two verses in which the word occurs. Upon encountering this troublesome word for a second time in the opening line of Q. 4:176, Ṭabarī clearly has no intention of subjecting his audience—or himself—to a repetition of the tedious controversy surrounding its exact definition. Instead, he simply reiterates his own conclusion and refers the interested reader back to his discussion of Q. 4:12b for details:

> We have already explained the meaning of the word *kalāla* on the basis of authoritative statements which indicate the validity of [our explanation]. We also referred to the disagreement of those who disagree about it. Therefore, it is unnecessary to repeat the matter. We have already explained that, in our opinion, the word *kalāla* refers to all those except parent and child.[19]

If Ṭabarī is to be believed, then all of the evidence bearing upon the meaning of the word *kalāla* has already been placed before the reader, and it is on the basis of this evidence, presumably complete, that he determines the "correct" definition of the word. In fact, however, Ṭabarī has failed to consider at least thirteen *shawāhid* whose contents have a direct bearing upon the meaning of the word. He does not refer to these *shawāhid* until the middle of his discussion of Q. 4:176, i.e., after he has already made up his own mind—and the reader's—as to the exact meaning of the word. By the time he mentions these texts, the reader has already been persuaded that the word *kalāla* means "all those except parent and child."

Ṭabarī's inclusion of the thirteen *shawāhid* in his commentary (most later commentators omit them) suggests that he may have been open to an alternative explanation of the meaning of Q. 4:12b and 4:176. This possibility deserves further consideration. Be that as it may, we turn now to an examination of several of these texts. To appreciate their significance fully, it will be helpful to disregard temporarily everything that has been said up to this point about the meaning of the word *kalāla*.

The tone of these thirteen *shawāhid* differs considerably from that of the twenty-seven already cited by Ṭabarī. They are noteworthy both for their vividness and for their failure to put forward a specific definition of the word *kalāla*. Instead, they suggest that the meaning of that word was clouded in mystery during the years immediately following the death of Muham-

19. Ṭabarī, *Jāmiʿ*, 6:40.

mad. In view of their nature, it will be convenient to refer to these *shawāhid* as "anecdotes."

Analysis of the chains of authorities appended to each anecdote may eventually make it possible to date each one to within perhaps a quarter of a century. At the present time, it can only be said that in all likelihood the anecdotes were created *after* what has been referred to as the "traditional" understanding of Q. 4:12b and 4:176 had already taken firm root in the consciousness of Muslim scholars. They were put into circulation by persons who clearly objected to the traditional interpretation, and who themselves viewed the two verses in an entirely different light. The issue was apparently so controversial that it was impossible to state openly the exact nature of the objection. Therefore, the persons in question resorted to indirection and innuendo, creating a number of carefully coded anecdotes. The clues contained in these anecdotes suggest an alternative reading of Q. 4:12b, a reading that radically transforms the meaning of that verse, as well as the nature of its relationship to Q. 4:176.

The anecdotes center upon the figure of ᶜUmar b. al-Khaṭṭāb (d. A.D. 644), one of Muhammad's closest companions, who later became the second successor to the Prophet. ᶜUmar was also referred to by the epithet *al-fārūq*, a word which came to be understood as "he who distinguishes truth from falsehood." It is perhaps no coincidence that several words derived from the root *f–r–q* are crucial to the following anecdotes in which ᶜUmar is portrayed as being deeply concerned about the meaning of the word *kalāla*. The following anecdote is typical:

> Abū Kurayb informed us saying: ᶜUththām informed us saying: al-Aᶜmash informed us saying: I heard them mention, and I think Ibrāhīm was among them, on the authority of ᶜUmar. He said: "That I should know about *al-kalāla* is dearer to me than possessing the equivalent of the poll tax of the fortresses of Byzantium."[20]

A second anecdote reinforces the implication that at the time of Muhammad's death, and for at least a short time thereafter, the meaning of the term remained uncertain:

> Yaᶜqūb b. Ibrāhīm informed me saying: Ibn ᶜUlayya informed us saying: Abū Ḥayyān informed us saying: Al-Shaᶜbī informed me, on the authority of Ibn ᶜUmar: I heard ᶜUmar b. al-Khaṭṭāb

20. Ibid., 6:43 (ll. 23–24).

preaching from the pulpit of Medina. He said: "O people, there are three things about which it was my desire that the Messenger of God not depart from us (*lam yufāriqnā*) before making an agreement to which final appeal could be made: the grandfather, *al-kalāla*, and the gates of usury."[21]

These two anecdotes suggest that the meaning of the word *kalāla* remained clouded in obscurity for at least a few years after the death of Muhammad.

A third anecdote indicates that the confusion with regard to *al-kalāla* was a problem during the lifetime of Muhammad himself. ʿUmar relates that he repeatedly asked the Prophet about the meaning of the word *kalāla*, eventually provoking a physical rebuke:

> Yaʿqūb informed me saying: Ibn ʿUlayya informed us, on the authority of Saʿīd b. Abī ʿArūba, on the authority of Qatāda, on the authority of Sālim b. Abī al-Jaʿd, on the authority of Maʿdān b. Abī Ṭalḥa, that ʿUmar b. al-Khaṭṭāb said: "There was nothing about which I queried the Messenger of God so frequently as *al-kalāla*, until he poked me in the chest and said: 'Let the summer verse which is at the end of *Sūrat al-Nisā'* be sufficient for you.'"[22]

In his response, Muhammad refers ʿUmar to Q. 4:176, the second verse in which the word *kalāla* occurs, so that it must have been the first occurrence of the word in Q. 4:12b that was the cause of ʿUmar's confusion. Clearly, this anecdote, as well as the ones to follow, are relevant to *both* Q. 4:12b and 4:176. Yet we hear nothing of them anywhere in the course of Ṭabarī's discussion of the former verse. And when Ṭabarī does finally cite the anecdotes, he misleads the reader into thinking that they are relevant to the assertion that the word *kalāla* signifies "all those except the father."[23] None of the anecdotes discussed here have anything to do with this assertion.

Muhammad's response to ʿUmar's repeated inquiries ("Let Q. 4:176 be sufficient for you") was apparently no answer at all. We have seen that ʿUmar was still uncertain about the meaning of the word *kalāla* after the Prophet's death. Muhammad's response apparently meant nothing to him, as the following anecdote makes clear:

21. Ibid., 6:43–44.
22. Ibid., 6:44 (ll. 3–5).
23. Ibid., 6:43 (ll. 1–2).

> Muhammad b. ʿAlī b. al-Ḥasan b. Shaqīq informed us saying: I heard my father say: Abū Ḥamza reported to us, on the authority of Jābir, on the authority of al-Ḥasan b. Masrūq, on the authority of his father. He said: I asked ʿUmar, while he was preaching to the people, about a relative of mine who was inherited by a *kalāla*. [ʿUmar] replied: "*Al-kalāla, al-kalāla, al-kalāla*!" And he grabbed his beard. Then [ʿUmar] said: "By God, I would rather know its meaning than possess anything on earth. I asked the Messenger of God about it and he replied: 'Did you not hear the verse that was revealed in the summer?'" So he repeated it three times.[24]

It is ironic that the same ʿUmar who had sought and received clarification from Muhammad about *al-kalāla* cannot explain the significance of the word when called upon to do so. Instead, he grabs his beard and repeats the word three times in apparent anguish, a response that suggests that he was extremely troubled by the term.

This anecdote contains the first substantial clue to the developing mystery. The word *kalāla* occurs only twice in the Qur'an, once in Q. 4:12b and again in 4:176, and these two verses are somehow related to one another. Are we to assume that the creator of the anecdote wanted to portray Muhammad as an obscurantist, answering questions with riddles? I think not. Rather, it may be that Q. 4:176 does in fact provide an answer to a question raised by 4:12b, but that the exact nature of this answer was no longer apparent at the time the anecdote was put into circulation. The creator of the anecdote may have been suggesting that the answer becomes apparent only when the two verses are understood as they were by Muhammad himself, and not as they were by Companions such as ʿUmar. How then did Muhammad understand Q. 4:12b and 4:176? How did his understanding differ from what became the traditional interpretation? Before answering these questions, let us examine three more anecdotes.

The mystery surrounding the word *kalāla* reaches a dramatic climax in a pair of anecdotes in which ʿUmar suddenly knows the meaning of the word. Determined to convey this knowledge to his associates, he is prevented from carrying out his intention by a phenomenon that he interprets as a sign of divine intervention:

> Abū Kurayb informed us saying: ʿUththām informed us saying: al-Aʿmash informed us, on the authority of Qays b. Muslim, on

24. Ibid., 6:44 (ll. 18–22).

> the authority of Ṭāriq b. Shihāb. He said: "ʿUmar took a shoulder blade (*katif*) and gathered the Companions of Muhammad. Then he said: 'Verily, I am about to issue a decree regarding *al-kalāla* that women will talk about in their private quarters.' At that very moment, a snake emerged from the house, causing everyone to scatter (*tafarraqū*). [ʿUmar] said: 'Had God wanted the matter to terminate, then he would have finished it.'"[25]

The wording of this anecdote is extremely suggestive. Even on the surface level it indicates that ʿUmar knew the meaning of the word *kalāla*, but was prevented from disclosing this information by the sudden appearance of a snake, which he interpreted as a sign of divine intervention.

The anecdote also operates on a deeper, symbolic level, by means of which its creator was able to express ideas that could not be spoken of openly. First, as the story opens, ʿUmar is holding a shoulder blade (*katif*) to which no further reference is made. The image of the *katif* would have evoked an immediate response among the persons to whom the anecdote was directed. Islamic tradition teaches that Muhammad's followers recorded the revelations upon whatever writing materials were available to them, such as scraps of parchment, palm branches, and shoulder blades.[26] The creator of the anecdote may have introduced this image so as to suggest that the real issue is not a speech by the Caliph, but the Qur'an itself. Secondly, before ʿUmar was silenced, and while he was still intent upon issuing a decree, he indicates that once the meaning of the word *kalāla* became known it would become a source of gossip or discussion among women. Although this reference might be nothing more than a rhetorical flourish characteristic of ʿUmar's speech, if we adopt the position that the story was consciously created and that the anecdote is nothing more than a pseudohistorical document, then the reference to women takes on added significance. In that case, whoever created the anecdote knew full well that ʿUmar would not reveal the true meaning of the word, and he (or she) may be alluding to the actual meaning of the word, "between the lines," as it were. Finally, the snake appears, causing all those gathered to scatter (*tafarraqū*). In retrospect, we may say that ʿUmar's failure to issue the intended decree promoted unity within the Islamic community with respect to the significance

25. Ibid., 6:43 (ll. 25–27).
26. Ibn Abī Dā'ūd, *Kitāb al-Maṣāḥif*, p. 20 (ll. 21–22).

of Q. 4:12b and 4:176. Besides "to scatter," the word *tafarraqa* also signifies "to break up into sects." It was to prevent the Islamic community from breaking up into competing sects that the Caliph ʿUthmān established a single, uniform text of the Qur'an, burning all other versions.[27] The confusion surrounding the significance of Q. 4:12b and Q. 4:176 may have been related to the establishment of a single text of the Qur'an. In that case, the use of the word *tafarraqa* may have been intended as a reference to the issue of the community's unity.

The next anecdote presents a slightly different version of the preceding one:

> Ibn Wakīʿ informed us saying: Muhammad b. Ḥumayd al-Miʿmarī informed us, on the authority of Maʿmar, on the authority of al-Zuhrī, on the authority of Saʿīd b. al-Musayyab, that ʿUmar b. al-Khaṭṭāb wrote a document (*kitāb*) regarding the grandfather and *al-kalāla*. He tarried so as to consult God about it saying: "O God, if you know anything good about it then advance it." Until, when he was stabbed, he called for the document and erased it. And no one knew what he had written thereon. [ʿUmar] said: "I had written a document concerning the grandfather and *al-kalāla*, and I consulted God about it. As a result I have decided to leave you [believing] what you already [believe]."[28]

This anecdote, like the previous one, can be read on two levels. On the surface level, the story explicitly refers to the suppression of information concerning the term *al-kalāla*: ʿUmar again knows something about this word but, rather than divulge this knowledge orally, he consigns it to writing. Subsequently, he himself destroys the document, in the very last moments of his life, after consulting with the Divinity. As for the contents of the erased document, "no one knew what he had written thereon." The last line of the anecdote indicates that the suppressed meaning of the word is different from its accepted signification; thus, the suppressed meaning must be something other than, "all those except parent and child" or "one who leaves neither parent nor child." It has already been suggested, on the basis of an examination of a previous anecdote, that the word *kalāla* is somehow related or of concern to women.

On the symbolic level, the preceding anecdote reaches a dra-

27. Ibid., pp. 18–19.

28. Ṭabarī, *Jāmiʿ*, 6:43 (ll. 14–18); see also ʿAbd al-Razzāq, *Muṣannaf*, 10: 301–02 (no. 19183).

matic climax when the dying caliph calls for the document and erases it: *Ḥattā idhā ṭuʿina daʿā bi'l-kitāb fa-maḥā.* The word *kitāb* here simply refers to a specific document. *Al-kitāb*, on the other hand, is another designation for the Qur'an. The reference to *al-kitāb*, like the reference to the *katif*, may indicate that the real problem is to be found not in the document destroyed by ʿUmar but in the Qur'an itself.

Let us consider one final anecdote:

> Muhammad b. Bashshār informed us saying: Ibn Abī ʿAdī informed us, on the authority of Saʿīd, on the authority of Qatāda, on the authority of Sālim b. Abī al-Jaʿd, on the authority of Maʿdān b. Abī Ṭalḥa, that ʿUmar b. al-Khaṭṭāb preached to the people on Friday, and he said: "By God, I will not leave after me anything which is of greater concern to me than the matter of *al-kalāla*. I asked the Messenger of God about it. He did not become as cross with me about anything as he did about [this matter], until he jabbed me in the throat and said: 'Let the summer verse which was revealed at the end of *Sūrat al-Nisā'* be sufficient for you.' And if I live I will issue a decree about it so that no one who recites the Qur'an (*qara'a 'l-qur'ān*) will disagree about it."[29]

The preceding anecdote, which repeats elements of several that have already been discussed, contains the final and perhaps the most important clue that makes it possible to postulate an alternative interpretation of Q. 4:12b and 4:176. In the final line of the anecdote, ʿUmar states: "And if I live I shall issue a decree so that no one who recites the Qur'an will disagree about it." Unfortunately, ʿUmar did not live long enough to carry out his promise, for he was assassinated on the Wednesday following this sermon. Once again, the creator of the anecdote knew that ʿUmar would not issue the promised decree, a fact which he turns to his advantage by making ʿUmar refer to disagreement among Qur'an reciters as to the proper manner in which to recite the verse in which the word *kalāla* occurs. In all likelihood, reference is being made to Q. 4:12b, which, as we have seen, is extremely equivocal. Ṭabarī indicates one possible variant reading, but insists that it has no effect whatsoever on the general meaning of the verse. Is there an alternative reading, overlooked or possibly even suppressed, that somehow transforms the accepted interpretation of Q. 4:12b?

Before turning to a consideration of this possibility, it may be

29. Ṭabarī, *Jāmiʿ*, 6:44 (ll. 11–17).

useful to summarize briefly the clues elicited from the preceding anecdotes. These anecdotes attest to considerable confusion and uncertainty among the Companions of the Prophet as to the meaning of Q. 4:12b and 4:176. This confusion centered upon the word *kalāla*, the meaning of which was unknown as late as the caliphate of ʿUmar. One anecdote hints that the word is somehow related to or of concern to women. There seems to have been disagreement among the Qur'an reciters as to the proper manner in which to recite Q. 4:12b. And several anecdotes suggest that Q. 4:176 will be seen to answer a question raised by Q. 4:12b once these two verses are understood as they were by Muhammad himself.

An Alternative Interpretation

We begin with the reading of Q. 4:12b. Simple examination of the consonantal text of the verse suggests an alternative vocalization, one that Muslim scholars have never considered. The consonantal text is written as follows:

وان كان رجل يورث كلالة او امراة و له اخ او اخت فلكل واحد

منهما السدس، فان كانوا اكثر من ذلك فهم شركاء في الثلث من بعد

وصية يوصي بها او دين غير مضار وصية من الله والله عليم حليم

An Arabist unfamiliar with the traditional reading of the verse, and approaching the text for the first time, might reason as follows: The masculine singular noun *rajulun* is the subject of the third-person singular, form IV, active verb *yūrithu*. This verb takes not one but two objects in the accusative case, i.e., *kalālatan aw imra'atan*. The masculine singular pronoun in the prepositional phrase *wa-lahu* correctly refers back to the masculine singular noun *rajulun*. The dual pronoun in the prepositional phrase *minhumā* also correctly refers back to the compound subject *akhun aw ukhtun*. Finally, the noun *rajulun* in the opening line of the verse also governs the active verb *yūṣī* towards the end of the verse. Q. 4:12b may therefore be read in the following manner:

> Wa-in kāna rajulun YŪRITHU kalālatan aw IMRA'ATAN wa-lahu akhun aw ukhtun fa-li-kulli wāḥidin minhumā al-sudusu.

> Fa-in kānū akthara min dhālika fa-hum shurakā' fi'l-thuluthi min ba'di waṣiyyatin YŪṢĪ bihā aw daynin ghayra muḍārrin waṣiyyatan min allāhi. Wallāhu 'alīmun ḥalīmun. (Emphasis added.)

The proposed reading differs from the traditional one at three points that are indicated by the upper-case letters in the above transliteration: Instead of the *yūrathu/imra'atun/yūṣā* complex we find a *yūrithu/imra'atan/yūṣī* complex. The proposed vocalization is perfectly unobjectionable from the standpoint of syntax; indeed, it resolves at once all of the syntactic problems confronted by Ṭabarī: The bifurcated compound subject *rajulun . . . aw imra'atun* disappears; the word *kalāla* now occurs in the accusative case for the simple reason that it is the initial direct object of the transitive verb *yūrithu*; the pronoun in the prepositional phrase *wa-lahu* no longer refers back, awkwardly, to a compound subject; and the active verb *yūṣī* governed by the noun *rajulun* makes better sense than the impersonal passive *yūṣā*.

Consideration of the meaning of Q. 4:12b when read in the above manner may help to explain why Muslim scholars have overlooked the *yūrithu/imra'atan/yūṣī* complex. Before translating the verse into English it will be necessary to consider the definitions of three words: *yūrithu, imra'a,* and *kalāla*.

The verb *yūrithu* can be seen only as the active imperfect of the form-IV perfect verb *awratha*, derived from the root *w–r–th*. The form-I verb *waritha* signifies "to inherit, to be an heir." Therefore, the form-IV verb *awratha* ought to mean "to make someone inherit or be an heir," or "to designate someone as heir."[30]

The root *k–l–l* occurs in several Semitic languages besides Arabic, including Akkadian, Aramaic, Syriac, and Hebrew. In all four of these languages the word corresponding to the Arabic *kalāla* functions as a female kinship term. The Akkadian *kallātu*, which occurs in numerous legal inscriptions, refers to a young woman acquired by the master of a household as a wife for his son living in this household, hence a "daughter-in-law." Under certain circumstances the word also signifies a "sister-in-law."[31]

30. The fact that the word *awratha* does not bear this meaning in the technical vocabulary of Islamic law is directly related to the phenomenon being considered here.

31. *The Assyrian Dictionary*, ed. by A. L. Oppenheim (Chicago, 1971), 8 (K): 82.

The Aramaic and Syriac *kalltā* and the Hebrew *kallāh* refer to a "daughter-in-law" and also to a "bride."[32]

The strong resemblance between the words *kallātu*, *kalltā*, and *kallāh*, on the one hand, and *kalāla* on the other raises the interesting possibility that the Arabic term, the meaning of which was unclear to the Caliph ʿUmar, was originally a loan word from another Semitic language.[33] In that case, during the lifetime of Muhammad and for a short time after his death, the word *kalāla* may have functioned as a feminine kinship term whose semantic value embraced one or more of the concepts "bride," "daughter-in-law," and "sister-in-law."

We may test this assumption by examining the context in which the word *kalāla* occurs in early Arabic texts, so as to determine the appropriateness or lack thereof of the proposed definition. (For the sake of simplicity, the word will be translated as "female in-law" in the following discussion.) It will be remembered that Ṭabarī settled upon the definition "all those except parent and child" on the basis of the following statement attributed to Jābir b. ʿAbd Allāh: "O Messenger of God, none but *kalāla* will inherit from me. So what about the inheritance?" In fact, the context here does not make it possible to define the word *kalāla* with any degree of specificity. Certainly, the word, as it is used here, must refer to the heir rather than to the deceased himself. But the definition "female in-law" suits the context just as well as "all those except parent and child," if not better; indeed, the phrase "none but a female in-law will inherit from me" makes much better sense than the awkward circumlocution "none but all those except parent and child will inherit from me." Ṭabarī cites several more statements in which the word *kalāla* occurs; in each case, the definition "female in-law" makes better sense of the text than the vague expression "all those except parent and child."[34]

Two verses of poetry provide a more meaningful context in

32. *A Dictionary of the Targumim, the Talmud Babli and Yerushalmi, and the Midrashic Literature*, 1:639; *Aramäisch-Neuhebräisches Handwörterbuch*, p. 200; *A Compendious Syriac Dictionary*, p. 216.

33. It is generally accepted among Western scholars that the Arabic of the Qur'an contains numerous borrowings from Aramaic, Syriac, and Hebrew. See, for example, A. Jeffery, *The Foreign Vocabulary of the Qur'an*.

34. See Ṭabarī, *Jāmiʿ*, 4:284 (ll. 27–29) and 4:286 (ll. 24–26) for two more examples.

which to evaluate the semantic value of the word *kalāla*. Consider, for example, the following verse:

> You did not inherit the staff of kingship from a *kalāla*
> [But] from the two sons of Manāf, ʿAbd Shams and Hāshim.

This verse is often cited in support of the assertion that the word *kalāla* means "all those except parent and child." The verse is therefore understood as indicating that kingship is inherited from close relatives rather than from distant ones.[35] In reality, kingship may be inherited from any member of the family, including brothers, cousins, and uncles. The assumption that the word *kalāla* originally signified a female in-law may bring us closer to the meaning of this verse of poetry. It is not the degree of kinship that is at issue, but the very fact of kinship. A dynasty collapses when someone who is not a member of the ruling family assumes power.

Another verse of poetry illustrates the same point:

> A man's father affords him protection
> But the client of a *kalāla* is not roused to anger.

The lexicographer Ibn Manẓūr glosses this verse as follows: "He means that a man's father expresses anger on his behalf if he is treated unjustly, whereas the clients of *kalāla*, namely brothers, uncles, cousins, and other relatives, do not become as angry as a father."[36] Now, according to the principle of *ʿaṣabiyya* (group

35. Ibn Manẓūr, *Lisān*, 11:592.

36. Ibid., 11:593. I have recently come across a text that uses the word "*kalāla*" in a manner that can only signify a "daughter-in-law." *Kitāb al-Aghānī*, 9: 2300–04, preserves the story of a love affair between the poet, Qays b. Dharīḥ, and Lubnā bint al-Ḥubāb al-Ḳaʿbiyya. Qays fell in love with Lubnā and married her against the wishes of his parents, who wanted him to marry one of his paternal cousins. Umm Qays became jealous of Lubnā, claiming that Qays had become more responsive to his wife than to his mother. After Qays recovered from a near-fatal illness, his mother seized upon Lubnā's barrenness as a pretext to get rid of the woman, saying to her husband, "I was afraid that Qays would die without leaving descendents, for that woman (viz., Lubnā) is barren. You are a wealthy man, so that [if Qays had died] your property would have passed to *al-kalāla*. Therefore, marry him to another woman—perhaps God will provide him with children" (p. 2303). The context here requires that "*kalāla*" refer to Lubnā, Umm Qays's *daughter-in-law*. Further, "*kalāla*" here cannot refer to "one who dies leaving neither parent nor child," the preferred meaning of the term among Muslim lexicographers, because then the sentence becomes tautological. And it is unlikely that "*kalāla*" signifies "all those ex-

feeling) analyzed so brilliantly by Ibn Khaldūn, one can expect as much support from a brother as from a father. The difficulty is once again resolved if we assume that the word *kalāla* was used in this verse in the sense of a female in-law, in which case the verse would indicate that one can expect greater support from one's father and, by extension, from one's blood relatives, than from the clients of an in-law.

Although there can be no neat or elegant solution to the type of historical reconstruction that is being attempted here,[37] a significant body of evidence supports the assumption that the word *kalāla* was originally a kinship term referring to a female in-law. Perhaps the strongest support for this assumption is to be found in Q. 4:12b itself. According to the proposed reading, the words *kalāla* and *imra'a* are juxtaposed to one another. The latter term is commonly used in Arabic to signify a "wife."[38] It is therefore

---

cept the parent and child," i.e., cousins, etc., because Qays's parents had originally tried to get him to marry one of his cousins. (A full translation of the text is provided in appendix B.)

37. I am grateful to colleagues who have raised several cogent objections to the preceding analysis, three of which are especially noteworthy: (1) The Arabic language already had a term for "daughter-in-law" and "sister-in-law," the early use of which is attested to in several *ḥadīth*, namely *kannatun*. (2) Although *kalāla* shares the same root (*k-l-l*) as the Semitic words *kallātu*, *kalltā*, and *kallāh*, it exhibits a different morphological pattern than the others, i.e., *faʿāla*. If we are, in fact, dealing with a loan word, one would have expected an Arabic term **kalla* instead of *kalāla*. (3) Finally, the *faʿāla* pattern itself is normally used in Arabic as an infinitive, denoting a state of being, e.g., *ḥaḍāra* ("the state of being settled"). See W. Wright, *A Grammar of the Arabic Language*, 1:113. The pattern is not normally used to indicate a substantive.

To these objections I would respond as follows: (1) The existence of two words for the same concept is not unusual. The Qur'an contains many synonyms, e.g., *ab* and *wālid* ("father"). Furthermore, modern lexicographers have suggested that the word *kanna* itself is ultimately derived from the Akkadian *kallātu* and the Aramaic *kalltā*. See *Wörterbuch der klassischen arabischen Sprache*, ed. by M. Ullmann, 1:372–73. (2) The original Semitic morphology may have been corrupted during the course of linguistic transmission. A hybrid *kalāla* may have served the interests of interdialectical distinctiveness better than a hypothetical **kalla*. (3) The vagaries of linguistic transmission may therefore account for the unexpected morphological pattern. Even if they do not, the objection to the use of a *faʿāla* pattern to signify a substantive should be addressed not only to the proposed definition of *kalāla*, but also to the accepted one. According to the Arabic lexicographers the word means "one who leaves neither parent nor child," "all those except parent and child," "a distant paternal cousin," or "a distant relative," all of which are substantives. (See Ibn Manẓūr, *Lisān*, 11:592–94). Thus, anyone who rejects the proposed definition on these grounds must also reject the accepted definition of the term.

38. E. Lane, *An Arabic-English Lexicon*, pt. 7, pp. 2702–03.

possible to translate the phrase *kalālatan aw imra'atan* as "a daughter-in-law or wife," i.e., a man's own wife or his son's wife.

It follows from the preceding discussion that Q. 4:12b, when read in the proposed manner, signifies:

> If a man designates a daughter-in-law or wife as heir, and he has a brother or sister, each one of them is entitled to one-sixth. If they are more than that, they are partners with respect to one-third, after any legacy he bequeaths or debt, without injury. A commandment from God. God is knowing, forbearing.

The proposed reading radically transforms the meaning of Q. 4:12b as compared with the traditional understanding of that verse. Q. 4:12b now refers not only to the award of a fractional share of the estate to siblings, but also to the designation of a daughter-in-law (*kalāla*) or wife as heir! In order to ascertain the primary objective of this legislation, it will be useful to work through the dynamics of the hypothetical situation described in the verse.

Suppose that a man writes a last will and testament in which he designates his wife to be his heir. And suppose further that at the time of his death he leaves his wife and two siblings, a brother and a sister. Each sibling receives one-sixth of the estate, as is specifically stated. The remaining two-thirds of the estate is presumably inherited by the wife. Had there been three or more siblings, in addition to the wife, the estate would have been divided in much the same manner: The siblings divide one-third of the estate among themselves on a *per capita* basis; the ceiling of one-third placed upon their entitlement insures that the wife will inherit a minimum of two-thirds of the estate. The outcome would be exactly the same if the man had designated his son's wife as his heir.

Both persons who are considered as potential testamentary heirs are related to the deceased by ties of marriage, whereas the siblings who are awarded a small fractional share of the estate are related to him by ties of blood. The failure of Q. 4:12b to mention the existence of either parents or children suggests that the siblings are the closest surviving relatives of the deceased. In other words, the verse implicitly assumes that the deceased leaves neither parent nor child.[39]

39. The initial obscurity of Q. 4:12b following the adoption of the *yūrathu/imra'atun/yūṣā* complex was resolved by transforming the implicit assump-

Why do the siblings receive a fractional share of the estate, no matter how small, even though the deceased indicated his desire that someone else, namely the daughter-in-law or wife, be his testamentary heir? Should not the designated heir inherit the entire estate? This may have been the very question that arose in the minds of Muhammad's companions, prompting one or more of them to approach him, seeking clarification of the issue. After learning of their concern, Muhammad received a revelation containing an answer to their inquiry: Q. 4:176.

It has already been suggested that Q. 4:176 will be seen to answer a question raised by Q. 4:12b when the latter verse is understood as it was by Muhammad himself. How then does Q. 4:176 explain why the siblings in Q. 4:12b receive a fractional share of the estate even though someone else has been designated as heir? I propose the following explanation of the relationship between these two verses: In Q. 4:12b the siblings are the testator's closest surviving blood relatives; the designated heir, whether she be a daughter-in-law or wife, is not related to the testator at all. In the absence of a will, the siblings of 4:12b would have inherited the entire estate (or the bulk of it if they were only females) according to the rules enumerated in Q. 4:176 (see appendix A). Thus, Q. 4:12b may award the siblings a small fractional share of the estate as compensation for their having been disinherited. The intent of the award seems to have been to prevent a testator from ruthlessly excluding from his will his closest surviving relatives, for whom he is obliged to provide. Persons disinherited in this manner have a legal claim against the estate for up to one-third of its total value. The law seeks to strike a balance between the personal wishes of the deceased and the needs of his immediate family.[40]

According to the proposed alternative explanation of the meaning of Q. 4:12b and 4:176, it is not the quality of siblings that changes from the first verse to the next, as is generally believed,

tion of the verse into the explicit definition of the word *kalāla*, which accordingly came to signify either "one who leaves neither parent nor child" or "all those except parent and child."

40. The share awarded to disinherited siblings in Q. 4:12b should be compared with the *actio ad supplendam legitimam*, a reform of the Roman law of inheritance instituted by Justinian less than a century before the revelation of the Qur'an. For an English translation of this reform, see William G. Hammond, *An Introduction to Sandar's Institutes of Justinian*, pp. 285–86.

but the circumstances in which a particular set of siblings find themselves. The former verse compensates disinherited siblings by awarding them a small fractional share of the estate; the latter justifies this award by delineating the inheritance rights of siblings upon intestacy. In both cases, reference is presumably being made to consanguine/germane siblings. The proposed explanation therefore disposes of the need to invoke the distinction between uterine and consanguine/germane siblings, by means of which Muslim scholars explain away the apparent contradiction between the two verses when Q. 4:12b is read in the traditional manner. The adoption of the *yūrithu/imra'atan/yūṣī* complex restores the natural relationship between the two verses.

Thus, each of the clues elicited from the anecdotes has made a significant contribution to the proposed alternative explanation of Q. 4:12b and 4:176: It is not the abortive speech by ʿUmar in which he holds a shoulder blade (*katif*) aloft, nor the document (*kitāb*) that he destroyed on his deathbed, but the reading and understanding of the Qur'anic text itself that is at issue. There is a significant reason why there should have been a dispute among the Qur'an reciters as to the proper manner in which to recite Q. 4:12b, and it is conceivable that the dispute involved two groups: Those who adhered to the *yūrithu/imra'atan/yūṣī* complex, and those who favored the *yūrathu/imra'atun/yūṣā* complex. The indication by ʿUmar that once the significance of the word *kalāla* became known women would "discuss it in their private quarters" may be related to the suggestion that the word was originally a female kinship term, and that Q. 4:12b referred to the designation of a daughter-in-law or wife as heir. Finally, Muhammad's response to ʿUmar's repeated inquiries about *al-kalāla* ("Let Q. 4:176 be sufficient for you") reveals itself as a clear and straightforward answer to the question, "Why do the siblings in Q. 4:12b receive a fractional share of the estate even though someone else has been designated as the heir?"

We began this chapter by examining the semantic and syntactic difficulties inherent in the opening line of Q. 4:12b when that verse is read and understood in the traditional manner. Next, we introduced a series of anecdotes that attest to significant early confusion regarding the meaning of Q. 4:12b and 4:176. These anecdotes contain several clues that suggest an alternative reading of Q. 4:12b as well as an alternative explanation of the meaning of that verse and its relationship to Q. 4:176. My conviction that the alternative reading/explanation reflects the original significance of these two verses is based upon three primary considerations.

The first consideration is the consonantal text of the Qur'an itself; the arguments are largely grammatical and linguistic. The *yūrithu/imra'atan/yūṣī* complex constitutes a simpler, less strained reading of Q. 4:12b than the traditional reading. The proposed alternative definition of the word *kalāla* facilitates the understanding, not only of Q. 4:12b and 4:176, but also of several other early texts in which the word occurs. Finally, the apparent contradiction between the explicit wording of Q. 4:12b and 4:176, when viewed in the traditional manner, is seen to be a secondary effect of the abandonment of the original reading of Q. 4:12b and the subsequent reinterpretation of the verse.

The second consideration is the existence of a forgotten counter-tradition; the arguments are historical. The anecdotes indicate that during the first century after the death of Muhammad, discussion of Q. 4:12b and 4:176 was considerably more open than it would become shortly thereafter. The anecdotes attest to considerable confusion and uncertainty among prominent early Muslims with regard to the proper recitation of Q. 4:12b, the meaning of the word *kalāla*, and the nature of the relationship between Q. 4:12b and 4:176. The fate of this counter-tradition is mirrored in the anecdotes themselves; like the document destroyed by ʿUmar on his deathbed, the anecdotes soon lost all meaning and passed into virtual oblivion.

Faced with two mutually exclusive interpretations of the meaning of Q. 4:12b and 4:176, Muslim scholars settled upon what would become the only accepted interpretation of these two verses. The force of consensus increased with the passage of time. The process whereby early uncertainty and confusion were downplayed and converted into an image of certain knowledge is neatly encapsulated in the following statement by the fourteenth-century commentator, Ibn Kathīr:

> *Al-kalāla* is derived from *al-iklīl* (crown), i.e., that which encloses the head from the sides. The intention here is those who inherit from him indirectly, not from above or below, as al-Shaʿbī related, on the authority of Abū Bakr al-Ṣiddīq, that he was asked about *al-kalāla* and he replied: "I have my own personal opinion (*ra'y*) on this matter. If it is correct then it is from God; if it is

mistaken then it is from Satan and neither God nor his Messenger is responsible. *Al-kalāla* [signifies] he who has neither parent nor child."

When ʿUmar became Caliph he said: "God forbid that I should go against an opinion held by Abū Bakr." Ibn Jarīr and others reported the same.

Ibn Abī Ḥātim said in his commentary: Muhammad b. [ʿAbd Allāh] b. Yazīd told us, on the authority of Sufyān, on the authority of Sulaymān al-Aḥwal, on the authority of Ṭā'ūs, who said: I heard Ibn ʿAbbās say: I was the last person to visit ʿUmar and I heard him say: "What did I say?" and "What did I say?" and "What did I say?". He said: "*Al-kalāla* is he who has neither parent nor child."

The same opinion was espoused by ʿAlī and Ibn Masʿūd, and it was judged correct on the authority of more than one, on the authority of Ibn ʿAbbās and Zayd b. Thābit. And this opinion is held by al-Shaʿbī, al-Nakhaʿī, al-Ḥasan, Qatāda, Jābir b. Zayd, and al-Ḥakam. It is held by the Medinans, Kufans, and Basrans. It is the opinion of the seven *fuqahā'*, the four *imām*s, and the majority of the ancients (*wa'l-khalaf*)—indeed all of them—and more than one has attributed consensus to it.

There is one report that is traced back to the prophet (*marfūʿ*): Abū al-Ḥusayn b. al-Labbān, reporting on the authority of Ibn ʿAbbās, held against [the above], saying that it signifies "he who has no child." The first [definition] is the correct one; perhaps the transmitter did not understand what he meant.[41]

There is no mention here of the counter-traditions discussed above. The "correct" definition of the word *kalāla* was put into the mouth of the first Caliph, Abū Bakr, in the form of a personal opinion. This opinion was confirmed by ʿUmar, presumably on the ground that Abū Bakr, as one of Muhammad's closest associates, was trustworthy. Despite the indication that ʿUmar himself remained uncertain of the meaning of the word until he died, the "correct" definition was circulated by numerous Companions, including ʿAlī, and by many Successors, several of whom appeared in the *isnād*s of our anecdotes. The "correct" definition circulated throughout the Islamic world, where it was virtually uncontested.

As this consensus became increasingly consolidated, the significance of the anecdotes discussed here declined. Given the certainty, correctness and authority of the arguments supporting the accepted interpretation, the anecdotes lost their original sig-

41. Ibn Kathīr, *Tafsīr al-qur'ān al-karīm*, 1:460.

nificance. It is perhaps not surprising that many commentators after Ṭabarī fail to mention them. When they are cited, it is suggested that ʿUmar's confusion resolved itself into the "correct" definition of the word *kalāla*.[42]

The third consideration is the control exercised by Muslim scholars over the proper recitation of the Qur'an. Once the traditional interpretation of Q. 4:12b and 4:176 had been hammered out on the basis of the doctrine of consensus, the very existence of the *yūrithu/imra'atan/yūṣī* complex was neglected, and eventually forgotten. To be more exact, the readings *yūṣī* and *yūrithu* were allowed to circulate, but in such a manner that they posed no threat to the accepted interpretation of the two verses. The history of the three words in the complex may be summarized as follows: (1) The *yūṣī* reading, which is trivial so far as the meaning of Q. 4:12b is concerned, was allowed to circulate freely as a canonical variant. It is routinely mentioned in most Qur'an commentaries, and is faithfully cited in the standard collections of the seven canonical variants.[43] (2) The *yūrithu* reading could also be brought into harmony with the traditional interpretation of Q. 4:12b, provided that the original meaning of the word *kalāla* remained unknown, and that the transitivity of the verb was not allowed to carry over to the word *imra'a*. It was therefore allowed to circulate, but only as a relatively unimportant, noncanonical variant; furthermore, no citation illustrating this variant ever extends beyond the word *kalāla*.[44] (3) Finally, the *imra'atan* reading could not possibly be reconciled with the traditional interpretation of Q. 4:12b. The designation of a wife as one's heir is inconceivable within the framework of the Is-

42. Zamakhsharī, *Kashshāf*, 1:485–87 and 598–99; Ṭabarsī, *Majmaʿ al-bayān li-ʿulūm al-qur'ān*, 3:30–42 and 3:294–98; Bayḍāwī, *Anwār al-tanzīl wa-asrār al-ta'wīl*, 1:199, 244; Nīsābūrī, *Gharā'ib*, 4:187–201 and 6:25–27; Ibn Juzayy, *al-Tashīl li-ʿulūm al-tanzīl*, 1:234–38, 297; al-Maḥallī and al-Suyūṭī, *Tafsīr*, pp. 83, 107; Nasafī, *Tafsīr*, 1:206–10 and 1:265–66; Qurṭubī, *al-Jāmiʿ li-aḥkām al-qur'ān*, 5:54–81 and 6:28–29; Alūsī, *Rūḥ al-maʿānī*, 4:349–54 and 6:61–72; Ṭabāṭabā'ī, *al-Mīzān fī tafsīr al-qur'ān*, 4:205–33 and 5:153–56.

43. Ibn Mujāhid, *Kitāb*, p. 228; Ibn Khālawayh, *al-Ḥujja fi'l-qirā'āt al-sabʿ*, p. 96; Dānī, *al-Taysīr fi'l-qirā'āt al-sabʿ*, p. 94; Qāḍī, *Sharḥ al-naẓm al-jāmiʿ li-qirā'āt al-imām Nāfiʿ*, p. 130; Muḥaysin, *al-Irshādāt al-jaliyya fi'l-qirā'āt al-sabʿ*, p. 102; Zamakhsharī, 1:486; Nīsābūrī, *Gharā'ib*, 4:189.

44. Ibn al-Anbārī, *al-Bayān fī gharīb al-qur'ān*, 1:245; Ibn Khālawayh, *Mukhtaṣar fī shawādhdh al-qur'ān*, p. 25; Ibn Jinnī, *al-Muḥtasib*, 1:182; Zamakhsharī, 1:485; Ṭabarsī, 3:36; Bayḍāwī, 1:199; Qurṭubī, 5:77; Ṭabāṭabā'ī, 4:212.

lamic law of inheritance, which imposes compulsory rules for the division of property. Therefore, the *imra'atan* reading was totally suppressed; to the best of my knowledge, no scholar, Sunnī or Shīʿī, Muslim or non-Muslim, has ever considered even the *possibility* of such a reading.[45]

It seems that the only way to preserve the integrity of the accepted interpretation of Q. 4:12b and 4:176 was to ignore the very existence of a problem. One searches the sources in vain for even a single reference to the *yūrithu/imra'atan/yūṣī* complex. Examination of the commentaries and the collections of canonical and noncanonical variants yields only two of the three readings. By ignoring the entire complex, and especially by not teaching the *imra'atan* reading, Muslim scholars have been able to avoid confronting the possibility that the original significance of Q. 4:12b was radically transformed by means of the imposition of a secondary reading of three words in that verse.[46]

I have attempted to demonstrate that it is possible to view Q. 4:12b in such a manner that it explicitly refers to a man's right to designate an heir. Although there may be objections to the proposed reading of that verse—and I anticipate that there will be—it cannot be denied that the Islamic sources bear witness, both positively and negatively, to the existence of a problem. Others may suggest a different interpretation of the verse, or another explanation of the significance of the anecdotes, but we may no longer continue to ignore the fact that a problem exists.

45. The postulated suppression of the *imra'atan* reading supports A. Jeffery's assertion of over forty years ago that "when we have assembled all the variants from these earlier Codices that can be gleaned from the works of the exegetes and philologers, we have only such readings as were useful for the purposes of *Tafsīr* and were considered to be sufficiently near orthodoxy to be allowed to survive." (*Materials for the History of the Text of the Qur'an*, p. 10.) For a convenient summary of the current state of our knowledge of Qur'an readings see R. Paret, "*Qirā'a*," in *EI*², 5:127–29.

46. The significance of the disregard for the *yūrithu/imra'atan/yūṣī* complex may be illustrated by the results of a simple experiment. I presented the consonantal text of Q. 4:12b to approximately twenty accomplished Arabists and, without indicating the nature of my interest, asked each one to read and translate the text. All but one produced the *yūrithu/imra'atan/yūṣī* complex, and none knew the meaning of the word *kalāla*. The fact that the first thought that comes to the mind of a disinterested party has never been considered by Muslim scholars is indicative of the extent of the threat that the proposed reading poses to the integrity of Islamic doctrine.

The One-Third Restriction: *al-waṣiyya fi'l-thulth*

My reinterpretation of Q. 4:12b prompts a reconsideration of the overall structure of the system of inheritance introduced by Muhammad. The relationship between the voluntary and compulsory aspects of the "science of the shares" is traditionally defined by the maxim, *al-waṣiyya fi'l-thulth* (a bequest may not exceed one-third), which was reportedly established when Muhammad told Saᶜd b. Abī Waqqāṣ that he might bequeath no more than one-third of his estate to legatees.[47] Muslim legists have interpreted the prophetic dictum as an effort to balance the entitlement of the compulsory heirs (minimum of two-thirds), on the one hand, and legatees (maximum of one-third), on the other. I maintain, however, that the phrase refers, not to the relative entitlement of compulsory heirs and legatees, but to that of the testamentary heir and legatees (the former being the primary heir, the latter secondary heirs). Although there is no clue of any of this in the report traditionally cited by the legists, I find an interesting detail in a variant version in which Saᶜd, wanting to know how much he could bequeath to legatees, consults Muhammad, *first making it clear that he is going to designate a testamentary heir* ("O Apostle of God, I have wealth and I am going to designate a female in-law as the testamentary heir [*ūrithu kalālatan*]"). Muhammad seems unruffled and tells Saᶜd that he may bequeath up to one-third of his estate to legatees.[48] Clearly, designating an heir was a common practice. If, as I have argued elsewhere, this was the earliest version of the report in question,[49] and if one accepts my reinterpretation of Q. 4:12b, it follows that the one-third restriction was originally introduced in order to strike a balance between the entitlement of the *testa-*

47. See introduction, note 35. R. M. Speight has collected and analyzed the numerous variant versions of this report in his "The Will of Saᶜd b. a. Waqqāṣ: The Growth of a Tradition." The authenticity of the report containing the one-third restriction became the subject of an exchange between Joseph Schacht and Noel J. Coulson. See Coulson, *A History of Islamic Law*, pp. 65–69; Schacht, "Modernism and Traditionalism in a History of Islamic Law," pp. 388–400; and Coulson, "Correspondence," pp. 195–203.

48. Ibn Ḥanbal, *Musnad* (Cairo), 4:60. See also Ibn Saᶜd, *al-Ṭabaqāt al-kubrā*, 3:146 (ll. 3–13); Ibn Shuᶜbah, *Kitāb al-sunan*, vol. 3, pt. 1, pp. 87–88 (nos. 331, 335).

49. See David S. Powers, "The Will of Saᶜd b. Abī Waqqāṣ: A Reassessment."

mentary heir (minimum of two-thirds), on the one-hand, and legatees (maximum of one-third), on the other.

The Bequest Verses

The proposed reinterpretation of Q. 4:12b also suggests that we reconsider the original relationship between Q. 2:180 and 2:240 ("the bequest verses") and 4:11–12 ("the inheritance verses"). Although this subject will be dealt with fully in chapter 5, it may be useful at this point to anticipate the results of the argument to be presented in that chapter, insofar as they bear on the overall structure of the proto-Islamic law of testate succession.

The bequest verses (see appendix A), which were reportedly revealed "at the beginning of Islam,"[50] encourage the person anticipating death to make provisions in his last will and testament for parents, relatives, and wives. But the testamentary freedom reflected in Q. 2:180 and 2:240 came to an abrupt end in the year 3/625 when God revealed Q. 4:11–12, which award specific fractional shares of the estate, *inter alia*, to parents and wives.[51] Muslim scholars, who had come to view these fractional shares as compulsory rules, saw an apparent overlap or contradiction between the two sets of verses; if one is entitled to both a fractional share and a bequest, then a parent or wife might receive a bequest of up to one-third of the estate in addition to the fractional shares mentioned in Q. 4:11–12.[52] It was in order to avoid this possibility that the jurists began to teach, beginning ca. A.D. 650, that the inheritance verses had superseded or abrogated (*nasakha*) the bequest verses,[53] a position that has been accepted by the overwhelming majority of Muslim scholars throughout the centuries.[54]

But the apparent contradiction between the two sets of verses disappears once we make the assumption of a clear-cut distinction between testate succession and intestacy. And just such a

50. Zamakhsharī, 1:289. For additional references, see introduction, note 31.

51. Zamakhsharī, 1:476–77.

52. Shāfiʿī, *Risāla*, p. 69, pars. 396–97; Khadduri, *Islamic Jurisprudence*, p. 141, par. 128.

53. Ṭabarī, *Jāmiʿ*, 2:116–19 (Q. 2:180) and 2:579–82 (Q. 2:240).

54. E.g., Ibn Kathīr, 1:211.

distinction is made by the proto-Islamic law of testate succession, the general outlines of which, as reconstructed on the preceding pages, may be characterized as follows: The testator was free to determine whom his heir(s) would be and to specify the property that the heir(s) would inherit; although the testator had the power to disinherit close blood-relatives, the latter might claim a small fractional share of the estate as compensation for the disherison (Q. 4:12b). The testator was also free to leave bequests for parents, relatives, and wives (Q. 2:180 and 2:240); indeed, he was encouraged to do so provided that the bequests did not exceed one-third of the estate's net value (*al-waṣiyya fi'l-thulth*). Only in the absence of a will did the fractional shares mentioned in the inheritance verses, that is to say, the rules of intestacy, properly speaking, take effect.[55]

The distinction between testate succession and intestacy disappeared during the years immediately following the death of Muhammad when, in connection with political, social, and economic factors to be discussed in chapter 4, the proto-Islamic law of inheritance was transformed into the *ʿilm al-farāʾiḍ*. The probable starting point of this transformation was the elimination, in Q. 4:12b, of the reference to the possibility of designating an heir. Concomitantly, the fractional shares mentioned in the inheritance verses came to be understood, not as rules of intestacy, but as compulsory rules to be applied at all times. These two changes created the apparent contradiction between the bequest and inheritance verses, and Muslim authorities resolved the contradiction, beginning no earlier than the middle of the first/seventh century, by invoking the doctrine of abrogation. The abrogation of these verses, then, was not the result of any change in the divine will, but of changed perceptions of the meaning of the divine word.[56]

55. The proto-Islamic law of intestacy will be dealt with at greater length in chap. 3.

56. For a systematic discussion of the abrogation of Q. 2:180 and 2:240, see chap. 5.

2

Husbands and Wives as Heirs in Early Islam

The Qur'an treats the rules of inheritance at greater length and in greater detail than it does perhaps any other area of the law. *Sūra*s two, four, and five of the Qur'an contain ten verses, often very long and complex, dealing directly with this subject.[1] The commentators tell us that the purpose of this legislation was to improve the status of women, whom the tribal customary law of pre-Islamic Arabia had deprived of the right to inherit: "The people of the *jāhiliyya* (age of ignorance) used to distribute the inheritance to males, to the exclusion of females."[2] According to the Islamic sources, the elevation of women to the status of full heirs took place in several stages: Prior to Islam, it was the custom of the Arabs "not to award any part of the inheritance to women and children. They used to say, 'Only those who fight and protect property are entitled to inherit.'"[3] Then, "at the beginning of Islam,"[4] God revealed Q. 2:180 and 2:240, which encourage men to leave legacies for, *inter alia*, mothers and wives. Next, in A.D. 624, a woman named Umm Kuḥḥa allegedly approached the Prophet and complained that her deceased husband's two paternal cousins had seized his estate and refused to give any part of it to her or her three daughters. Muhammad told

1. Q. 2:180–82, 2:240, 4:8, 4:11–12, 4:176, 5:106–107.

2. Ṭabarī, *Jāmiʿ al-bayān*, 4:262. See also Zamakhsharī, *Kashshāf*, 1:476; Ṭabarsī, *Majmaʿ al-bayān*, 3:24; Rāzī, *al-Tafsīr al-kabīr*, 9:194; Qurṭubī, *al-Jāmiʿ li-aḥkām al-qur'ān*, 5:46; Bayḍāwī, *Anwār al-tanzīl*, 1:196.

3. Bayḍāwī, 1:196. See also Ṭabarī, 4:262; Zamakhsharī, 1:476; Ṭabarsī, 3:24; Rāzī, 9:194; Qurṭubī, 5:46; Nasafī, *Tafsīr*, 1:205–06; Nīsābūrī, *Gharā'ib al-qur'ān*, 4:182–83; Ibn Kathīr, *Tafsīr al-qur'ān*, 1:454–55.

4. Zamakhsharī, 1:289; Bayḍāwī, 1:100–101; Nasafī, 1:88.

the woman to withdraw "so that he might see what God would introduce." Then, we are told, God revealed Q. 4:8, which establishes that both men and women are entitled to inherit. But this verse still does not specify the exact entitlement of females, and soon thereafter God revealed Q. 4:11–12, which award specific shares of the estate to daughters, mothers, sisters, and wives.[5]

This representation, accepted uncritically by French Orientalists writing at the turn of the century, served as the basis for their contention that the Qur'anic inheritance legislation was "superimposed" on the tribal customary law of pre-Islamic Arabia, and that these two heterogeneous elements were fused together to form the *ʿilm al-farāʾiḍ*.[6] The "superimposition theory" was subsequently adopted by most western legal historians.[7]

But the historical accuracy of this representation is highly suspect. It is based on anecdotes belonging to the genre of literature known as *asbāb al-nuzūl* which, as a recent study has argued, preserve little, if any, genuine historical information.[8] Furthermore, the idealized picture presented by the sources glosses over the socioeconomic complexity of the Hijaz, such as the distinction between nomads and sedentary peoples,[9] and is difficult to reconcile with some widely accepted facts of pre-Islamic history.[10] Finally, the failure of the traditional representation to ac-

5. For source references, see notes 2 and 3 above.

6. See Marçais, *Des parents et alliés successibles en droit musulman*, and Bousquet and Peltier, *Les successions agnatiques mitigées*, pp. 97–108. For a detailed critique of the superimposition theory see chap. 3.

7. See, for example, Joseph Schacht, "*Mīrāth*," *EI*[1] and Coulson, *Succession in the Muslim Family*, pp. 29–30.

8. In "The Quranic *Asbāb al-Nuzūl* Material: An Analysis of its Use and Development in Exegesis," Andrew L. Rippin demonstrates that the primary aim of the *asbāb* reports was to create an edifying narrative context for the interpretation of a given Qur'anic verse. This genre of literature will be discussed in greater detail in chap. 6.

9. Although it may be true that certain women in pre-Islamic Arabia did not inherit, this was not necessarily the case with all women. The *jāhiliyya*–Islam dichotomy invoked by the commentators should be taken not as an accurate statement of socioeconomic conditions in the Hijaz on the eve of Islam but as an ideologically inspired statement designed to contrast the backwardness of the *jāhiliyya* with the progressiveness of Islam. For an excellent discussion of this issue from the perspective of an anthropologist studying modern conditions, see Martha Mundy, "Women's Inheritance of Land in Highland Yemen," pp. 161–87.

10. Muhammad's first wife, Khadīja, for example, led an independent life as a rich widow engaged in the lucrative caravan trade, years before Muhammad re-

count for several early developments in the law of inheritance, one of which will be discussed below, casts further doubt on its historical accuracy.[11]

Perhaps the most questionable feature of the traditional account concerns the status of wives as heirs. The commentators tell us that prior to Islam, a widow formed part of her husband's estate and was herself subject to inheritance. This situation was reportedly put to an end by Q. 4:19 ("O believers, it is not lawful for you to inherit women against their will").[12] But, in addition to terminating her status as chattel, Q. 4:12a suddenly raises the widow to the level of a full legal heir, awarding her either one-fourth or one-eighth (the variation depending on whether or not there are any children) of her husband's estate. Now, I find it striking that a woman in seventh-century Arabia—whether living in a town or among the nomads, either before Islam or after—should inherit in her capacity as a wife. Of all the legal systems of the Near East, only Islamic law treats a wife as a legal heir upon intestacy. In ancient Babylonia, a wife did not inherit unless her husband expressly designated her as an heir in a last will and testament.[13] In Jewish law, the husband is heir to his wife, but the wife is not a legal heir to her husband, although she does enjoy a number of rights which afford her a share in her husband's estate and which ensure provision for her sustenance and essential needs until her death or remarriage.[14] In Egypt, the

ceived his first revelation. See *The Life of Muhammad*, tr. A. Guillaume, p. 82. W. Robertson Smith, in his *Kinship and Marriage in Early Arabia*, pp. 119–21, attempts to reconcile the apparent contradiction between Khadīja's wealth and the assertion that women could not inherit by suggesting that she may have acquired her property by means of either a gift *inter vivos* or a last will and testament. For another example of female wealth in pre-Islamic Arabia see Irfan Shahid, *The Martyrs of Najran: New Documents*, p. 57, where the female Christian martyr, Ruhayma, estimates her personal fortune at 40,000 *denarii*, not including precious jewels.

11. See chap. 6.

12. Ṭabarī, *Jāmiʿ*, 4:304–13; Zamakhsharī, 1:490–91; Ṭabarsī, 3:50–54; Qurṭubī, 5:94–98; Bayḍāwī, 1:201; Ibn Kathīr, 1:464–68. (Note, however, that in his *al-Ṭabaqāt al-kubrā*, 8:153, Ibn Saʿd mentions that Ḍibāʿa bint ʿĀmir inherited from her husband, Hawdha b. ʿAlī al-Ḥanafī, a pre-Islamic figure active in Persia [*fa-halaka ʿanhā fa-warathathu mālan kathīran*]. I am indebted to Patricia Crone for this reference.)

13. *The Ancient Near East: An Anthology of Texts and Pictures*, ed. J. B. Pritchard, pp. 138–67.

14. S. Shilo, "Succession," *Encyclopedia Judaica*.

principle was that a husband and wife inherit from their respective families, but not from each other.[15] The same principle was applied in Roman law and, probably, in the Syrian provinces of the Roman Empire.[16] Why is it that the Qur'anic legislation deviated from the prevailing sociolegal situation in the Near East, manifesting a more "progressive" attitude toward wives than any other indigenous legal system?

It is to this question that the present chapter is addressed. A close examination of several problematic aspects of the Qur'anic inheritance laws raises the possibility that the traditional understanding of Q. 4:12a, i.e., that a surviving spouse is a full legal heir with rights equal to those of the deceased's blood relatives, is not identical to the original significance of that verse. Rather, it is my contention that during the lifetime of Muhammad and perhaps for a short time after his death, inheritance upon intestacy was contingent upon blood relationship, so that a wife and husband did not, under normal circumstances, inherit from one another. The award in Q. 4:12a of a fractional share of the estate to a surviving spouse was meant, originally, to apply to an exceptional case. But, for reasons that remain to be determined, the Muslim community, in the years immediately following Muhammad's death, mistook the exceptional nature of the award so that it came to be taken as the norm. This conceptualization, I maintain, explains a wide range of historical data better than either the traditional Islamic account or the "superimposition theory." At the same time, I want to stress the tentative and provisional nature of my hypothesis, which, given the nature of the sources, cannot be proven conclusively.

Three Problems in the Islamic Law of Inheritance

I propose to begin by drawing the reader's attention to a curious phenomenon which, although generally recognized, has never, to my mind, been adequately explained. Apparent contradictions

15. P. W. Pestman, "The Law of Succession in Ancient Egypt," pp. 71–72.

16. Roman law: Barry Nicholas, *An Introduction to Roman Law*, pp. 87–89. Syro-Roman law: *Syrisch-römisches Rechtsbuch aus dem fünften Jahrhundert*, ed. Bruns and Sachau, p. 70.

in Q. 4:11–12, as traditionally understood, forced Muslim legists, when working out the details of the Islamic law of inheritance, to adopt a position which on at least three occasions deviates from the explicit wording of the Qur'an, and these discrepancies between the *fiqh* (law) and the Qur'an were the subject of considerable discussion among the scholars. I shall attempt to demonstrate that the apparent contradictions in the Qur'an result from an early shift in the understanding of Q. 4:12a, which awards a fractional share of the estate to a surviving spouse.

The ᶜUmariyyatān

Nonliteralist position. The first inheritance case that I propose to consider, the so-called *ᶜUmariyyatān* (two decisions of ᶜUmar), focuses upon the entitlement of a mother when the deceased, who is childless, leaves both parents. The Qur'an is quite explicit about the mother's entitlement in this circumstance: "If he does not have a child, and his parents are his heirs, then his mother is entitled to one-third." The father, here, inherits the remaining two-thirds of the estate as the closest surviving *ᶜāṣib*. The division of the estate between the father and mother in the proportion of two to one confirms the phrase that occurs at the outset of Q. 4:11, "a male is entitled to the share of two females."

The *fuqahā'* (legists) treat this last phrase, which they take as referring to males and females of the same class and degree of relationship to the deceased (e.g., son/daughter and father/mother), as an inviolable principle.[17] But the addition of a surviving husband or wife to the equation upsets the arithmetic. Suppose, for example, that a man dies, leaving his wife and both parents. The wife and mother inherit one-fourth and one-third of

17. Rāzī (9:213–14) states that "the principle of inheritance (*qāᶜidat al-mīrāth*) is that, when a male and female of the same class (*jins*) inherit together, the male is entitled to the share of two females." In support of this statement, he refers to the two instances in which the phrase "a male is entitled to the share of two females" occurs in the Qur'an (Q. 4:11a and 4:176), but fails to mention two cases in which the Qur'an awards males and females of the same class *equal* shares of the estate. For more on this alleged principle, see below, p. 65.

the estate, respectively, in their capacity as *ahl al-farā'iḍ*, and the father, it would seem, should inherit the remaining five-twelfths of the estate as the closest surviving *ʿāṣib*. Notice, however, that his share (five-twelfths) is not, in this case, twice as large as that of the mother (one-third). Clearly, the solution just outlined violates the "principle" that a male is entitled to twice the share of a female of the same class and degree of relationship to the deceased.

The alleged principle is also violated when a woman dies, leaving her husband and both parents. According to the Islamic law of inheritance, the husband and mother inherit one-half and one-third, respectively, in their capacity as "sharers," and the father inherits the remaining one-sixth as the closest surviving male agnate. However, the mother's share (one-third) is now twice as large as the father's (one-sixth), thereby turning on its head the principle that "a male is entitled to the share of two females."

The legal and historical sources do not indicate any awareness of these two problems within the Muslim community in the period between the revelation of the inheritance verses in A.D. 624 and the death of Muhammad eight years later. It is, instead, in the generation immediately following the Prophet's death that the problems seem to have presented themselves. Different Companions are reported to have proposed a solution to each problem. (Thus the appellation "*ʿUmariyyatān*," applied to these two problems by the later Islamic sources[18] and accepted by Coulson,[19] is actually a misnomer. Although ʿUmar's name is mentioned in connection with the case of a husband, father and mother, his name is never mentioned in connection with the other case.[20] However, inasmuch as no substantive issues are in-

18. See Ibn Qudāma, *Mughnī*, 6:237, where the author states that "these two cases are referred to as the *ʿUmariyyatān* because ʿUmar decided them in this manner, and he was followed in this by ʿUthmān, Zayd b. Thābit and Ibn Masʿūd." Note, however, that Ibn Rushd (*Bidāyat al-mujtahid wa-nihāyat al-muqtaṣid*, 2:371) refers to these two cases as *al-gharrāwayān* (the two marvels).

19. Coulson, *Succession*, p. 45. Schacht, on the other hand, refers to these two cases as *al-Gharībatān* (the two strange cases) in "*Mīrāth*," *EI*[1].

20. The only Companion whose name is mentioned in connection with both cases is Zayd b. Thābit, so that the designation *Zaydiyyatān* would be more correct than *ʿUmariyyatān*.

volved here, it will be convenient to refer to these two problems as the "*ʿUmariyyatān*.")

The following statement, attributed to Ibn Masʿūd (d. 653), suggests that in fact ʿUmar was the first person to propose a solution to the case of a man who dies, leaving a wife and both parents: "Whenever ʿUmar b. al-Khaṭṭāb cleared a path for us, and we followed it, we found it easy. He was asked about a wife and two parents and he said, '[Give] to the wife one-fourth, to the mother one-third *of what remains*, and to the father whatever is left'"[21] (emphasis added). ʿUmar's successful resolution of this case depends entirely on the phrase "of what remains," which does not occur in Q. 4:11, but is an interpolation proposed in an effort to harmonize the Qur'an and the *fiqh*. This solution preserves the Qur'anic principle that "a male is entitled to the share of two females" (the father inherits one-half of the estate and the mother one-fourth), but only at the expense of the explicit wording of another Qur'anic statement indicating that the mother is entitled to a full one-third of the estate.

Ibn Masʿūd subsequently spelled out the reasoning underlying ʿUmar's solution: If the wife were to receive one-fourth of the estate, and the mother one-third, then the father would inherit only five-twelfths. This would contradict the principle that "a male is entitled to the share of two females." Ibn Masʿūd's refusal to accept such a result compelled him to adopt the solution established earlier by ʿUmar: "God never saw me give preference to a mother over a father."[22] Ibn Masʿūd, ʿUmar, and Zayd b. Thābit (d. A.D. 666)—who is also reported to have adopted this solution[23]—seem not to have been bothered by the fact that, in direct violation of what the Qur'an specifies, the mother receives one-fourth of the estate instead of one-third.

The solution to the case in which a woman dies leaving her husband, mother and father is attributed, variously, to ʿAlī (d. A.D. 661), al-Ḥārith al-Aʿwar (d. A.D. 684), and Zayd b. Thā-

21. Ibn Shuʿbah, *Kitāb al-sunan*, vol. 3, pt. i, pp. 12–13 (nos. 6–8); Bayhaqī, *al-Sunan al-kubrā*, 6:228 (ll. 4–6).

22. Hans-Peter Raddatz, "Frühislamisches Erbrecht nach dem *Kitāb al-Farā'iḍ* der Sufyān at-Taurī," p. 37. See also Dhahabī, *Talkhīṣ al-Mustadrak*, 4:336 (l. 20); and Bayhaqī, 6:228, l. 24 (where the statement is attributed to Zayd b. Thābit).

23. Raddatz, p. 37; Bayhaqī, 6:228 (ll. 9–15).

bit.[24] Here, the husband takes one-half of the estate and the father and mother divide the remaining half in the proportion of two to one, so that the father takes one-third and the mother one-sixth. Again, the Qur'anic principle that "a male is entitled to the share of two females" is upheld at the expense of the explicit wording of the Qur'an, which states that the mother is entitled to one-third of the estate.

The solution embodied in the *ʿUmariyyatān* manages to salvage the Qur'anic principle that "a male is entitled to the share of two females," but only at the expense of the explicit wording of Q. 4:11b, which states, "If he does not have a child, and his parents are his heirs, then his mother is entitled to one-third." In the two cases that we have examined, the mother inherits first one-fourth of the estate, and then one-sixth. This discrepancy between the *fiqh* and the Qur'an was subsequently explained away by the legists. Mālik (d. A.D. 795), for example, indicated that the two cases in question constitute an exception to the general rule that a mother is entitled to one-third of the estate when the deceased leaves no children:

> If the deceased did not leave either a child, grandchild, or two or more brothers, then the mother is entitled to a full one-third, except in two cases (*illā fī farīḍatayn*): (1) If a man dies leaving his wife and both parents, then his wife is entitled to one-fourth, and his mother is entitled to one-third of what remains, i.e., one-fourth of the entire estate. (2) If a woman dies leaving her husband and both parents, then her husband is entitled to one-half, and her mother is entitled to one-third of what remains, i.e., one-sixth of the entire estate.[25]

Mālik concludes his discussion by quoting Q. 4:11b, which, as we have seen, states that the mother is entitled to one-third of the estate, but he passes over the discrepancy between the *fiqh* and the Qur'an with no further comment. He makes no attempt to explain why these two cases should constitute an exception to the general rule.

The task of explaining this phenomenon was taken up by the commentators. Zamakhsharī (d. A.D. 1144), whose discussion of

24. Ibn Shuʿbah, vol. 3, pt. i, pp. 13–14 (nos. 11–15, 17); Bayhaqī, 6:228 (ll. 11–16, 19–24); Ibn Rushd, 2:371; Ibn Qudāma, 6:237.

25. Mālik b. Anas, *Muwaṭṭa'*, 2:506. See also Ibn Shuʿbah, vol. 3, pt. i, p. 3 (no. 5b); Bayhaqī, 6:228 (ll. 9–15).

the *ʿUmariyyatān* exemplifies the efforts made to narrow the gap between the *fiqh* and the Qur'an, proposes the following explanatory gloss which has the effect of limiting the cases to which the Qur'anic award of one-third to mothers applies:

> It means, "If he does not have a child, and his parents are his only heirs then his mother is entitled to one-third." Because, if his parents, together with a husband or wife, are his heirs, then the mother is entitled to one-third of what remains after allocation of the spouse's share, not to one-third of what he leaves . . . The meaning [of the verse] is that the father and mother, when alone, divide the inheritance in the proportion of two shares for the male to one for the female.[26]

Zamakhsharī explains that the mother is entitled to the full one-third of the estate in the case in which the parents are the *only* surviving heirs of the deceased (*wa-warithahu abawāhu fa-ḥasbu*), but she is not entitled to this share when the deceased leaves a spouse. Surely Zamakhsharī's reasoning here is circular: he argues that the Qur'anic statement does not apply universally because there are two cases in which it cannot be satisfied; these two "exceptions" are then read back into the Qur'anic text by means of an explanatory gloss which explains hardly anything.

Some justification had to be provided for the claim that in these two exceptional cases the mother inherits one-third *of what remains* after the spouse receives his/her share, rather than one-third of the entire estate. Zamakhsharī addresses this problem in the following terms:

> There are two ways to interpret this:
>
> (1) The spouse is only entitled to his/her award by virtue of a contract, not [by virtue] of blood relationship. Therefore, with regard to the division of the estate after [the spouse has been awarded his/her share], it [viz., the division] resembles a bequest.
>
> (2) The father is stronger than the mother in [matters of] inheritance by virtue of the fact that he receives twice as much as she does when they are alone, in which case he inherits in the dual capacity of a "sharer" and a male agnate. But if she were given a full one-third, that would lead to the reduction of his share below hers. Obviously, if a woman dies leaving her husband and both parents, and the husband receives one-half, the mother one-third, and the father what remains, then the mother would take two shares and the father only one! Thus, the principle would be in-

26. Zamakhsharī, 1:483.

verted in such a way that the female would take the share of two males.[27]

Zamakhsharī, in his first point, draws a distinction between a spouse and a mother as heirs. Islamic law defines an "heir" as any person to whom the Qur'an awards a fractional share of the estate. But Zamakhsharī, here, ignores this definition and argues that the entitlement of the mother, who is a blood relation of the deceased, is somehow stronger than the entitlement of the spouse, who is not. He harmonizes the *fiqh* and Qur'an by likening the spouse's award (by definition, an inheritance) to a bequest (*fa-ashbaha 'l-waṣiyya*). It is a principle of Islamic law (which Zamakhsharī chooses to recognize) that heirs only inherit after debts have been paid and bequests distributed. Thus, if the surviving spouse is considered to be a legatee rather than an heir, it becomes clear why the mother takes one-third of what remains after the spouse has taken his/her share.[28] This explanation succeeds, however, only because Zamakhsharī insists on viewing the spouse in terms contrary to those defined by Islamic law.

Zamakhsharī bases his second point on the assumption that the Qur'anic phrase, "a male is entitled to the share of two females," constitutes an inviolable principle which must be applied to all males and females of the same class and degree of relationship to the deceased. As we shall soon see, this assumption is demonstrably false: the principle is not a principle.

Literalist position. The deviation from the explicit wording of the Qur'an in the *ʿUmariyyatān* did not pass unnoticed or unchallenged. The sources preserve a number of reports in which various Companions insist upon a literal interpretation of the Qur'an. ʿAlī is reported to have said, with regard to the case of a woman who died leaving her husband and both parents, that "the mother is entitled to one-third of the entire estate."[29] An even

27. Ibid.

28. Zamakhsharī touches here on the issue that lies at the heart of this chapter, to wit, the status of wives as heirs in early Islam. By drawing a distinction between the entitlement of affinal relatives and blood relatives, he is unwittingly appealing to a principle of inheritance that, as I shall attempt to demonstrate, was in effect during the lifetime of Muhammad, but was neglected soon after the Prophet's death.

29. Ibn Shuʿbah, vol. 3, pt. i, p. 14 (no. 16): *"li'l-umm thulth al-aṣl."* See also Bayhaqī, 6:228 (ll. 14–16). Note that ʿAlī has already been identified as a proponent of the nonliteralist position.

more emphatic statement of this position is attributed to Ibn ʿAbbās (d. A.D. 687), who is reported to have participated in the following exchange between ʿIkrima (d. A.D. 723 or 725) and Zayd b. Thābit:

> [ʿIkrima] said: Ibn ʿAbbās sent me to Zayd b. Thābit to ask him about [the case of] a husband and two parents. Zayd said, "To the husband one-half, and to the mother one-third of what remains, and to the father the remainder of the property."
>
> [ʿIkrima] said: So I came to Ibn ʿAbbās and informed him of [Zayd's response]. He said, "Go back to him and say to him, 'Have you issued your opinion on the basis of the Book of God or on the basis of your independent reasoning (*ra'y*)?'"
>
> [ʿIkrima] said: So I went to him and he said, "On the basis of my independent reasoning." I returned to Ibn ʿAbbās and told him [this]. Ibn ʿAbbās said, "I issue my opinion on the basis of my independent reasoning: to the mother a full one-third."[30]

Ibn ʿAbbās forces Zayd to admit that his decision to award the mother one-third of what remains is based entirely upon his independent reasoning, for which there is absolutely no Qur'anic support. In another version of the anecdote, Ibn ʿAbbās exclaims, "I do not find in the Book of God 'one-third of what remains!'",[31] thereby highlighting the absence in the Qur'an of any textual support for Zayd's proposed solution. The text of the Qur'an clearly indicates that the mother is entitled to a full one-third of the estate, not one-third *of what remains* after the husband receives his share of the estate, and Ibn ʿAbbās solves the *ʿUmariyyatān* on the basis of a literal reading of the text.

The Ẓāhirī (literalist) school sided with Ibn ʿAbbās on the question of the *ʿUmariyyatān*.[32] Dā'ūd b. ʿAlī al-Ẓāhirī (d. A.D. 884), the founder of the school, is reported to have held the literalist position, but unfortunately his writings have not come down to us. We do, however, possess the *Muḥallā* of Ibn Ḥazm al-Qurṭubī (d. A.D. 1064), one of the outstanding representatives of the Ẓāhirī law school.[33] This treatise contains a long discus-

30. Bayhaqī, 6:228 (ll. 20–28). See also Qurṭubī, 5:56 (bottom).

31. Rāzī, 9:213.

32. On the Ẓāhirīs, see Ignaz Goldziher, *The Ẓāhirī's: Their Doctrine and History*.

33. Ibn Ḥazm, *Muḥallā*, ed. Ḥasan Zaydān Ṭulbah (12 vols.; Cairo: Maktabat al-Jumhūriyya al-ʿArabiyya, 1390/1970). On Ibn Ḥazm, see R. Arnaldez, *Grammaire et théologie chez Ibn Ḥazm de Cordoue*, and Anwar G. Chejne, *Ibn Ḥazm*.

sion of the *ʿUmariyyatān* in which Ibn Ḥazm systematically sets out the arguments of the majority position and proceeds to refute them one by one. His refutation may be summarized as follows:

1. The proponents of the majority position base their argument, in part, on statements attributed to various Companions, viz., ʿUmar, Ibn Masʿūd, and ʿUthmān, and not upon the *sunna* of the Prophet. Such statements, Ibn Ḥazm maintains, do not constitute a valid *ḥujja* (proof text), which can be established only by a prophetic *sunna*.[34]
2. Among the statements attributed to the various Companions, Ibn Ḥazm singles out Ibn Masʿūd's justification for the majority position: "God never saw me give preference to a mother over a father."[35] Ibn Ḥazm manages to undermine the strength of this statement by producing a report in which Muhammad informs an inquirer that his mother should hold first place in his affections, to be followed by his father.[36] Surely the *sunna* of the Prophet, which indicates that a mother takes preference over a father, is of greater force than the contrary opinion of Ibn Masʿūd.[37]
3. Even if Ibn Masʿūd's statement did constitute a *ḥujja*, the proponents of the majority position are not consistent, for they award a female a larger share of the estate than a male of the same class in certain inheritance cases noted by Ibn Ḥazm.[38] Ibn Ḥazm concludes this point with an indignant reference to the hypocrisy of his opponents: "Then they denounce us for giving preference to a mother over a father in a case in which God imposes that result!"[39]

34. *Muḥallā*, 10:326 (bottom)–327 (l. 6).

35. See note 22.

36. The full text of the report reads as follows: "O Messenger of God, who is most entitled to my reverence?" The Apostle of God said, "Your mother." He said, "Then who, O Apostle of God?" He said, "Your mother." He said, "Then who, O Apostle of God?" He said, "Your mother." He said, "Then who, O Apostle of God?" He said, "Then your father." See Bukhārī, *Kitāb al-jāmiʿ al-ṣaḥīḥ*, 4:108 (no. 2); Ibn Māja, *Sunan*, 2:1207 (no. 3658); and Tirmidhī, *Sunan*, 3:206 (no. 1909). The nonlegal nature of this report weakens the strength of Ibn Ḥazm's argument.

37. *Muḥallā*, 10:327–28.

38. Ibid., 10:327 (ll. 20–22).

39. Ibid., 10:328 (l. 6).

4. The proponents of the majority position maintain that the Qur'anic phrase "a male is entitled to the share of two females" establishes the principle that a male is entitled to the share of two females of the same class and degree of relationship to the deceased. It is for this reason that they are troubled by the solution in which the mother inherits one-third and the father five-twelfths, or, worse yet, in which the mother inherits one-third and the father one-sixth. Ibn Ḥazm demonstrates, however, that the "principle" that his opponents are so jealous of upholding is no principle at all, for he notes that Q. 4:11 mentions a case in which a father and mother receive equal shares of the estate: "Each one of his parents is entitled to one-sixth of what he leaves, if he has a child."[40] (Ibn Ḥazm might also have cited the section of Q. 4:12 which awards a brother and sister—again a male and female of the same class and degree of relationship to the deceased—equal shares of the estate: "If a man or woman dies leaving neither parent nor child, and has a [uterine] brother or sister, each one of them is entitled to one-sixth.")
5. Finally, Ibn Ḥazm declares that the glosses suggested by the commentators ("if his parents are his [only] heirs" and "to his mother one-third [of what remains]") are invalid for the following reasons: First, in the exchange between Ibn ʿAbbās and Zayd b. Thābit cited earlier, Ibn ʿAbbās specifically asks Zayd if he can support his position on the basis of a Qur'anic text. Zayd's failure to mention the gloss proposed by the commentators suggests to Ibn Ḥazm that it did not exist at the time; furthermore, Zayd openly admits that he has arrived at his decision on the basis of his independent reasoning, which, *ipso facto*, constitutes grounds for rejection. Secondly, the same people who claim that the mother is entitled to one-third of what remains, in the case of the *ʿUmariyyatān*, take the very next line of the Qur'an ("if he has brothers, then his mother is entitled to one-sixth") literally, i.e., one-sixth of the entire estate. Why, Ibn Ḥazm asks, do they take "one-third" in the sense of "one-third of what remains" in the one case but not in the other? He condemns his opponents for interpreting the Qur'an in an inconsistent and arbitrary manner and for sug-

40. Ibid., 10:327 (ll. 13–15).

gesting emendations here and there according to need, without any methodological justification.[41]

The controversy surrounding the *ʿUmariyyatān* was settled, ultimately, by the doctrine of consensus. The majority of the Muslim commentators and legists preferred the nonliteralist position. The literalist position, despite its soundness and its adherence to the explicit wording of the Qur'an, attracted only limited support and was reduced to an unsuccessful minority opinion.[42]

ʿAwl

Nonliteralist position. The second inheritance case that I propose to consider involves one of the most peculiar features of the Islamic law of inheritance. In certain circumstances, the deceased may leave a particular constellation of heirs, all of whom are *ahl al-farā'iḍ*, and yet, when they are awarded their fractional shares, the resultant sum exceeds 100 percent of the estate. For example, suppose a man dies leaving three daughters, both parents, and a wife. All six persons qualify as "sharers," but the sum of the shares mentioned in the Qur'an (two-thirds, one-third, and one-eighth, respectively) equals 27/24 of the estate. The legists hold that the share of each heir should be reduced on a *pro rata* basis (hence, the appellation *ʿawl* or "proportional reduction"), in order to arrive at unity. This procedure, however, has the unfortunate result of reducing the share of each heir below the level specified by the Qur'an.[43]

Once again, there is no mention of this problem in any of the sources dealing with the lifetime of Muhammad; Ibn al-ʿArabī

41. Ibid., 10:329 (ll. 5–9).

42. This was apparently one of the few instances in which "Ibn ʿAbbās disagreed with all of the people." (Bayhaqī, 6:228 [11. 28–30]). The following jurists are reported to have supported the literalist position: Shurayḥ al-Qāḍī (d. between A.D. 695 and 717), Muʿādh b. Jabal (d. 640), Dā'ūd b. ʿAlī al-Ẓāhirī (d. 884), and Ibn al-Labbān (d. 1012). Muhammad b. Sīrīn (d. 729) straddled the fence on this issue, favoring the minority position in the case of a wife, mother, and father but the majority position in the case of a husband, mother, and father. See Ibn Rushd, 2:371; Qurṭubī, 5:56–57; Ibn Kathīr, 1:458.

43. See the article "*ʿAwl*," in *EI*[1] and Coulson, *Succession*, pp. 45–47, for further details on this procedure.

(d. A.D. 1148) explicitly states that it presented itself for the first time during the caliphate of ʿUmar b. al-Khaṭṭāb (r. A.D. 634–44): "When God—praised be He—decreed the amounts of the shares and established their values, and some time went by after that, a case arose, during the caliphate of ʿUmar, namely, the crowding of the 'sharers' and the oversubscription of the estate."[44] There is no agreement, however, regarding the identity of the first person to introduce the procedure of proportional reduction. According to some it was ʿUmar himself; when Zufar[45] asked Ibn ʿAbbās who was the first person to reduce the shares by *ʿawl*, the latter replied, "ʿUmar b. al-Khaṭṭāb, may God be pleased with him."[46] Another source indicates that Zayd b. Thābit "was the first person to apply *ʿawl* to the shares."[47] Still another source confers the honor upon ʿAlī who, while delivering a sermon, was reportedly interrupted by someone who asked how the estate should be divided when a man died, leaving his wife, father, mother and two daughters (Qur'anic shares = one-eighth, one-sixth, one-sixth, and two-thirds, respectively). ʿAlī reportedly replied, without a moment's hesitation, "The wife's one-eighth becomes one-ninth."[48]

The *ʿawl* procedure creates a theological problem at the same time that it solves a mathematical one, for the result of reducing the shares of each heir is that no heir receives the fractional share specified in the Qur'an. In the *Minbariyya* or "sermon case" mentioned above, the wife (whose Qur'anic share is one-eighth) inherits one-ninth, the two daughters (whose combined Qur'anic share is two-thirds) inherit 16/27, and the parents (whose combined Qur'anic share is one-third) inherit 8/27.

ʿUbayd Allāh b. ʿAbd Allāh b. ʿUtba b. Masʿūd (d. A.D. 716) reports that Ibn ʿAbbās, again a champion of the literalist position, proposed an alternative solution to the cases in which the Qur'anic portions exceed unity:

44. Ibn al-ʿArabī, *Aḥkām al-qur'ān*, 1:353.

45. This is either Zufar b. Aws b. al-Ḥadathānī (see Bayhaqī, 6:253 [l. 11]; al-Muttaqī al-Hindī, *Kanz al-ʿummāl fī sunan al-aqwāl wa'l-afʿāl*, 11:19 [l. 13]); or Zufar b. al-Ḥārith al-Baṣrī, who died ca. A.D. 695 (Ibn al-ʿArabī, 1:353 [l. 16]).

46. Bayhaqī, 6:253 (ll. 11–12); see also al-Ḥākim al-Nīsābūrī, *al-Mustadrak ʿalā al-ṣaḥīḥayn fi'l-ḥadīth*, 4:340 (l. 12).

47. Ibn Shuʿbah, vol. 3, pt. i, pp. 18–19 (no. 33); see also Bayhaqī, 6:253 (ll. 1–3).

48. Coulson, *Succession*, p. 47; Ibn Shuʿbah, vol. 3, pt. i, p. 19 (no. 34); Bayhaqī, 6:253 (ll. 4–5).

I [ʿUbayd Allāh], together with Zufar b. Aws b. al-Ḥadathānī, visited Ibn ʿAbbās after he had gone blind. We discussed the shares of inheritance. He said, "Do you think that the One who counted the innumerable sands of Arabia did not count one-half, one-half, and one-third? When both halves are gone, where is the place for the one-third?"

Zufar said to him, "O Ibn ʿAbbās, who was the first person to reduce the shares by *ʿawl*?"

He said, "ʿUmar b. al-Khaṭṭāb, may God be pleased with him."

He said, "Why?"

He said, "When they contended with one another, and one of them was on top of the other, [ʿUmar] said, 'By God, I do not know what to do with you. And, by God, I do not know which of you God put first and which of you he put last.' [ʿUmar] said, 'I find no better solution than to divide the property among you proportionally.'"

Then Ibn ʿAbbās said, "By God, had he put first the ones God had put first and put last the ones that God had put last, no share would have been reduced."

Zufar said to him, "Which of them did God put first and which of them [did He] put last?"

He said, "Every share which is reducible to a [lower share]—these are the ones God put first, i.e., the husband receives one-half, which is reducible to one-fourth but not any lower; the wife receives one-fourth, which is reducible to one-eighth but not any lower. The sisters receive two-thirds, and one sister receives one-half, but if there are daughters, they get what remains—these are the ones God put last. If [ʿUmar] had given the ones that God put first a full share, and then divided what remained among those he put last on a *pro rata* basis, no share would have been reduced."

Zufar said to him, "What prevented you from advising ʿUmar of this opinion?"

He said, "By God, fear of him."[49]

The anecdote opens with Ibn ʿAbbās expressing shock at the idea that God—"who counted the innumerable sands of Arabia"—could not handle simple fractions. He identifies ʿUmar as the first person to reduce the shares, thereby demonstrating *ʿawl* to be a post-Prophetic innovation, and proceeds to place this innovation in its proper historical context. As the leader of the

49. Bayhaqī, 6:253 (ll. 7–19). See also Ibn Shuʿbah, vol. 3, pt. i, p. 19 (no. 36); al-Hākim al-Nīsābūrī, *Mustadrak*, 4:340 (ll. 10–17); Ibn Rushd, 2:376–77; Ibn al-ʿArabī, 1:353; al-Mutaqqī al-Hindī, 11:19–20 (no. 121). Ibn ʿAbbās' reluctance to challenge ʿUmar openly on the question of *ʿawl* may be related to the severe treatment that ʿUmar accorded to Muslims who expressed excessive interest in the *mutashābihāt* or "ambiguous verses." See Nabia Abbott, *SALP*, 2:107–11.

Umma, ʿUmar was often called upon to settle disputes, and it stands to reason that inheritance disputes occurred frequently. On this particular occasion ʿUmar was approached by a group of heirs who were arguing among themselves, apparently over the division of an estate that had been oversubscribed. ʿUmar first tried to discover some criterion by which to rank them, but was forced to admit that he did not know "which of you God put first and which of you He put last." Unable to eliminate any of the heirs, ʿUmar decided to reduce the share of each one on a *pro rata* basis.

Ibn ʿAbbās claims to have succeeded where ʿUmar failed. He noticed that the "sharers" fall into two distinct categories. One group (spouses, parents, and uterine siblings) is assured of a minimum share of the estate in all circumstances. To hold that this minimum prescribed portion could be further reduced, argued Ibn ʿAbbās, was to contradict the very purpose of the Qur'an. The shares allotted to the second group (daughters, germane and/or consanguine sisters), on the other hand, do not represent a minimum entitlement, for the Qur'an indicates that in the presence of their respective brothers, these females inherit as residuaries, thereby reducing their shares of the estate below the Qur'anic portion. Ibn ʿAbbās argues that, since the fixed portions of the second group are not guaranteed in the same way as those of the first, their shares may be reduced, when necessary. He therefore concludes that when an estate is oversubscribed, the burden of the necessary reduction should fall on the daughters and sisters.[50]

The solution proposed by Ibn ʿAbbās was rejected by the majority of his contemporaries and relegated to the status of an unsuccessful minority opinion.[51] But ʿAṭā' b. Abī Rabāḥ (d. A.D. 732), one of the few early authorities to side with Ibn ʿAbbās on this issue, is reported to have made a highly suggestive statement in which he indicates to Ibn ʿAbbās that when they die, the early and presumably authentic *fiqh* will die with them: "The people do not follow either you or me; if we die, they will not divide the inheritance according to your method." To this Ibn ʿAbbās reportedly replied, "Let them gather, and let us put our hand on

50. I rely, here, on Coulson, *Succession*, p. 48.

51. Ibn al-ʿArabī, 1:353 (l. 19): "The *umma* accepted ʿUmar's opinion, and no one paid any attention to what Ibn ʿAbbās said."

the corner of the Kaᶜba (*rukn*). Then let us beseech God and invoke the curse of God upon the liars: God did not decree what they say."[52]

At the outset of a lengthy discussion of *ᶜawl*, Ibn Ḥazm categorically states his position in opposition to the mainstream of Islamic thought: "There is absolutely no proportional reduction of shares in matters of inheritance."[53] He proceeds, as with the *ᶜUmariyyatān*, to review systematically the arguments for and against the procedure. The proponents of *ᶜawl*, he notes, do not even attempt to find support for their position in the *sunna* of the Prophet; rather, they openly admit that proportional reduction was applied for the first time by either Zayd b. Thābit or ᶜUmar b. al-Khaṭṭāb. Such claims prove nothing, Ibn Ḥazm maintains, except that the procedure was an innovation introduced by the Companions.[54] ᶜUmar, as we have seen, resorted to the procedure of *ᶜawl* because he did "not know which of them God put first and which of them he put last." This admission of ignorance plays right into the hands of Ibn Ḥazm:

> ᶜUmar spoke the truth, and he usually refrained from making a decision so long as the matter had not been made clear to him. Are we not certain that God did not impose anything on us without explaining the reason? But if [the question of priority] was concealed from ᶜUmar, it was not concealed from Ibn ᶜAbbās, and the ignorance of the former does not constitute a valid argument against the latter. [Many things] were concealed from ᶜUmar: Knowledge of the permissibility of a large dower, and the death of the Apostle of God, and the meaning of *kalāla*.[55]

After refuting the case advanced by the proponents of *ᶜawl*, Ibn Ḥazm reviews the arguments of those, like Ibn ᶜAbbās, who oppose the procedure. Unlike ᶜUmar, who based his decision on the strength of his personal opinion, Ibn ᶜAbbās based his opinion on the text of the Qur'an.[56] "Any person of sound judgment," Ibn Ḥazm concludes, "cannot doubt that God never intended to award shares of the estate that would exceed the size of the

52. Ibn Shuᶜbah, vol. 3, pt. i, p. 19 (no. 37).
53. *Muḥallā*, 10:330 (l. 8).
54. Ibid., 10:332 (ll. 1–3).
55. Ibid., 10:334 (ll. 10–16). I have discussed in chap. 1 ᶜUmar's confusion with regard to the meaning of *al-kalāla*.
56. Ibid., 10:335 (ll. 16–17).

estate . . . It is necessary to hold according to the text of the Qur'an, not according to the opinions of those who would oppose it."[57]

"After any bequest he bequeaths or debt"

The third inheritance case to be considered involves a phrase that occurs once in Q. 4:11 and three times in Q. 4:12. The Qur'an awards a share of the estate to the mother, husband, wife, and (uterine) sibling "after any bequest he bequeaths or debt" (*min baʿdi waṣiyyatin yūṣī bihā aw dayn*). According to Islamic law, shares of the estate are not distributed to the heirs until, first, all debts have been paid and, second, bequests have been distributed. The early authorities sought to find support for the precedence of debts over bequests in the Qur'anic phrase "after any bequest he bequeaths or debt," but noticed that, in this phrase, bequests are mentioned before debts. ʿAlī b. Abī Ṭālib, upon becoming aware of this discrepancy, reportedly made the following statement to a group of Qur'an reciters: "The Apostle of God paid off debts before bequests, but you recite *'al-waṣiyya'* before *'al-dayn.'*"[58]

ʿAlī's statement, which establishes a correspondence between the *fiqh* and *sunna* of the Prophet, was instrumental in the arguments put forward by the classical jurists. Shāfiʿī states that Muhammad "made it clear that the debt is [paid] before bequests and inheritance and that there may be no bequest or inheritance until the creditors receive full payment of the debt."[59] Shāfiʿī underscores the crucial role played by the *sunna* of the Prophet in determining the *fiqh*, noting that "were it not for the indication of the *sunna*, then the *ijmāʿ* (consensus), it would be impossible to tell whether debts should be paid before bequests or vice-versa."[60]

57. Ibid., 10:335 (ll. 19–21).

58. Ḥumaydī, *Musnad*, 1:30–31 (no. 56); Tirmidhī, 3:294 (no. 2205); Ibn Māja, 2:906 (no. 2715); al-Ḥākim al-Nīsābūrī, *Mustadrak*, 4:336 (ll. 13–17); Bayhaqī, 6:267 (ll. 27–29); al-Mutaqqī al-Hindī, 22:164 (no. 1075) and 168 (no. 2002).

59. Shāfiʿī, *Risāla*, p. 40, par. 218.

60. Ibid., p. 40, par. 219. Shāfiʿī refers here to the *sunna* of the Prophet without citing the above-mentioned *ḥadīth*. This particular report had a troubled his-

The *ahl al-ḥadīth* (traditionists) succeeded in overcoming the discrepancy between the Qur'an and the *fiqh* by appealing to the *sunna* of the Prophet. They salvage the *fiqh* by grounding it in the *sunna* of the Prophet, but that only complicates matters, for now both the *fiqh* and the *sunna* are at variance with the Qur'an. If the payment of debts should precede the distribution of bequests, why does the Qur'an mention bequests before debts? The commentators devote considerable energy to answering this question, and it is interesting to observe how they manage to transform an apparent defect into a virtue. In a dazzling display of hermeneutical ingenuity, they argue that God had many excellent reasons for mentioning bequests before debts. A sampling of these arguments follows:

1. Some commentators explain that the wording of the phrase in question was conditioned by a legal consideration. A bequest resembles a share of inheritance in the sense that both are unilateral transfers made without anything being given in return. Heirs and legatees are in direct competition with one another for the estate of the deceased; since bequests reduce the *quantum* that remains for the heirs, it is in their interest to ignore or invalidate bequests. A debt, on the other hand, cannot be ignored, because of the presence of powerful credi-

---

tory that may explain why Shāfiʿī does not cite it. We learn from Bayhaqī (6:267) that Shāfiʿī, elsewhere, cites the report with the following *isnād*: Sufyān—Abū Isḥāq—al-Ḥārith—ʿAlī—the Prophet. This *isnād*, Shāfiʿī argues, fails to meet the standards of *ḥadīth* criticism for two reasons: First, it is one of the *āḥād* or "isolated" reports, since al-Ḥārith (al-Aʿwar) is the only person to transmit it from ʿAlī; secondly, reports transmitted on the authority of al-Ḥārith are not acceptable as proof texts, since the *ḥadīth* critics impugn his personality (see, for example, Ibn Ḥibbān, *Kitāb al-majrūḥīn min al-muḥaddithīn*, 1:216–17; and Ibn Kathīr, 1:459). The weakness of the *isnād* helps to explain the subsequent history of this report: Muslim does not include it in his *Ṣaḥīḥ*; Bukhārī (*Ṣaḥīḥ*, 2:188) mentions the *sunna* of the Prophet in *bāb* 9 of his chapter on bequests ("Explanation of His word 'after any bequest he bequeaths or debt,' and it is mentioned that the Prophet paid off debts before bequests"), but then fails to cite the relevant report (see also Nasā'ī, *Sunan*, 6:205); Tirmidhī, (3:294 [no. 2205]) cites the report in full, but, according to al-Mutaqqī al-Hindī (22:294 [no. 1075]), he considered it to be weak; Ibn Māja (2:906 [no. 2715]) cites the report in full, with no comment. It may be significant that in none of the standard *ḥadīth* collections do we find evidence of any attempt to make this particular report more acceptable by improving its *isnād*. Note, however, that Bayhaqī (6:267 [l. 31]) transmits a version of the report in which ʿĀṣim b. Ḍamra replaces al-Ḥārith al-Aʿwar.

tors who will press their demands. God therefore mentioned bequests before debts, so the argument runs, in order to encourage the heirs to honor their obligation.[61]

2. The syntax of the phrase "after any bequest he bequeaths or debt" provides additional support for the preceding legal consideration. The words "bequest" and "debt" are linked together by the disjunctive particle *aw* (or). Unlike the conjunction *waw* (and), which yields a sequence (*tartīb*) of items, the particle *aw* links two items that are considered to be of equal value. Thus, the mention of bequests before debts does not, the commentators argue, mean that bequests take precedence over debts in the division of an estate.[62]
3. Several commentators appeal to rhetorical considerations. Unlike a debt, which exists independently of the wishes of the testator, the existence of a bequest is contingent upon an indication by the testator, either orally or in writing, of his intention to leave a gift. The Qur'an mentions bequests first, the argument runs, because of their tenuous nature,[63] or because that which is problematic (*mushkil*) and requires clarification should be placed before that which is certain.[64] According to another, similar explanation, bequests are more numerous than debts because, thanks to the encouragement of the *Sharīʿa*, they have become quasi-obligatory (*ka'l-lāzim*). Bequests are mentioned before debts because it is proper to mention that which is imperative before that which is contingent.[65]
4. Other commentators prefer an ethical explanation. Bequests are made—in theory, at least—to the poor and weak members of society. Debts, on the other hand, are owed to creditors who demand payment on the basis of their strength and power. The Qur'an mentions bequests before debts out of concern for the interest of the weaker members of society.[66]

61. Zamakhsharī, 1:483–84; Rāzī, 9:216; Nasafī, 1:208; Nīsābūrī, *Gharā'ib*, 4:196.

62. Zamakhsharī, 1:483–84; Ibn al-ʿArabī, 1:343–44; Ṭabarsī, 3:35; Rāzī, 9:216; Qurṭubī, 5:24; Bayḍāwī, 1:198; Nasafī, 1:208; Nīsābūrī, *Gharā'ib*, 4:196.

63. Ibn al-ʿArabī, 1:343–44; Qurṭubī, 5:74; Bayḍāwī, 1:198.

64. Ibn al-ʿArabī, 1:344 (ll. 3–4).

65. Qurṭubī, 5:73–74.

66. Qurṭubī, 5:73–74; Ibn Juzayy, *Kitāb al-tashīl li-ʿulūm al-tanzīl*, 1:236–37.

5. A final example is related, again, to a legal consideration. The Qur'anic verses prescribing bequests for parents, relatives, and wives (Q. 2:180 and 2:240) are considered to have been partially abrogated by Q. 4:11–12, which, as we have seen, award fixed shares of the estate to those same persons.[67] Ibn al-ʿArabī explains that bequests are mentioned before debts in order to strengthen them after their having been weakened by the doctrine of abrogation.[68]

Apparent contradictions in the Qur'an, then, forced the Muslim authorities to deviate from the explicit wording of the text in two instances (*ʿUmariyyatān* and *ʿawl*), and the Qur'an deviates from the *fiqh* in yet a third ("after any bequest he bequeaths or debt"). Ibn ʿAbbās, in the first two instances, and ʿAlī, in the third, called for a literal interpretation of the Qur'an, but to no avail, as the nonliteralist position gained general acceptance. Some attempts were later made to bridge the gap between the Qur'an and the *fiqh* by means of various hermeneutical devices; for the most part, however, the later legists and commentators do not seem to have been greatly troubled by the gap. And nobody asks, "Why does the Qur'an contradict itself?" or "Why does the Qur'an deviate from the *fiqh*?" It is to these questions that we now direct our attention.

The Status of Husbands and Wives as Heirs

Hypothesis

The apparent contradictions in the Qur'an may have been caused by early, hitherto unrecognized, changes in the understanding of the inheritance verses. Specifically, it is possible that the original intention of these verses was to make inheritance contingent upon kinship, i.e., relationship by blood, so that a husband and wife did not, under normal circumstances, inherit from one another.[69] Support for this principle can be found in Q. 4:8, which

67. For more on this, see chap. 5.

68. Ibn al-ʿArabī, 1:344: "*Fa-lammā daʿafahā al-naskh quwiyat bi-taqdīm al-dhikr.*"

69. This would mean, within the terms of the Islamic law of inheritance, that a husband and wife could not inherit from one another under any circumstances—the "science of the shares" does not permit one spouse to designate

reads as follows: "To men a share of what parents and kindred leave, and to women a share of what parents and kindred leave, whether it be little or much, an apportioned share." The Muslim commentators routinely assert that the purpose of this verse was to extend the right to inherit to females.[70] But who are the "women" mentioned in Q. 4:8? The commentators identify them as the daughters, mothers, sisters, and *wives* who are awarded a share of the estate in Q. 4:11–12. However, by linking the revelation of Q. 4:8 to that of 4:11–12, the commentators distort the meaning of the former verse, which clearly says nothing about a wife inheriting from her husband, or vice versa.[71] If we examine Q. 4:8 independently of 4:11–12 and ask, once again, who the ("men" and) "women" mentioned in that verse are, the answer can only be that men inherit as sons, fathers, and brothers, whereas women inherit as daughters, mothers, and sisters. Q. 4:8 establishes the principle that inheritance is limited to the blood relatives of the deceased; it says nothing about affinal relatives. Indeed, several commentators identify this principle. Qurṭubī states that Q. 4:8 clarifies the *ratio legis* of inheritance, blood-relationship.[72] Similarly, Bayḍāwī and Nasafī identify the "men" and "women" mentioned in the verse as "those who inherit by virtue of blood-relationship."[73]

If Q. 4:8 establishes the principle that inheritance upon intestacy is limited to the blood relatives of the deceased, then what is the meaning of Q. 4:12a, which awards a share of the estate to a surviving husband or wife? A consideration of the institution of marriage may shed some light on this question. In premodern societies, women were often unable to support themselves economically and, therefore, found themselves in a difficult situation when a husband died. The institution of the bride-price was

---

the other as a testamentary heir, or to leave him/her a bequest. It is my contention that in the system of inheritance introduced by Muhammad it was, in fact, possible for a man to designate his wife as a testamentary heir (see chap. 1) or, alternatively, to leave her a bequest (see chap. 5); the reverse may also have been true.

70. See notes 2 and 3, above.

71. The linkage of Q. 4:8 and 4:11–12 exemplifies the hermeneutical principle of *ta'khīr al-bayān ʿan waqt al-khiṭāb* (delay of specification until after the time of address). See Bayḍāwī, 1:196.

72. *Jāmiʿ*, 5:46: "*bayān ʿillat al-mīrāth wa-hiya al-qarāba.*"

73. Bayḍāwī, 1:196; Nasafī, 1:205–06. See also Ṭabarsī, 3:24; Rāzī, 9:195; Nīsābūrī, *Gharā'ib*, 4:182–83.

designed, in part, to address this problem.[74] It was customary to pay part of the bride-price immediately and to postpone payment of the rest, which became due in the event of divorce, or upon the death of one of the spouses. The unpaid portion of the bride-price thus served as insurance against the possibility that a husband might predecease his wife without leaving a will. But the bride-price was stipulated at the time the marriage took place, and if the husband died intestate or without providing for the wife in his will, then she had no claim whatsoever against the estate.

Numerous Near Eastern societies, dating back as far as the fourth millenium B.C., have confronted the problem of the "unendowed" wife.[75] Roman law, which was applied in the provinces of the Near East,[76] and which may have exerted an influence on the formation of Islamic law,[77] provides a particularly illustrative example. Roman law recognized two forms of marriage, a normal form, in which the husband paid a bride-price and acquired marital power over the wife, and an exceptional form in which no bride-price was paid. The legal position of the wife vis-à-vis her husband was vastly inferior in the exceptional form of marriage, for the unendowed wife had no legal claim against her husband's estate if he failed to provide for her in his will, or died intestate. In A.D. 537 (less than one hundred years before the revelation of the Qur'an), the Emperor Justinian enacted a law that was designed to alleviate the predicament of unendowed wives. This law, found in *Novella* 53.6, is entitled "Concerning a Poor Woman Who is Unendowed." The first section of this law treats the case in which the deceased made no provision whatsoever for his wife or died intestate:

74. On bride-price, see Jack Goody and S. J. Tambiah, *Bridewealth and Dowry*; also *The Meaning of Marriage Payments*, ed. J. Comaroff.

75. See *The Ancient Near East*, ed. Pritchard, pp. 156–57, par. 172, for the situation in ancient Mesopotamia.

76. The Roman law of inheritance, for example, was adopted in sixth-century Armenia. See Nicholas Adontz, *Armenia in the Period of Justinian*, pp. 141–54.

77. For the copious literature on the problem of Byzantine-Roman influence on Muslim law, see Ignaz Goldziher, *Muslim Studies*, 2:79; Santillana, *Code Civil et Commercial Tunisien* (Tunis, 1899); Schmidt, *Die Occupatio im islamischen Recht* (Strasbourg, 1910), p. 1, note 1; Heffening, *Das islamische Fremdenrecht* (Hanover, 1925), pp. 3–4; Volterra, *Diritto Romano e diritti Orientali* (Bologna, 1937), pp. 60–66; Nallino, "Considerazioni sui rapporti fra diritto musulmano," in *Raccolta di scritti editi e inediti*, 4:85–94.

> As every law enacted by Us is based upon clemency, and We see that when men married to women who have brought no dowry die, the children alone are legally called to the succession of their father's estates, while their widows, even though they may remain in the condition of lawful wives, for the reason that they have not brought any dowry, and no ante-nuptial donation has been given them, can obtain nothing from the estates of their deceased husbands, and are compelled to live in the greatest poverty, We wish to provide for their maintenance by enabling them to succeed to them, and be called to share their estates conjointly with the children. But as We have already enacted a law which provides that when a husband divorces his wife, whom he married without any dowry, she shall receive the fourth of his estate, just as in the present instance, whether there are few or many children, the wife shall be entitled to the fourth of the property of the deceased.

The legislator, at this point, inserted a clause defining the widow's entitlement in the case in which she has received a legacy from her husband:

> If, however, a husband has left a legacy to his wife and this amounts to less than a fourth of his estate, this amount shall be made up out of the same. Hence, as We come to the relief of women who have not been endowed, or divorced by their husbands, so We assist them where they have constantly lived with them, and We grant them the same privilege.

The law ends with a clause indicating that the legislation applies to unendowed husbands as well as to unendowed wives:

> Again, everything that We have stated in the present law with reference to the fourth to which a poor woman is entitled shall equally apply to a husband, for like the former one, We make this law applicable to both.[78]

Novella 53.6 bears a ṣtriking resemblance to Q. 4:12a. Both enactments award a fractional share of the estate to a surviving husband or wife and both take into account any legacy that the deceased may have left.[79] There are differences, too. The Roman law treats husbands and wives on a basis of equality, whereas the Islamic law awards a husband twice the share of a wife. *Novella*

78. *Corpus Iuris Civilis*, ed. R. Schoell, 3:304–05; *The Civil Law*, tr. S. P. Scott, 16:229–30; W. W. Buckland, *A Text-Book of Roman Law From Augustus to Justinian*, p. 327.

79. On legacies, see chap. 5.

53.6 makes no distinction between a couple with or without children, but Q. 4:12a awards a childless spouse half the share of one with children. And *Novella* 53.6, of course, expressly states the circumstances in which the award is to be made, whereas Q. 4:12a does not.

Although it is unlikely that Muhammad or any of his followers were directly familiar with Roman law, it is possible that Justinian's reforms found their way into the Hijaz by way of the Byzantine provinces in the Near East.[80] Leaving aside the question of transmission, let us assume, for the sake of argument, that Q. 4:12a, like *Novella* 53.6, was originally intended to apply in the case of unendowed husbands and wives and that, during the lifetime of Muhammad, inheritance upon intestacy was restricted to the blood relatives of the deceased. Is there any evidence in the Islamic sources that would tend to support this hypothesis, and does this hypothesis make better sense of the data than does the traditional interpretation of Q. 4:12a?

Supporting Evidence

The three inheritance cases. First, the hypothesis explains why the Qur'an appears to contradict itself in the three cases discussed in the first part of this chapter. If the award of a fractional share of the estate to a surviving spouse was meant, originally, to apply in the exceptional case of an unendowed spouse, then the transformation of the exception into a norm would have had the effect of "overloading" the delicate mathematical balance upon which the inheritance verses are predicated, causing them to "short-circuit" at a number of points.

In the case of the *ʿUmariyyatān* (a childless person dies, leaving a spouse and both parents), the Muslim authorities faced a dilemma because they attempted to satisfy three conditions

80. The assertion that Roman law may have provided the ultimate source for certain Qur'anic laws runs counter to the general consensus of western legal historians on this question. In defense of this claim, I would point out that, not only does my proposed reinterpretation of Q. 4:12a bear a distinct resemblance to Justinian's "Law Concerning an Unendowed Wife," but also, my rereading of Q. 4:12b (chap. 1) bears a distinct resemblance to the *actio ad supplendam legitimam*, another of Justinian's legal reforms. Is it merely a coincidence that two Roman legal reforms should find their way, albeit in disguised form, into a single Qur'anic verse?

which cannot all be satisfied at once: (1) The surviving spouse must receive his/her share of the estate; (2) the mother must receive one-third of the estate; (3) the father's share must be twice as large as the mother's. Although it is possible to satisfy any two of these conditions at once, it is mathematically impossible to satisfy all three simultaneously. The Muslim authorities therefore had to sacrifice one of the three conditions. Ruling out (1) would have been a bad choice because that would leave a surviving spouse without any way of inheriting from the deceased. The possibility of sacrificing (3) may have been ruled out because of the patriarchal, *ʿaṣabī*, nature of the society. The sacrifice of (2), then, may have constituted the least of three evils: the mother still inherits, but she receives less than she would have otherwise.

The assumption that a surviving spouse normally does not inherit a fractional share of the estate makes it possible to satisfy the other two conditions: the mother inherits one-third of the estate, whereas the father inherits two-thirds. (Of course, the problem would reappear in the case of an unendowed spouse, but such cases, in all likelihood, would occur only rarely.) The hypothesis also eliminates the problem of an oversubscribed estate (e.g., a person dies, leaving a husband [Qur'anic share = one-fourth] or wife [Qur'anic share = one-eighth], three daughters [Qur'anic share = two-ninths, each], and both parents [Qur'anic share = one-sixth, each]). Clearly, it is the share awarded to the surviving spouse that upsets the calculation, and the elimination of this share reduces the sum total to 100 percent of the estate. (It would be necessary to invoke the procedure of proportional reduction in those exceptional cases in which an unendowed spouse was involved, but this would happen only rarely.)

Finally, the hypothesis explains why the Muslim authorities ran into trouble when they sought Qur'anic support, in the phrase "after any bequest he bequeaths or debt," for the *fiqh* procedure of giving debts precedence over bequests. This phrase was not meant to establish any such order of priorities. Rather it was intended to indicate that, in the exceptional case of an unendowed spouse, if the deceased had left a bequest for the surviving spouse, and this bequest amounted to less than the fractional share mentioned in Q. 4:12a, the surviving spouse was entitled to the difference between the two amounts. After the award made in Q. 4:12a had been transformed from an exception into a norm, the legists sought to stretch the meaning of this phrase, now archaic, to fit the requirements of the law. They failed in this endeavor and turned, instead, to the *sunna* of the Prophet to find support for the *fiqh*.

The Sunna of the Prophet. The following report, which pertains to the revelation of Q. 2:240, portrays Muhammad as drawing a clear distinction between the rights of a wife, on the one hand, and heirs, on the other:

> A man from Ṭā'if, who had sons and daughters, came to Medina, accompanied by his parents and his wife. He died in Medina and [the case] was brought before the Prophet. He gave the parents and the children the customary amount, but he did not give [anything] to the wife—except to order them [viz., the heirs] to maintain her out of her husband's estate for a year.[81]

The evidence of this report is not conclusive, however, because the incident reportedly occurred prior to the revelation of Q. 4: 12a.

The events surrounding the death of Muhammad provide further support for our hypothesis. If the traditional interpretation of Q. 4:12a was in effect during the lifetime of the Prophet, then Muhammad's wives were entitled to inherit one-eighth of his estate in their capacity as *ahl al-farā'iḍ*. But the sources indicate that Muhammad's wives did not inherit anything from him, and that he did not consider them to be his heirs. Muhammad is reported to have said, "My heirs will not divide a *dīnār*. Whatever I leave, after maintenance for my wives and provisions for my *ʿāmil* (agent), is for charity."[82] Here, Muhammad's desire to frustrate his heirs is juxtaposed with his concern for the well-being of his wives. Wives are entitled to maintenance but do not inherit, exactly as our hypothesis suggests. The following report, attributed to ʿĀ'isha, again makes the point that Muhammad did not consider his wives to be his heirs:

> The wives of the Prophet, at the time of the death of the Apostle of God, wanted to send ʿUthmān b. ʿAffān to Abū Bakr in order to

81. Wāḥidī, *Asbāb nuzūl al-qur'ān*, p. 76 (no. 234); Maḥallī, *Tafsīr al-qur'ān al-karīm*, p. 57 (margin).

82. Mālik, 2:993 (no. 28). See also Ibn Ḥanbal, *Musnad* (Cairo), 13:25–26 (no. 7301); Muslim, *Ṣaḥīḥ*, 2:55; Bukhārī, *Ṣaḥīḥ*, 4:284.

> ask him about their inheritance from the Apostle of God. But ʿĀ'isha said to them, "Did not the Apostle of God say, 'We do not leave any inheritance; what we leave is for charity?'"[83]

The orthography, syntax, and meaning of the Arabic phrase which I have translated as "We do not leave any inheritance; what we leave is for charity" has been the subject of considerable discussion among Muslim scholars.[84] For our purposes, it is sufficient to point out that the wives of the Prophet do not invoke Q. 4:12a in support of their inheritance claims. Yet, if the traditional interpretation of this verse had been in effect, there could have been no better support for their claim.

Bride-price. The sources also manifest sensitivity to the distinction between marriages with and without bride-price (*ṣadāq*). On the one hand, the Qur'an repeatedly refers to the payment of a bride-price as an essential condition for a valid marriage.[85] In the *ḥadīth* literature, on the other hand, there are numerous references to cases in which marriages were arranged without the payment of a bride-price.[86] ʿĀ'isha is reported to have condemned this practice, reproaching women who offered themselves to the Prophet without requesting a bride-price.[87]

The legal status of an unendowed wife whose husband predeceased her was a subject of considerable controversy during the first century of Islam. The early authorities held three different positions on the issue. The first position is attributed to Muhammad, who decreed that a woman whose husband had died without assigning her a *ṣadāq* was entitled to the fair bride-price.[88] Muhammad, in this case, said nothing about the wife's receiving a share of her husband's estate.

The second position, according to which the unendowed

83. Mālik, 2:993 (no. 27). See also Bukhārī, *Ṣaḥīḥ*, 4:284. According to Islamic tradition, Muhammad's estate was not subject to the normal rules of inheritance, because of his special status as a Prophet. See chap. 4 for more on this.

84. See Goldziher, *Muslim Studies*, 2:101–103.

85. The Qur'an uses the terms *farīḍa* (Q. 2:236–37), *ṣadāq* (Q. 4:3), and *'ujūr* (Q. 4:24, 5:6, 60:10).

86. Ibn Shuʿbah, vol. 3, pt. i, pp. 223–26 (nos. 922–31, 933–34); Ibn Ḥanbal, *Musnad* (Beirut), 3:480 and 4:279–80; 6:158; Abū Dā'ūd, *Sunan*, 6:147–51 (nos. 2100–3); Bayhaqī, 7:244–47; Mālik, 2:527; Nasā'ī, 6:98–99; Tirmidhī, 2:406 (nos. 1154–55); Ibn Māja, 1:609 (no. 1891); Shāfiʿī, *Umm*, 8:181.

87. Ibn Ḥanbal (Beirut), 6:158: *"taʿriḍ nafsahā bi-ghayr ṣadāq."*

88. Ibn Shuʿbah, vol. 3, pt. i, p. 226: *"lahā mithlu ṣadāqi nisā'ihā."*

widow is entitled to a share of the inheritance but not to any bride-price, is attributed to three different Companions: (a) ʿAlī, when asked about a woman whose husband had died without assigning her a bride-price, is reported to have said, "She is entitled to the inheritance, and she must observe the waiting-period, but she gets no bride-price."[89] (b) The same position is attributed to Zayd b. Thābit: One of ʿAbd Allāh b. ʿUmar's sons was betrothed to a daughter of ʿUbayd Allāh b. ʿUmar. The boy died without either consummating the marriage or assigning her a bride-price. When the widow's mother attempted to claim the bride-price for her daughter, ʿAbd Allāh b. ʿUmar said, "She is not entitled to the *ṣadāq*. Had she been entitled to it, we would not have kept it or wronged her." The mother, not satisfied with this answer, called for adjudication. The judge, Zayd b. Thābit, sustained the father's contention that the widow was not entitled to the bride-price, but awarded her a share of the inheritance.[90] Notice, here, that Zayd awards the widow a share of the inheritance in the *exceptional* case in which no bride-price was stipulated at the time the marriage took place. The situation presented in this case reflects, exactly, my proposed reinterpretation of Q. 4:12a.[91] Masrūq, commenting on Zayd's decision, reportedly said, "There had never before been an award of inheritance without there being a *ṣadāq* first."[92] (c) This position is also attributed to ʿAbd Allāh b. ʿUmar himself.[93]

According to the third position, attributed to ʿAbd Allāh b. Masʿūd, the unendowed widow is entitled to both a share of the inheritance and a bride-price:

> A group of people came to [ʿAbd Allāh b. Masʿūd] and said, "One of our men married a woman, but did not assign her a bride-price, and died before having intercourse with her."
>
> ʿAbd Allāh said, "I have not been asked, ever since I left the Apostle of God, a more difficult question than this one. So, go ask someone else."

89. Ibn Shuʿbah, vol. 3, pt. i, p. 224; Bayhaqī, 7:247 (ll. 4–9).

90. Mālik, 2:527; Ibn Shuʿbah, vol. 3, pt. i, pp. 224–25 (nos. 925–26, 928); Bayhaqī, 7:246–47.

91. It should be noted that Zayd supervised the redaction of the ʿUthmānic recension of the Qur'an, was fluent in Syriac, and, as mentioned in chap. 4, p. 142, was the first person to write a treatise on the "science of the shares." See Fuat Sezgin, *GAS*, 1:395–96, 401.

92. Ibn Shuʿbah, vol. 3, pt. i, pp. 224–25 (nos. 926–27).

93. Ibn Shuʿbah, vol. 3, pt. i, p. 224 (no. 926).

They argued with him about it for a month, at the end of which they said to him, "Whom shall we ask if we do not ask you? You are one of the greatest Companions of Muhammad in this country. We shall not find anyone except you."

He said, "I will issue an opinion on this, on the basis of my independent reasoning. If it is correct, then it is from God alone, He has no partner; but if it is mistaken, then it is from me and from Satan, and God and His Apostle are not responsible for it. I think I would give her the fair *ṣadāq*—no more and no less—and she is entitled to inherit, and she must observe the waiting period of four months and ten days."

[ᶜAlqama] said, "This was said within earshot of men from the tribe of Ashjaᶜ, so they stood up and said, 'We bear witness that your decree is the same as that of the Apostle of God in the case of one of our women, Barwaᶜ bint Wāshiq.'"

[ᶜAlqama] said, "ᶜAbd Allāh was never seen to rejoice as greatly as he did on that day, except [on the day] he became a Muslim."[94]

The status of the unendowed wife is presented as an extremely difficult question. At the outset of the report, Ibn Masᶜūd is apparently unaware of any relevant *sunna* of the Prophet and refuses, at first, to make any statement. When, after a month, he is persuaded to issue an opinion, he prefaces his response with a disclaimer frequently invoked by the Companions when exercising their independent judgment on difficult issues.[95] The unendowed wife, according to Ibn Masᶜūd, is entitled to both a share of the inheritance and a bride-price. Upon hearing this judgment, several men from the tribe of Ashjaᶜ[96] informed Ibn Masᶜūd that

94. Nasā'ī, 6: 100. See also Ibn Shuᶜbah, vol. 3, pt. i, pp. 225–26 (nos. 929–31); Ibn Ḥanbal (Beirut), 3: 480 and 4: 279–80; Ibn Ḥanbal (Cairo), 6: 74–75 (nos. 4099–4100) and 6: 137–38 (nos. 4276–77); Tirmidhī, 2: 406 (nos. 1154–55); Ibn Māja, 1: 609 (no. 1891); Abū Dā'ūd, 6: 147–49 (nos. 2100–2); Bayhaqī, 7: 245–49. The authenticity of these reports has been questioned by both Muslim and Western scholars; see Goldziher, *Muslim Studies*, 2: 139–40.

95. Abū Bakr, for example, is reported to have made the following statement with regard to the meaning of the word *kalāla*: "I have my own personal opinion on this matter. If it is correct, then it is from God; if it is mistaken, then it is from Satan, and neither God nor his Apostle is responsible. *Al-kalāla* [signifies] 'he who has neither parent nor child.'" (Ibn Kathīr, 1: 460.) For a discussion of the theological significance of this disclaimer, see Aẓīmābādī, *Sharḥ sunan Abī Dā'ūd*, 6: 148–49.

96. The names and number of men from the tribe of Ashjaᶜ who were present on this occasion vary from one version of the report to another. Some versions refer to only one man: "a man from Ashjaᶜ" (Nasā'ī, 6: 98–99); "al-Ashjaᶜī" (Bayhaqī, 7: 245 [l. 32]); "Abū Sinān al-Ashjaᶜī" (Ibn Shuᶜbah, vol. 3, pt. i, p. 225 [no. 929]); "Maᶜqil b. Sinān" (Ibn Shuᶜbah, vol. 3, pt. i, pp. 225–26 [no. 930]); "Maᶜqil b. Yasār" (Bayhaqī, 7: 245 [ll. 15–21]); "Salāma b. Yazīd" (Ibn Ḥanbal

his decision was in conformity with the *sunna* of the Prophet in a case involving a woman belonging to their tribe.[97]

The position represented by Ibn Masʿūd eventually prevailed over the other two positions. The *sunna* of the Prophet, as represented in position one, was superseded by the prophetic *sunna* established in position three. As for the second position, it is reported that ʿAlī attempted to discredit the testimony of the Ashjaʿī tribesman, proclaiming, "The opinion of a Bedouin should not be accepted over the Book of God."[98] But ʿAlī does not cite any relevant Qur'anic verse and his position eventually succumbed to the force and authority of the *sunna* of the Prophet.[99] The matter was still in flux during the lifetime of Shāfiʿī (d. A.D. 820), who is reported to have followed the opinion of ʿAlī at first, but then to have switched to the opinion of Ibn Masʿūd after becoming convinced of the soundness of the Ibn Masʿūd report.[100]

Miscellaneous considerations. If my hypothesis is correct, then the elevation of a surviving spouse to the status of a full legal heir marked a radical departure from the system of inheritance introduced by Muhammad. Whatever the causes of this change

---

[Beirut], 3:279–80). Other versions indicate that two or more men were involved: "Abū Sinān and al-Jarrāḥ" (Ibn Ḥanbal [Cairo], 6:75 [no. 4100] and 6:137–38 [no. 4276]); "A man from Ashjaʿ and Abū al-Jarrāḥ" (Ibn Ḥanbal [Cairo], 6:74–75 [no. 4099]); "A man from Ashjaʿ and Abū al-Jarrāḥ and Abū Sinān" (Abū Dā'ūd, 6:148–49 [no. 2102]); "A group of people from Ashjaʿ, including al-Jarrāḥ and Abū Sinān" (Bayhaqī, 7:246); "Men from Ashjaʿ" (Bayhaqī, 7:245 [ll. 22–31]).

The variations in the names do not, according to Bayhaqī (7:246), invalidate the authenticity of this report: "This disagreement over the name of the person who transmitted the story of Barwaʿ bint Wāshiq, on the authority of the Prophet, does not weaken the report, for the *isnād*s of all forms of the report are sound, even if some of them indicate that 'a group from Ashjā' testified, others give the name of one of them, others give the name of two, and still others give only a general indication, without naming names. A report is not to be rejected for such a reason. Were it not for the trustworthiness of the person who transmitted [the story] from the Prophet, there would be no sense to the joy expressed by ʿAbd Allāh b. Masʿūd. But God knows best." See also ʿAẓīmābādī, 6:150; and Ibn al-Turkomānī, *al-Jawhar al-naqī*, 7:245–246.

97. This may be an instance of back-projection of legal doctrine, in the Schachtian sense.

98. Bayhaqī, 7:247 (ll. 6–10). See also Ibn Shuʿbah, vol. 3, pt. i, p. 226 (no. 931).

99. Furthermore, the *isnād* of the report containing ʿAlī's statement was rejected on technical grounds. See Ibn al-Turkomānī, 7:247 (ll. 22–28).

100. Shāfiʿī, *Umm*, 8:181; Tirmidhī, 2:407; Bayhaqī, 7:244–45.

may have been, it is clear that the reinterpretation of Q. 4:12a posed a threat to the social and economic cohesion of the Muslim family, for the award of a fractional share of the estate to an affinal relative, such as a spouse, weakens the control of the family over valuable economic resources. Although I cannot, at present, fix the exact time at which the change took place, I am inclined to place it during the generation immediately following the death of Muhammad. Once the change occurred, it was, in theory, irreversible, but we do find a number of attempts to circumvent or minimize the effects of the new interpretation of Q. 4:12a: (1) ᶜUmar held that a wife is not entitled to inherit any part of the blood money (*diya*) of her husband, which is distributed among the blood relatives (*ᶜāqila*) of the deceased.[101] (2) In certain cases, the only surviving relatives of the deceased are *ahl al-farā'iḍ*, whose prescribed portions do not exhaust the estate. In such circumstances, the orthodox law schools (with the exception of the Mālikis) apply the doctrine of *radd*, returning the surplus to the "sharers" on a *pro rata* basis. Significantly, however, an exception is made for the surviving spouse, who is not allowed to participate in *radd* on the grounds that he or she is not a blood relative of the deceased.[102] (3) The Shīᶜīs hold that a childless wife inherits no share in her husband's land; furthermore, she does not inherit the immovable property—buildings, trees, etc.—*in specie*, but is entitled to receive the value of her share therein.[103] (4) A survey of the ethnographic literature reveals that Muslims throughout the world have tended to disregard the Qur'anic verses awarding shares of inheritance to women, in general, and wives, in particular.[104] A wife does, occasionally, press claims against her husband's estate, but this tends to be the exception, rather than the rule.[105] These four examples, which appear to be attempts to neutralize the undesirable effects of the

101. Tirmidhī, 3:288 (no. 2193); Ibn Māja, 2:803 (no. 2642) and 2:914 (no. 2736); Abū Dā'ūd, 8:144–45 (no. 2911).

102. Coulson, *Succession*, pp. 49–51.

103. Ibid., pp. 113–14.

104. *Women in the Muslim World*, ed. L. Beck and N. Keddie, index, s.v. "inheritance"; Gabriel Baer, *Population and Society in the Arab East*, pp. 38–40; P. Stirling, *Turkish Village*, p. 123; B. Aswad, *Property Control and Social Strategies*, p. 54.

105. Aharon Layish, *Women and Islamic Law in a Non-Muslim State*, pp. 301–06.

change in the legal status of a widow, provide further, indirect, support for our hypothesis.

I began this chapter by asking why Islamic law, unlike the other legal systems of the Near East, accords a surviving spouse the status of a full legal heir. I have argued that: (a) in the system of inheritance introduced by Muhammad, a husband and wife did not inherit from one another upon intestacy; (b) Q. 4:12a is related, indirectly, to a reform in the Roman law of inheritance instituted less than a century before the revelation of the Qur'an; (c) the award of a fractional share of the estate to a surviving spouse was intended, originally, to apply to an exceptional case; and (d) the exception was transformed into a norm, in all likelihood during the generation following the death of the Prophet, and the original function of the award came to be forgotten.

This hypothesis explains a wide range of phenomena better than the traditional understanding of Q. 4:12a does. First, the assumption that, during the lifetime of Muhammad, inheritance upon intestacy was limited to the blood relatives of the deceased brings the Qur'anic inheritance legislation into line with the other legal systems of the Near East and explains why the Prophet did not award the widow from Ṭā'if a share of her husband's estate,[106] and why the Prophet's wives made no appeal to Q. 4:12a when claiming a share of his estate.[107] Second, a shift in the interpretation of Q. 4:12a (from exception to norm) explains why the Qur'an came to appear to contradict itself and why the early Muslim authorities, when working out the details of the inheritance verses, were forced to deviate from the explicit wording of the Qur'an. Finally, subsequent efforts to circumvent or minimize the undesirable effects of awarding a share of the estate to a surviving spouse can be seen as attempts to reestablish the socioeconomic equilibrium that had been upset by the reinterpretation of Q. 4:12a.[108]

106. See above, p. 80.

107. See above, pp. 80–81.

108. The hypothesis also generates a number of new questions: What were the exact lines of transmission along which a Roman law found its way into the Qur'an? Why is the text of Q. 4:12a, which is supposed to refer to an exceptional case, worded in general terms? Exactly when did the proposed transformation take place, and for what reasons? And, finally, how is it possible that the original meaning of Q. 4:12b was forgotten? These questions are perhaps best left for a subsequent investigation.

3

The Law of Intestacy

Western scholars have sought to provide answers to two important questions regarding the formation of the Islamic law of inheritance, to wit, "What was the prevailing system of inheritance in the Hijaz prior to the revelation of the Qur'anic inheritance legislation?" and "What are the material sources of this legislation?" Scholars tend to view the Islamic law of inheritance as a creation *sui generis* which bears no relation to contemporary systems of inheritance in the Arabian peninsula or adjacent areas. According to the superimposition theory, (1) prior to the revelation of the Qur'an, matters of inheritance were regulated by the tribal customary law of pre-Islamic Arabia which limited the right to inherit to the active male members of the tribe (the *ʿaṣaba*); (2) the Qur'anic inheritance laws do not, in and of themselves, constitute a complete, comprehensive system of inheritance, but simply modify the tribal customary law by extending the right to inherit to females and relatives through females (the *ahl al-farāʾiḍ*);[1] and (3) the Qur'anic legislation was superimposed on the tribal customary law, and Muslim legists later fused together these two heterogeneous elements to form the *ʿilm al-farāʾiḍ*.[2]

1. Robert Roberts, *Social Laws of the Qoran*, p. 26, writes that "[i]t must be admitted that these laws concerning inheritance, in spite of the fact that they were promulgated with the best intention, and in spite of the fact also that they appear on first sight most minute and definite, yet are but little adapted as a basis for the formation of a complete and proper succession-law." See also Coulson, *Succession in the Muslim Family*, p. 30.

2. See W. R. Smith, *Kinship and Marriage in Early Arabia*, pp. 64–67; Marçais, *Des parents et alliés successibles en droit musulman*; Bousquet and Peltier, *Les successions agnatiques mitigées*, pp. 83–120; Coulson, *Succession*, pp. 29–30.

I maintain that the Islamic law of inheritance developed in a manner very different from that postulated by Western scholars. In the present chapter I shall attempt to substantiate the following points: (1) the *ʿaṣaba* of pre-Islamic Arabia are not identical to the *ʿaṣaba* of Islamic law; (2) the Qur'anic inheritance laws do, in fact, constitute a complete and comprehensive system of inheritance; (3) the primary purpose of this legislation was to redefine the order of priorities according to which the various classes of heirs inherit, not to extend the right of inheritance to females; and (4) the Qur'anic inheritance laws totally replaced the tribal customary law of pre-Islamic Arabia, rather than supplementing or modifying that law.

The Meaning of the Term "*ʿAṣaba*"

Western scholars routinely assert that the *ʿaṣaba* of Islamic law are a carry-over from the tribal customary law of pre-Islamic Arabia, and they attempt to reconstruct this tribal law by appealing to the Islamic term. Coulson, for example, describes the tribal customary law of pre-Islamic Arabia in the following terms:

> [I]n order to keep property within the tribe, the rights of inheritance belonged solely to the male agnate relatives (*ʿaṣaba*) of the deceased. Furthermore, it was the "nearest" such relative alone who inherited, the order of priority being the descendants of the deceased, followed by his father, his brothers, and their issue, his paternal grandfather, and finally his uncles and descendants.[3]

This statement, if correct, suggests that in pre-Islamic Arabia the child of the deceased took precedence over the latter's father and brothers in matters of inheritance; in other words, the transmission of property from one generation to the next was governed by the principle of direct descent. There is reason to believe, however, that the intergenerational transmission of property in pre-Islamic Arabia was governed, not by the rule of direct descent, but by the principle of seniority. Before attempting to substantiate this claim, I shall examine the historiographical background of Coulson's assertion regarding the *ʿaṣaba* in order to assess the nature and value of the evidence upon which it is based.

3. Coulson, *A History of Islamic Law*, p. 16.

It was W. Robertson Smith who first identified the *ʿaṣaba* as a carryover from the tribal customary law of pre-Islamic Arabia:

> But it is the limits of heirship that indicate the original basis of the system of inheritance, and these, even in Mohammedan law, are defined in a way which shews that the right of inheritance originally lay with the *ḥayy* as a whole, or rather with the active members of it. For Mohammed enjoins that after the fixed shares are paid a gratuity shall be given to every kinsman who is present at the distribution of a dead man's estate. And when there are no heirs, or something remains over after they have got their due, the reversion falls to the *ʿaṣaba*, a word which primarily means those who go to battle together, i.e. have a common blood-feud. Similarly, in the old law of Medina, women were excluded from inheritance on the principle that "none can be heirs who do not take part in battle, drive booty and protect property." (Bayḍāwī, 1 : 196)[4]

By juxtaposing the word *ʿaṣaba*, which he defines as "those who go to battle together," with Bayḍāwī's statement to the effect that the right to inherit in pre-Islamic Arabia was limited to the active male members of the tribe, Smith implies that the *ʿaṣaba* of Islamic law were the male heirs of pre-Islamic Arabia. Notice, however, that Bayḍāwī himself does not use the word *ʿaṣaba* to describe these heirs. It is only Smith, perhaps because of his familiarity with the Islamic law of inheritance, who introduces the term into the discussion.

The identification, whatever its cause, struck firm roots in scholarly discourse. Marçais later reconstructed the inheritance practices of pre-Islamic Medina by invoking the *ʿaṣaba* of Islamic law:

> Two points merit attention as being characteristic of the inheritance law of Medina: First, the exclusive right of the *ʿaṣaba*, male relatives through males, and the corresponding incapacity of females and relatives through females; second, a likely rule of individual devolution according to which the closest male relatives exclude the more distant ones.[5]

Clearly, however, Marçais's reconstruction of Medinese law is based upon the assumption of an identity between the *ʿaṣaba* of Islamic law and those of pre-Islamic Arabia, an assumption for which he provides no evidence.

4. Smith, *Kinship*, pp. 65–66.

5. Marçais, p. 35; Bousquet and Peltier, p. 84.

This assumption was later made explicit by G.-H. Bousquet when he sought to revive the Marçais thesis after it had been renounced (see my introduction) by its author:

> The entire Islamic law of inheritance is composed of the juxtaposition of two ideas: (1) That the succession must devolve upon the *ʿāṣib* relatives, males through males; (2) but that, nevertheless, a fixed share must be first allotted to certain females, or relatives through females. Since we know that which, in the elaboration of the system, is due to the Qur'an—the allocation of the fixed shares—it seems certain that the other cornerstone of the law of inheritance—agnatic devolution—is pre-Islamic.[6]

In other words, if we take the Islamic law of inheritance as the starting-point of our investigation, and subtract from it the modifications introduced by the Qur'an, the residue should approximate the tribal customary law of pre-Islamic Arabia.[7]

Curiously, the Qur'an makes no reference to the *ʿaṣaba*, the group whose rights were supposedly being modified. Bousquet, sensitive to this omission, countered by arguing that the general renown of the group made it unnecessary to mention them.[8] Indeed, Bousquet argued that the very silence of the Qur'an with regard to the *ʿaṣaba* proves that they were the heirs of pre-Islamic Arabia:

> The Qur'an presumes the existence of many institutions of which it makes no mention . . . Muslim law superimposes the *farḍ* heirs, solely instituted by the Prophet in the Qur'an, upon the male heirs. The very silence of [the Qur'an] on the subject of the *ʿaṣaba* confirms that they were the original heirs whose rights were in the process of being curtailed.[9]

The thinking of Smith, Marçais, and Bousquet, i.e., that it is possible to distill the tribal customary law of pre-Islamic Arabia out of the Islamic law of inheritance, came to represent the general consensus of western scholars on the subject, a consensus that lasted for almost twenty years before being subjected to a serious challenge. In 1949, an examination of a corpus of early *ḥadīth* led R. Brunschvig to argue that the *ʿaṣaba* of pre-Islamic

6. Bousquet and Peltier, p. 99.
7. See also Schacht, "The Law," p. 66.
8. Bousquet and Peltier, pp. 108–09.
9. Ibid., p. 109.

Arabia were not identical to the *ʿaṣaba* of Islamic times.[10] Brunschvig claimed to have discovered a more archaic form of the order of *ʿaṣaba* in the rules governing the transmission of the right to patronage (*walāʾ*). The underlying principle is expressed in the formula *al-walāʾ liʾl-kubr*, "patronage belongs to the eldest." Brunschvig suggested that the intergenerational transmission of property in pre-Islamic Arabia was governed, not by the principle of direct descent, but by the principle of seniority. His theory may be summarized as follows: A group of brothers form a kind of fraternal corporation (*fratriarcat*). As individual members of a group of brothers die, these rights become concentrated in fewer and fewer hands, until, finally, the longest-lived brother acquires a monopoly over everything. Upon his death, the next generation assumes control, and the process repeats itself. Brunschvig saw this process as a vestige of the tribal customary law of pre-Islamic Arabia which, he contended, governed the inheritance practices of the Arabs at a "remote epoch"; he did not attempt to determine when the principle of seniority gave way to that of direct descent.

Historical, linguistic, and ethnographic considerations provide support for Brunschvig's theory: (1) Strabo, describing Yemen in the first century A.D., indicates that control over property and the exercise of political office were both governed by the principle of seniority.[11] (2) It is related, on the authority of Ibn ʿAbbās, that it was customary for the Arabs of the *jāhiliyya* to award the inheritance to the eldest members of the tribe.[12] (3) The word *ʿuṣba*, which displays the same consonantal structure as the word *ʿaṣaba*, occurs frequently in pre-Islamic poetry, always in the sense of a group of men belonging to the same tribe;[13] the

10. R. Brunschvig, "Un système peu connu de succession agnatique dans le droit musulman," *Revue Historique de Droit Français Etranger* 27 (1950): 23–34; reprinted in his *Etudes d'Islamologie*, 2:53–64.

11. "Brothers have precedence over children; the kingship also and other offices of authority are filled by members of the stock in order of seniority. All the kindred have their property in common, the eldest being lord; all have one wife and it is first come first serve . . ." (*Geographus*, ed. by G. Kramer. Berlin, 1844–52, 16:4; quoted in Smith, *Kinship*, p. 158.)

12. Alūsī, *Rūḥ al-maʿānī*, 4:347: "*Annahum kānu yuʿṭūna ʾl-mīrāth al-akbar faʾl-akbar.*"

13. Azharī, *Tahdhīb al-lugha*, 1:455 (l. 15a); 2:316; Krenkow (ed.), *Ḥamāsat ibn al-Shajarī*, p. 12 (l. 19); Ahlwardt (ed.), *Der Dīwān des Regezdichters Rūba*

same term occurs four times in the Qur'an, again in the sense of "a group or band of brothers."[14] (4) Chelhod, in his study of law among the Bedouin, notes that the principle of seniority governs the transmission of property upon death:

> If the father of the deceased is still alive, and the latter has children, it is the former, nevertheless, who has the right to inherit. Upon his death, the property does not devolve upon his grandchildren, the direct heirs of the original deceased, but upon his own children, i.e., the brothers of the original deceased. This injustice is nicely conveyed by the following saying of the Bedouin: "The height of misfortune is to lose one's father before one's grandfather."[15]

Brunschvig's reconstruction of the tribal customary law of pre-Islamic Arabia did not attract the attention it deserves. Schacht indicated his general approval of the thesis, extending it to cover the period up to the Prophet.[16] But Coulson, who writes extensively about the tribal customary law of pre-Islamic Arabia, appears to have been totally unaware of Brunschvig's theory—at least, he mentions it nowhere. In what follows I shall attempt to show that Brunschvig's thesis not only facilitates a better understanding of the relationship between the tribal customary law of

---

ben El-'aggāg, p. 20 (l. 1); Ṭabarī, *Annales* (De Goeje), I/2:956 (l. 17); 4:1964 (l. 9); 5:2365 (l. 3); II/1:154 (l. 7); 1:641 (l. 7); 1:340 (l. 7); and 3:1923 (l. 13); Cheikho (ed.), *Le Kitāb al-Hamāsah de Abū Ubādat al-Buḥturī*, p. 88 (l. 1); p. 267 (l. 11); B. Lewin, *A Vocabulary of Hudailian Poems*, p. 289; Bevan (ed.), *The Naqā'iḍ of Jarīr and al-Farazdak*, p. 546 (l. 12); p. 716 (ll. 3 and 6); p. 988 (l. 9); p. 1078 (l. 11); Freytag (ed.), *Hamasae Carmina*, p. 71 (l. 26); p. 389 (l. 11); p. 640 (l. 11); p. 654 (l. 18); Balādhurī, *Ansāb al-ashrāf*, 4b:96 (l. 19); 4b:149 (l. 19); Baghdādī, *Kitāb al-Munammaq fī Akhbār Quraish*, p. 58 (l. 3); Ibn Hishām, *Sīra*, p. 44 (l. 13); p. 438 (l. 17); p. 526 (l. 5); p. 705 (l. 11); p. 707 (l. 18); p. 710 (l. 12); Ibn Qutayba, *al-Shiʿr wa'l-shuʿarā*, 2:589; Ahlwardt (ed.), *The Diwans of the Six Ancient Arabic Poets*, p. 16 (l. 14); Abū Zayd al-Anṣārī, *Kitāb al-nawādir fi'l-lugha*, p. 230 (l. 3); MacCartney (ed.), *The Dīwān of Ghailān b. ʿUqbah, known as Dhū' r-Rumma*, p. 168 (l. 6); p. 405 (l. 15); Bukhārī, *Ṣaḥīḥ*, 4:193. I would like to thank Ms. Zmira Cohen for making available to me the resources of the Jerusalem Concordance of Pre-Islamic Poetry.

14. Q. 12:8 reads: "When they said: 'Surely Joseph and his brothers are dearer to our father than we, though we are a band (*ʿuṣba*).'" The term is used in the same sense six verses later in the same chapter: "They said: 'If the wolf eats him, though we are a band (*ʿuṣba*), then surely we are lost.'" Cf. Q. 24:11 and 28:76. The word *ʿaṣaba* does not occur in the Qur'an.

15. J. Chelhod, *Le droit dans la société bédouine*, p. 135.

16. Schacht, "The Law," p. 67.

pre-Islamic Arabia and the Qur'anic legislation, but also sheds light on the significance of a hitherto obscure Qur'anic phrase.

The Law of Intestacy

Islamic tradition teaches that Q. 4:11, 4:12, and 4:176, which award shares of the estate to the daughter(s), father, mother, husband, wife, uterine sibling(s), and consanguine and/or germane sister(s), were revealed in order to extend the right to inherit to females.[17] I see this in a different light.

The length and density of these three verses raises the interesting—and, I believe, essential—question of versification. I have already demonstrated that Q. 4:12, which is traditionally "sandwiched" between Q. 4:11 and 4:176, can be broken down into two distinct subverses: the first, Q. 4:12a, awards a small fractional share of the estate to an unendowed spouse; the second, Q. 4:12b, awards a fractional share of the estate to a disinherited sibling.[18] Originally, neither subverse had anything to do with either compulsory rules or rules of intestacy, and I have therefore "removed" them from their traditional position between Q. 4:11 and 4:176 (see chapters 1 and 2). Q. 4:11 (see appendix A), like 4:12, can also be broken down into two subverses. Muslim scholars, when reading the verse, focus exclusively on *shares*, a perspective which causes it to appear as a single unit awarding shares of the estate, first to the daughter(s) and then to the mother. But if one focuses instead on the *heirs*, two distinct subverses become apparent. The first four sentences (hereafter 4:11a), up to and including, "Each one of his parents is entitled to one-sixth of what he leaves, if he has a child," all treat cases in which the deceased leaves at least one child. The next two sentences (hereafter 4:11b), beginning with, "If he does not have a

17. The presence of the husband and uterine brother among the *ahl al-farā'iḍ*, although problematic, can perhaps be explained by a desire to extend the right to inherit to male affines and certain relatives through females. But the presence of the father, one of the male heirs of pre-Islamic Arabia, is not so easily explained. Why award a fractional share of the estate to someone who already enjoyed the right to inherit? See Schacht, *An Introduction to Islamic Law*, pp. 171–72.

18. See chaps. 1 and 2.

child, and his parents are his heirs," both deal with cases in which the deceased leaves no children, and his parents are his closest surviving relatives.[19]

The division of Q. 4:11 and 4:12 into four subverses compels us, when attempting to explain the relation between these four units, to make assumptions that differ from those of the Islamic law of inheritance, and generates, in the process, a new system of inheritance—proto-Islamic law. In chapter 1, I reconstructed the proto-Islamic law of *testate* succession, using my reinterpretation of Q. 4:12b as the starting point, and in chapter 2 I argued for the exceptional nature of the award, in Q. 4:12a, to a surviving spouse. That leaves Q. 4:11a, 4:11b, and 4:176.[20] I shall attempt to demonstrate here that these three units form the core of the proto-Islamic law of *intestacy*, a system based upon simple mathematical rules that generate few, if any, of the difficulties characteristic of the Islamic law of inheritance. (The Islamic law of inheritance, it will be remembered, does not distinguish between testate succession and intestacy, but rather imposes compulsory rules for the division of property.)

These three units each contain between two and five sentences that can be viewed as discrete cases to be solved individually. A given case may involve anywhere from one to five (or more) heirs. The Qur'an frequently conveys the solution to these cases in a shorthand manner by stating the entitlement of only one of the heirs, usually a female. The text, however, contains rules that make it possible to determine the inheritance of the other heirs who, although mentioned, are not awarded a specific fractional share of the estate.[21] By working through Q. 4:11a, 4:11b, and 4:176 sentence by sentence, I shall attempt to recon-

19. Muslim legists also find it convenient to divide Q. 4:11 into two sections, but their fixation on "shares" causes them to do so at a different point than we do. The first three sentences of Q. 4:11 award fractional shares of the estate to daughters, and the next three sentences award fractional shares to the mother. Mālik (d. A.D. 795), *Muwaṭṭa'*, 2:504 and 506–07, divides the verse into two sections at the point where the award of shares to daughters gives way to the award of shares to the mother, thus blurring the distinction between the first two classes of heirs in proto-Islamic law, children and parents.

20. Q. 4:176 contains five sentences, all of which treat the case in which the deceased's closest surviving relative is a brother or sister. Unlike Q. 4:11 and 4:12, it cannot be broken down into subverses.

21. Muslim exegetes and legists ignore these persons.

struct the general outlines, and much of the detail, of the proto-Islamic law of intestacy.

Q. 4:11a: Children as Primary Heirs

Q. 4:11a treats the first class of heirs upon intestacy, children. It is composed of four sentences, all of which deal with cases in which the deceased leaves at least one child. Each sentence can be read as a discrete case which illustrates the rules of intestacy for a different combination of heirs. In the following translation, the sentences have been numbered for the sake of convenient reference:

> (1) God commands you concerning your children: A male is entitled to the share of two females. (2) If they are females above two, then they are entitled to two-thirds of what he leaves. (3) If there is one, then she is entitled to half. (4) Each one of his parents is entitled to one-sixth of what he leaves, if he has a child.

Sentence 1 is phrased in general terms ("a male is entitled to the share of two females") so as to make it possible to determine the solution for any combination of sons and daughters. Suppose, for example, that the deceased leaves one son and one daughter: the son inherits two-thirds of the estate and the daughter one-third. It is unnecessary to specify the cases in which the deceased leaves two sons and one daughter, two daughters and one son, etc., because the solution to them is governed by the principle, "a male is entitled to the share of two females."[22]

Sentences 2 and 3 treat the cases in which the deceased leaves one or more daughters, but no son. Sentence 3 indicates that one daughter inherits half of the estate, i.e., half the maximum entitlement of an only son (see below). The remaining half of the estate, the destination of which is unspecified, presumably falls to the "secondary heirs" (see below), if any. Sentence 2 states that

22. Mālik, who must reserve a fairly large portion of the estate for the other "sharers," is less explicit about the entitlement of sons and daughters: "If someone inherits together with them, by virtue of a specified share, and the [children] include a male, one begins with the 'sharers', and whatever remains after that is divided among the children according to their rights of inheritance." Thus, in Islamic law, the son and daughter inherit only *after* the satisfaction of the claims of the qualifying *ahl al-farā'iḍ*. See Mālik, 2:503.

three or more daughters divide a maximum of two-thirds of the estate on a per capita basis.[23] Once again, the residue presumably falls to the secondary heir(s), if any.[24]

Q. 4:11a does not specifically mention the case in which the deceased leaves one or more sons, perhaps because the Qur'an is primarily concerned with clarifying the more problematic aspects of inheritance, especially the rights of females. But the entitlement of an only son is easily derived from the information contained in the verse. If a male is entitled to the share of two females, and if an only daughter inherits half of the estate, then an only son must inherit the entire estate; two sons would presumably divide the estate in half; and so on.[25]

Parents may enter the inheritance together with a child, but only as "secondary heirs" for whom a maximum of one-third is reserved. Sentence 4 treats such a case: "Each one of his parents is entitled to one-sixth of what he leaves, if he has a child." Suppose, for example, that the deceased leaves his son, mother, and father. Each parent inherits one-sixth of the estate, and the son (the "primary heir") inherits the remaining two-thirds.[26] Notice that the father and mother divide the one-third of the estate reserved for secondary heirs on a per capita basis, irrespective of sex, a blatant contradiction of the principle that "a male is entitled to the share of two females." Muslim scholars, unable to explain this anomaly, pass over it in silence.[27]

The distinction between primary and secondary heirs may provide an explanation for the apparent contradiction between

23. The inheritance of *two* daughters can be derived either from the *sunna* of the Prophet, who awarded two-thirds of the estate to the two daughters of Umm Kuḥḥa and Saʿd b. al-Rabīʿ, or by analogy to Q. 4:176, which awards two-thirds of the estate to two sisters.

24. My conclusions, here, do not differ significantly from those of Muslim legists. See, for example, Mālik, 2:504.

25. Mālik cannot pursue this line of reasoning because he must reserve up to seven-twelfths of the estate for the qualifying *ahl al-farā'iḍ*, i.e., the father, mother, and husband or wife.

26. Mālik (2:506–07) expresses no interest whatsoever in the son; he cannot conclude that the son inherits the remaining two-thirds of the estate because he must reserve as much as half the estate for a surviving spouse. (Note the shorthand manner in which the Qur'an conveys the solution to a case in which there are three heirs by stating the entitlement of the two secondary heirs, leaving the reader to determine the entitlement of the primary heir.)

27. The principle is also violated in Q. 4:12b, which awards one-sixth of the estate to a (uterine) brother or sister. See chap. 1 for further details on this.

Table 1.
Children and Parents

Primary heirs				*Secondary heirs*	
Sons	*Share*	*Daughters*	*Share*	*Parents*	*Share*
One	All	x	x	x	x
One	2/3	One	1/3	x	x
One	1/2	Two	1/4 each	x	x
Two	1/2 each	x	x	x	x
Two	2/5 each	One	1/5	x	x
One	2/3	x	x	Both	1/6 each
One	4/9	One	2/9	Both	1/6 each
One	2/6	Two	1/6 each	Both	1/6 each
Two	2/6 each	x	x	Both	1/6 each
Two	4/15 each	One	2/15	Both	1/6 each

the two Qur'anic statements. The principle that "a male is entitled to the share of two females" applies only in those cases in which a male and female of the same class, e.g., son and daughter, inherit as primary heirs. But when a male and female of the same class, such as a father and mother, or brother and sister, inherit as secondary heirs, the rule is ignored and the heirs inherit on a per capita basis. The case of a father and mother, who may inherit either as secondary heirs (as in sentence 4 of Q. 4:11a) or as primary heirs (as in sentence 1 of Q. 4:11b), provides an excellent illustration of this point: In the former case the father and mother inherit one-sixth each, whereas in the latter (see below) the father inherits two-thirds and the mother one-third. (The results of my investigation of Q. 4:11a are summarized in table 1.)

Q. 4:11b: Parents and Siblings as Primary Heirs

A man or woman may die childless for any of a number of reasons, such as bachelorhood or spinsterhood, celibacy, sterility, infant mortality, death through injury or disease, and so on. But a person who dies childless may be survived by parents, siblings, uncles, cousins, and the like, and the law must establish a set of priorities to determine which of these will inherit upon intestacy.

The second class of legal heirs, after children, is composed of parents and siblings. Three different combinations are possible: parent(s) only, parent(s) and sibling(s), and sibling(s) only. Q. 4:11b treats the first two combinations; Q. 4:176 treats the third.

Q. 4:11b reads as follows:

> (1) If he does not have a child, and his parents are his heirs, then his mother is entitled to one-third. (2) If he has brothers, then his mother is entitled to one-sixth, after any bequest he bequeaths, or debt.

Sentence 1 treats the case in which the deceased dies childless, leaving both parents but no siblings. The Qur'an states that the mother inherits one-third, and it leaves the reader to ascertain easily the entitlement of the father (two-thirds) on the basis of the principle that "a male is entitled to the share of two females."[28] Although Q. 4:11b does not mention the case in which the deceased is survived by one parent, the solution can be derived by analogy to the similar cases mentioned in Q. 4:11a: A father, as the only heir, inherits the entire estate, whereas a mother, as the only heir, inherits half.

Sentence 2 poses some difficulty. It might refer to a man who dies leaving a mother and brothers, or to a man who dies leaving a mother, father, and brothers. I find the latter possibility more plausible because sentence 2 appears to be a special case of sentence 1, the difference being the addition of brothers to the constellation of heirs. Let us assume, then, that a man dies leaving his father, mother, and one or more brothers. Do the father and brother both inherit and, if so, how much do they receive? The following report provides a possible answer to this question:

> Zayd b. Thābit wrote to [Muʿāwiyā b. Abī Sufyān]: "You have written me asking about the grandfather. God knows best! That is one of the issues upon which only the commanders (*umarā'*), i.e.,

28. Mālik (2:506) again cannot pursue this line of reasoning because he must reserve between one-eighth and one-half of the estate for a surviving spouse. He indicates, moreover, that the father may inherit as little as one-sixth: "If the deceased leaves neither a child nor a male grandchild, then the 'sharers' who inherit together with the father are given precedence, and they are given their shares. If one-sixth or more of the property remains, it is for the father. If one-sixth or more does not remain, then the father is awarded one-sixth as a share."

> the caliphs, have passed judgment. I attended the two caliphs who preceded you when they gave him [viz., the grandfather] one-half in competition with an only brother, and one-third in competition with two brothers. If there are many brothers, they did not give him less than one-third."[29]

This report suggests that the grandfather and brothers do not bar one another from entering the inheritance. The grandfather and the siblings inherit on a per capita basis, unless there are three or more siblings, in which case a minimum of one-third is reserved for the grandfather, and the siblings divide the remaining two-thirds among themselves.[30] Inasmuch as the grandfather inherits by analogy to the father, rules that apply to the former no doubt also apply to the latter. This assumption makes it possible to derive the solution to sentence 2.

Let us begin with simple cases. If a man dies leaving his father and one brother, the two men divide the estate in half. If the deceased leaves his father and two brothers, each heir takes one-third of the estate. And if he dies leaving his father and three brothers, the father takes one-third and the brothers divide the remaining two-thirds on a per capita basis, taking two-ninths each.

The addition of the mother to the calculation complicates matters somewhat. Suppose, for example, that a man dies leaving his mother, father, and three brothers. Sentence 2 awards the mother one-sixth of the estate; the father (according to the principle, "a male is entitled to the share of two females") inherits one-third; and the brothers, on the basis of the Zayd report, divide the remaining half of the estate on a per capita basis, taking one-sixth each. Two brothers would inherit one-fourth each and one brother, half. (The results of this investigation of Q. 4:11b are summarized in table 2.)

Q. 4:176: Siblings as Sole Primary Heirs

The second class of heirs is composed of parents and/or siblings. As noted above, there are three possible combinations of heirs.

29. Mālik, 2:510. (*Isnād*: Yaḥyā b. Saʿīd—Muʿāwiya b. Abī Sufyān—Zayd b. Thābit.)

30. The report cited by Mālik is invoked to justify an exception to the rule, in Islamic law, that ascendents exclude collaterals.

Table 2.
Parents and Siblings

Primary heirs				*Secondary heirs*	
Father	All	x		x	x
Father	⅔	Mother	⅓	x	x
x		Mother	½	x	x
Father	½	x		Brother	½
Father	⅓	Mother	⅙	Brother	½
Father	⅓	x		2 brothers	⅓ each
Father	⅓	Mother	⅙	2 brothers	¼ each
Father	⅓	x		3 brothers	2/9 each
Father	⅓	Mother	⅙	3 brothers	⅙ each

Table 3.
Siblings Alone

Brothers	*Share*	*Sisters*	*Share*
One	All	x	x
Two	½ each	x	x
One	⅔	One	⅓
Two	⅖ each	One	⅕
One	½	Two	¼ each
x	x	One	½
x	x	Two	⅓ each

The first two, parent(s) alone, and parent(s) and sibling(s), are dealt with in Q. 4:11b; the third, sibling(s) alone, is dealt with in Q. 4:176, which reads as follows:

> When they ask you for a decision, say: God decrees for you in the case of *al-kalāla*: (1) If a man dies without a child, and he has a sister, then she is entitled to half of what he leaves. (2) He is her heir if she does not have a child. (3) If they (f.) are two, then they are entitled to two-thirds of what he leaves. (4) If they are brothers and sisters, then a male is entitled to the share of two females. God makes clear for you [lest] you go astray. God is all-knowing.

Q. 4:176, which specifies the rules of inheritance for siblings, is virtually identical to Q. 4:11a, which does the same for children. A sole surviving sister (sentence 1) inherits half of the estate.[31] Two or more sisters (sentence 3) inherit two-thirds of the estate.[32] Finally, whenever a combination of brothers and sisters inherit, the estate is divided up in accordance with the principle, "a male is entitled to the share of two females."[33]

Q. 4:176 contains an additional provision which, incidentally, confirms an assumption made above. When working out the details of Q. 4:11a, which does not specify the entitlement of an only son, I assumed that, since an only daughter inherits half the estate, and a male is entitled to the share of two females, an only son inherits the entire estate. This assumption is corroborated by sentence 2 of Q. 4:176, which treats the analogous case of a brother who is the sole surviving heir of his sister, and states, "he is her heir," i.e., he inherits the entire estate.[34] (The results of my investigation of Q. 4:176 are summarized in table 3.)

Summary: The Proto-Islamic Law of Intestacy

The proto-Islamic law of intestacy limits the right to inherit to the blood relatives of the deceased.[35] Husbands and wives do not, under normal circumstances, inherit from one another.[36] The deceased's legal heirs are his blood relatives, arranged in hierarchically related classes, irrespective of sex: (1) children; (2) parents and/or siblings; (3) siblings alone. Uncles, cousins, and the like, although not specifically mentioned in the Qur'an, presumably fill the classes below siblings. Members of a higher class bar any and all members of a lower class from entering the inheritance as primary heirs, e.g., children bar parents and siblings from entering the inheritance as primary heirs. Members of a lower class may, nevertheless, enter the inheritance as secondary heirs.

31. Cf. sentence (3) of Q. 4:11a.

32. Cf. sentence (2) of Q. 4:11a.

33. Cf. sentence (1) of Q. 4:11a.

34. See Shāfiʿī (*Risāla*, p. 255) who glosses sentences (2) and (3) of Q. 4:176 as follows: "Thus [God] prescribed that if the sister is the only survivor, she is to receive half; if the brother is the only survivor, he is to receive the entire estate."

35. See chap. 2, where I argue that this principle is established by Q. 4:8.

36. Only in the case of an unendowed spouse (see chap. 2) does a husband or wife inherit upon intestacy.

The primary heirs (except when there is only one, and she is female), inherit a minimum of two-thirds of the estate. If the primary heir is a single female, she inherits half as much as a male would have taken in similar circumstances. Two or more female primary heirs inherit a maximum of two-thirds of the estate. A maximum of one-third is reserved for the secondary heirs.

The rule that "a male is entitled to the share of two females" applies only to males and females of the same class who inherit as primary heirs: A father and mother, for example, inherit in the proportion of two shares for the male to one for the female when they inherit as primary heirs. But when the father and mother inherit as secondary heirs, e.g., when the deceased leaves his son and both parents, they inherit equal shares of the estate.

Sons and daughters have an unqualified right of inheritance. They automatically bar parents and siblings from entering the inheritance as primary heirs. Thus, children are the primary heirs of the proto-Islamic law of intestacy. Parents and siblings inherit, sometimes as primary heirs, sometimes as secondary heirs, depending upon the circumstances.

The proto-Islamic law of intestacy, then, differs radically from the "science of the shares." The latter grants the right of inheritance to affincs, makes no distinction between primary and secondary heirs (and therefore cannot account for the violation of the rule, "a male is entitled to the share of two females"), frequently requires complex mathematical calculations in order to determine the relative entitlement of the various heirs, and does not accord a position of primacy to the children of the deceased.

"Your Fathers and Your Sons"

Towards the end of Q. 4:11, immediately after awarding shares of the estate to the daughter(s), father, and mother, the Divinity states: *"Abā'ukum wa-abnā'ukum lā tadrūna ayyuhum aqrabu lakum naf'an . . ."* Muslim exegetes focus their attention on two aspects of this sentence. Is it addressed to the person anticipating death, or to the heirs? And does the word "usefulness" (*naf'an*) refer to usefulness in this world or in the next? Most exegetes consider the sentence to have been addressed to the person contemplating death,[37] but there is considerable variety of opinion regarding the temporal significance of the sentence. Some see it as referring to this world: (a) The most frequently mentioned explanation emphasizes the gap between the supreme wisdom of the Creator and the ignorance of man. Man, because of the limitations of his knowledge, cannot know which of his relatives is really most useful to him; nevertheless, he may attempt to distribute his estate in accordance with his personal estimation of their worth. This approach is doomed to failure because man does not know where his best interests actually lie, and it is for this reason that God, in His supreme wisdom, imposed standard, compulsory shares.[38] (b) More specifically, it is impossible for man to determine which is more useful, i.e., deserves greater compensation—the parents' upbringing of their children or the child's support for his parents in their old age.[39] (c) Alternatively, the confusion may refer to man's inability to know who will die first, his father or his son; God imposed the shares so that he will not hope for the possible material advantage that may result from one or the other of these circumstances.[40]

But it is also possible to read other-worldly significance into the sentence, as other exegetes do. Some link the sentence to the immediately preceding reference to bequests ("after any bequest he bequeaths") and teach that the rewards in the next world are greater than the rewards in this one. They argue as follows: You (the heir) do not know who is more useful to you, the relative who leaves a bequest for others, or the one who does not. The former makes you eligible for recompense in the next world in return for your having carried out the terms of the bequest, whereas the latter leaves you to enjoy the goods of this world. Although you may be attracted to the goods of this world, know that the reward you will receive in the next is actually greater.[41]

37. But see Ṭabāṭabā'ī, *al-Mīzān fī tafsīr al-qur'ān*, 4:209–10.

38. Ṭabarī, *Jāmiʿ*, 4:282; Zamakhsharī, *Kashshāf*, 1:484; Ṭabarsī, *Majmaʿ al-bayān*, 3:35; Rāzī, *al-Tafsīr al-kabīr*, 9:217–18; Ibn al-ʿArabī, *Aḥkām al-qur'ān*, 1:345; Bayḍāwī, *Anwār al-tanzīl*, 1:198; Nasafī, *Tafsīr*, 1:208; Nīsābūrī, *Gharā'ib*, 4:196.

39. Zamakhsharī, 1:484; Ṭabarsī, 3:35; Rāzī, 9:217–18; Nīsābūrī, *Gharā'ib*, 4:196; Alūsī, 4:345.

40. Ṭabarsī, 3:35; Rāzī, 9:217–18; Nīsābūrī, *Gharā'ib*, 4:196.

41. Bayḍāwī, 1:198; Nīsābūrī, *Gharā'ib*, 4:196; Alūsī, 4:345.

Other exegetes link the sentence to the erroneous belief that a father, because of his age, wisdom, and strength, is more useful than a son. The exegetes again convey the lesson that the appearances of this world should not be confused with the realities of the next. The story is told, in this connection, of a son who occupied a higher level in Paradise than his father and interceded on behalf of the latter to have him raised to the higher level.[42]

But what the exegetes do not successfully explain is the fact that the sentence *"Abā'ukum wa-abnā'ukum . . ."* occurs at the end of a verse which, according to Islamic tradition, extends the right to inherit to *females* by awarding fractional shares of the estate to the daughter(s), mother, and so on. This sentence, which properly means, "Your *fathers* and your *sons*, you know not which of them is closer to you in usefulness" (emphasis added),[43] makes little sense when viewed in the context of the Islamic law of inheritance. Translators of the Qur'an have glossed over the problem by rendering the opening phrase of the sentence as "Your parents and your children" rather than "Your fathers and your sons."[44] But this translation is both misleading and wholly inaccurate. *Abā'* means "fathers," not "parents," and *abnā'* means "sons," not "children."[45]

This problematic sentence ceases to be problematic, however, when viewed within the framework of the proto-Islamic law of intestacy. The legislation introduced in Q. 4:11a and 4:11b performs two primary functions: first, it establishes the order of priorities according to which the relatives of the deceased enter the

42. Ṭabarī, *Jāmiʿ*, 4:282; Zamakhsharī, 1:484; Ṭabarsī, 3:35; Rāzī, 9:217–18; Qurṭubī, *Jāmiʿ*, 5:74–75; Bayḍāwī, 1:198; Nīsābūrī, *Gharā'ib*, 4:196; Ibn Juzayy, *Kitāb al-tashīl*, 1:236–37; Alūsī, 4:345.

43. *Abā'* is the plural of *ab*, which signifies "father." *Abnā'* is the plural of *ibn*, which means "son."

44. See, for example, *The Koran*, tr. George Sale (London, 1850), p. 61; *The Qur'an*, tr. E. H. Palmer (Oxford, 1900): 1:73; and *The Koran*, tr. N. J. Dawood (Penguin, 1956), p. 367. J. M. Rodwell (*The Koran*, London, 1909, p. 43) adopted an intermediate position: "As for your fathers and your children . . ." To the best of my knowledge, only R. Bell (*The Qur'an*, Edinburgh, 1937, 1:69) and A. J. Arberry (*The Koran Interpreted*, London, 1955, 1:106) render the phrase as "Your fathers and your sons . . ."

45. The concept of "parents" is expressed in the Qur'an by the terms *abawāni* (Q. 4:11, 7:27, 12:6, 12:99–100; and 18:80) and *wālidāni* (e.g., Q. 2:83, 2:180, 2:215, 4:7, 4:33, 4:36, 4:135, 6:151, 17:23). The concept "children" is expressed by the plural noun *awlād* (e.g., Q. 2:233, 4:11, 6:151, 8:28, 17:31, 24:37, 60:3, 63:9, 64:14–15).

inheritance; second, it regulates the relative entitlement of males and females. The phrase "Your fathers and your sons" would appear to relate to the first of these two functions.

Brunschvig has argued that in pre-Islamic Arabia the transmission of property from one generation to the next was governed by the principle of seniority. Chelhod came to the same conclusion in his study of contemporary Bedouin tribes, adding that this principle often leads to intergenerational conflict between fathers and sons. If Brunschvig is correct, and if my reconstruction of the proto-Islamic law of intestacy is sound, then the Qur'anic rules governing the transmission of property via inheritance were intended to establish the principle of *direct descent* from father to son. In my reconstruction, the son not only inherits directly from his father but also excludes his grandfather and uncles from entering the inheritance as primary heirs. In other words, the proto-Islamic law of intestacy reduces the primary heirs of tribal customary law to the status of secondary heirs, while elevating the secondary heirs, children, to a position of primacy. The sentence, "Your fathers and your sons, you know not which of them is closer to you in usefulness," it seems to me, is a divine admonishment of those Arabs who continued to practice the old rules of inheritance. It would appear, then, that the Qur'anic inheritance legislation was meant, not to supplement the tribal customary law, as the superimposition theory indicates, but to replace that law in its entirety.

Western scholars, in their attempts to trace the formation of the Islamic law of inheritance, have argued that the right to inherit in pre-Islamic Arabia was limited to the active male members of the tribe, arranged in a series of hierarchically related classes, with sons occupying the first class; the Qur'anic legislation modified this situation by extending the right to inherit to females, and, subsequently, these two heterogeneous elements—the tribal customary law of pre-Islamic Arabia and the Qur'anic legislation—were fused together to form the "science of the shares."

This representation, in my opinion, must now be discarded. The transmission of property from one generation to the next in pre-Islamic Arabia was, in all likelihood, governed by the principle of seniority, not direct descent. Muhammad introduced a system of inheritance (what I call "proto-Islamic law") which was more or less complete. This system, which has few of the entanglements of the "science of the shares," was intended, not to modify the tribal customary law of pre-Islamic Arabia, but in fact to replace it.[46]

Conclusion: The Proto-Islamic Law of Inheritance

In part one of this study I have attempted to work backwards from the traditional understanding of several Qur'anic verses and prophetic *ḥadīth* to what I believe to have been their original significance. This approach has led me to postulate the existence of a hitherto unknown stage in the development of the Islamic law of inheritance which I refer to as "proto-Islamic law." I maintain that Muhammad introduced proto-Islamic, not Islamic, law and, further, that this system (1) came to replace the tribal customary law of pre-Islamic Arabia and (2) placed only minimal constraints upon the individual's freedom to determine the ultimate devolution of his/her property. In part two I shall argue (3) that the proto-Islamic law of inheritance was transformed, during the years following the death of Muhammad, into what would become known as the *ʿilm al-farāʾiḍ*. But first it may be helpful to summarize the provisions for testate succession and intestacy introduced by the proto-Islamic law of inheritance.

46. Although an investigation of the material sources of the proto-Islamic law of intestacy lies beyond the scope of this study, I suspect that a comparison of proto-Islamic law and other systems of inheritance operating in the Near East at approximately the same time will yield fruitful results. Egyptian, Syro-Roman, and Jewish law, for example, all limit inheritance upon intestacy to blood relatives of the deceased, arrange these relatives in a series of hierarchically related classes, and award shares of the estate to both males and females. There are differences, too. Egyptian law awards a double portion to the eldest son, whereas the daughter and all younger sons receive equal shares. Syro-Roman law treats sons and daughters on a basis of equality. According to Jewish law, the first son receives a double share and daughters inherit only in the absence of a son. There are also differences with respect to the classes of heirs. In Egyptian, Jewish, and Syro-Roman law, the first three classes, in order of priority, are children, parents, and siblings. But the differences, which may reflect regional and cultural variations, do not outweigh the overall similarity of these systems, and, in the future, scholars will have to pay serious attention to the possibility of Near Eastern influence on the Qur'anic legislation. (See Pestman, "The Law of Succession in Ancient Egypt"; K. Bruns (ed.), *Syrisch-römisches Rechtsbuch aus dem fünften Jahrhundert*; and Shilo, "Succession," in *The Encyclopedia Judaica*.)

The law of testate succession allowed a person anticipating death to designate as his/her heir a son, daughter, or other close relative, or an affine such as a spouse or in-law; in the latter case, however, relatives who would have inherited in the absence of the will are awarded a small fractional share of the estate as compensation for the disherison (Q. 4:12b). The testator might, in addition, bequeath up to one-third of the estate (*al-waṣiyya fi'l-thulth*) to parents and/or other close relatives (Q. 2:180). To be valid, a last will and testament had to be drawn up or dictated in the presence of two trustworthy witnesses (Q. 5:105–106). Tampering with the provisions of a will was discouraged (Q. 2:181), and disagreements over the provisions of a will were to be referred to a third party for settlement (Q. 2:182).

The law of intestacy took effect only in the absence of a valid last will and testament. The right to inherit upon intestacy was limited to blood relatives of the deceased (Q. 4:8); husbands and wives did not inherit from one another, except in the case of the unendowed spouse (Q. 4:12a). Heirs were divided into different classes—children, parents, and siblings—as established by Q. 4:11a, 4:11b and 4:176; these three units illustrate the application of the rules of intestacy to a select number of cases. A distinction can be drawn between primary heirs who inherit between 50 and 100 percent of the estate and secondary heirs who inherit a maximum of one-third. Children always inherit as primary heirs; parents and siblings inherit either as primary or secondary heirs, depending on the circumstances.

My theory accounts for a wide range of disparate phenomena for which neither Muslim nor western scholars have been able to provide a satisfactory explanation. Those who dispute my theory may want to advance an alternative explanation for the following five points:

(1) The early Islamic sources preserve a series of anecdotes that point to uncertainty regarding the meaning of the word *kalāla*, anecdotes in which the second caliph, ʿUmar b. al-Khaṭṭāb, plays a prominent role. ʿUmar is reported to have said, "The Messenger of God did not become as cross with me about anything as he did in the matter of *al-kalāla*." When a man approached ʿUmar and asked him about the meaning of this word, the caliph responded by grabbing his beard, repeating the word three times, and exclaiming, "By God, I would rather know its meaning than possess anything on earth." On another occasion

ʿUmar announced his intention to issue a public decree regarding *al-kalāla*, but reneged on his promise after a snake appeared, causing all the people who had gathered in the mosque to scatter. It is also reported that ʿUmar, on his deathbed, called for and erased a document that he had written about *al-kalāla*. These anecdotes make little or no sense when viewed in the context of the Islamic law of inheritance, for what could have been so controversial or mysterious about a word that means either "a man who dies leaving neither parent nor child" or "all those except the parent and child," or about a verse that awards a small fractional share of the estate to siblings? The commentators and legists, not surprisingly, paid little attention to the anecdotes, which began to pass out of circulation after the tenth century A.D.

These anecdotes, I maintain, were put into circulation by persons who objected to the traditional interpretation of Q. 4:12b, but who could not openly state the nature of this objection—and with good reason, for to do so would be tantamount to admitting that the early Muslim community had tampered with the recitation and interpretation of the Qur'an.[47] These people did manage, however, to circulate a series of carefully coded anecdotes that allude, between the lines, to the original significance of Q. 4:12b.

(2) Muslim scholars take the phrase "a male is entitled to the share of two females" which occurs once in Q. 4:11 and again in 4:176 as a general principle applying to all males and females of the same class and degree of relationship to the deceased. It is therefore difficult for these scholars to explain why the mother and father in Q. 4:11 and the brother and sister in Q. 4:12 are awarded equal shares of the estate. But the distinction I have made between primary and secondary heirs provides a simple explanation of this phenomenon. In proto-Islamic law the relative entitlement of a father/mother or brother/sister varies depending on whether they inherit as primary or secondary heirs. When they inherit as primary heirs, the male takes twice the share of a female, but when they inherit as secondary heirs, they take equal shares of the estate. This explanation covers all of the cases cited in Q. 4:11, 4:12 and 4:176.

(3) The Qur'an commentators perceive a number of semantic

47. Islamic doctrine maintains that the Jews and Christians tampered with the texts of their respective scriptures, whereas the Muslims are supposedly in possession of a pure, unadulterated text.

and grammatical difficulties with Q. 4:12b, including the definition and function of the word *kalāla*, the bifurcated subject, "a man . . . or a woman," and the inappropriateness of the pronoun reference, "he," referring back to this compound subject. Although it is possible to resolve each of these problems on an individual basis, as the commentators do, the very existence of the problems is, in my opinion, explained by the replacement of the original reading of the verse with a secondary reading. Restoring the original reading has the effect of eliminating all of these problems at one blow.

(4) Q. 4:12b and 4:176, as generally understood by Muslim scholars, appear to contradict one another, the former awarding siblings a different share of the estate than the latter does. The commentators resolve this discrepancy by drawing an arbitrary distinction between the type of sibling that is supposedly mentioned in the two verses, i.e., uterines in the former and consanguine and/or germane siblings in the latter. Again, the restoration to Q. 4:12b of its original reading eliminates the problem because, when viewed in this manner, the verse deals with a specific application of the law of testate succession, whereas Q. 4:176 defines the rights of siblings upon intestacy.

(5) Muslim legists, when working out the details of the "science of the shares," encountered a number of problems that forced them to deviate from the explicit wording of the Qur'an. In certain circumstances, for example, the sum of the shares to which the "sharers" are entitled exceeds 100 percent of the estate. In such cases, the legists decided to reduce the share of each heir on a pro rata basis (*ʿawl*); this technique, although resolving the mathematical difficulty, yields a solution in which none of the heirs receives his/her exact Qur'anic allotment. A similar problem occurs in connection with the entitlement of a mother. The Qur'an states that if a man dies leaving both parents, the mother is entitled to one-third of the estate. But the presence of a husband or wife has the effect of making it impossible for the mother to receive her full share, leaving her as little as one-fourth or one-sixth of the estate. I have argued that, originally, a surviving spouse was not entitled to inherit upon intestacy; it is only the elevation of the spouse to the status of a full legal heir that upsets the delicate mathematical balance upon which the proto-Islamic law of intestacy was predicated. In both cases the removal of the spouse from the calculation causes the problem to disappear.

Part Two

THE FORMATION OF THE ISLAMIC LAW OF INHERITANCE

4

Wealth, Power, and Politics in Early Islam

In part one of this study I argued that the Muslim community, in the years following the death of Muhammad, instituted a series of changes in the reading and/or interpretation of certain Qur'anic verses and at least one prophetic *ḥadīth*, all of which deal with inheritance. As a result, what came to be the traditional understanding of these texts differs considerably from what I believe to have been their original significance. These changes, if I may anticipate the conclusion of the present study, had the effect of transforming the system of inheritance introduced by Muhammad—a system that left the individual free to determine the ultimate devolution of his property—into the *ʿilm al-farā'iḍ*, which imposes compulsory rules for the division of a minimum of two-thirds of any estate. It may be useful, at this point, to pause and consider some larger historical issues, to wit, what the immediate and secondary causes of this transformation were, who stood to benefit from it, how they might have gone about instituting these changes, and what role they played in the formation of the Islamic law of inheritance. I shall consider the following three matters that may be related to these issues: the dispute over the caliphate, claims against Muhammad's estate by members of his family, and wealth, property, and inheritance in the first century A.H.

Succession and Inheritance

Inheritance rules sometimes reflect ideas about political succession. It is generally accepted, for example, that certain details of the Shīʿī law of inheritance were formulated in order to buttress Shīʿī claims regarding leadership of the community. Specifically, the rule that the son of a germane paternal uncle excludes from inheritance a consanguine paternal uncle seems to have been introduced in order to establish the superiority of ʿAlī over al-ʿAbbās as a possible leader of the community;[1] as one western scholar has put it, "the founders of Imāmī law were concerned that the right of inheritance should parallel the right of succession to the Prophet."[2] To the best of my knowledge, however, historians of Islam have never entertained the possibility that the exact form taken by the Sunnī law of inheritance may also have been conditioned by considerations related to the issue of political succession. I find it striking, for example, that Islamic law does not permit a person to designate a testamentary heir and that the split between the Sunnīs and the Shīʿīs was caused by a dispute over whether or not Muhammad had designated a political successor. I shall explore here the possibility that there may be a connection between the dispute over the caliphate and the form taken by the Islamic law of inheritance.

Muhammad's Political Testament

In view of the great importance placed upon testamentary dispositions in both the Qur'an and *ḥadīth*,[3] it is reasonable to assume that Muhammad, himself, would have taken care to draw up a last will and testament before he died. The Sunnī sources indicate that Muhammad did attempt to dictate a last will and testament shortly before his death but was prevented from carrying out his intention by the actions of several Companions:

> Ḥasan—Shaybān—Layth—Ṭā'ūs—Ibn ʿAbbās said: "When the Messenger of God was on the point of death (*lammā ḥuḍira rasūl allāh*) he said, 'Bring me a shoulder blade (*katif*) and I shall dictate for you a document (*kitāb*) on it, so that no two men will disagree after me.'" [Ibn ʿAbbās] said, "The people approached shouting loudly, and the woman said, 'Beware the testament (*ʿahd*) of the Messenger of God.'"[4]

1. See Coulson, *Succession in the Muslim Family*, p. 128.
2. W. Madelung, "Shīʿī Attitudes Towards Women as Reflected in Fiqh," p. 75.
3. See introduction, pp. 10–11, and chap. 5, pp. 145–49.
4. Ibn Ḥanbal, *Musnad* (Cairo), 4:235 (no. 2676).

The phrase *lammā ḥuḍira rasūl allāh* at the beginning of the report may signal a connection to Q. 2:180, the first of the two bequest verses, which opens with the phrase *idhā ḥaḍara aḥadakum al-mawt* (when death approaches one of you). The phrasing of this statement suggests that the time had come for Muhammad to draw up a last will and testament, an assumption that finds support in the continuation of the report, first when Muhammad asks his Companions to bring him some writing material so that he might dictate a document, and again in the statement uttered by the anonymous woman at the end of the report ("Beware the testament of the Messenger of God"); the term *ʿahd*, in classical Arabic, is frequently used to denote a succession covenant. It is not surprising, especially in light of subsequent events, that certain of Muhammad's Companions would have viewed with suspicion the prospect of his drawing up a last will and testament.

The response to Muhammad's request for writing material is striking. Although the Companions (here unidentified) were certainly familiar with the Qur'anic injunction to "obey God and His Prophet" (e.g., Q. 4:68, 4:82, and 24:51), no one present was moved to comply with Muhammad's request. The references to the shoulder blade (*katif*) and document (*kitāb*) bring to mind the reports (cited in chapter 1) that center on ʿUmar and the meaning of *al-kalāla*. In one of these reports, ʿUmar holds a shoulder blade in his hand while announcing his intention to issue a decree about *al-kalāla*, an intention which he fails to carry out. In another report, the dying caliph calls for and erases a document that he had written about *al-kalāla*.[5] We may be dealing here with a *topos*, for in all three of the reports in which a *katif* or a *kitāb*, or both, are mentioned, the central figure fails to issue a statement that he had intended to make.

ʿUmar's involvement in the opposition to Muhammad's attempt to dictate a final statement is made explicit in the following variant of the preceding report:

> Wahb b. Jarīr—Ubayy—Yūnus—al-Zuhrī—ʿUbayd Allāh b. ʿAbd Allāh—Ibn ʿAbbās said: "When death drew near to the Messenger of God (*lammā ḥadarat rasūl allāh al-wafāt*) he said, 'Come to me, and I will dictate for you a document so that you will not go astray after it.' There were [several] men in the house, among them ʿUmar b. al-Khaṭṭāb. ʿUmar said, 'The pain has overcome the Messenger of God. The Qur'an is in your possession. Let

5. See chap. 1, pp. 35–37.

the Book of God be sufficient for us.'" [Ibn ʿAbbās] said, "The people of the house disagreed and quarreled. Some of them said, 'The Messenger of God is dictating for you,' or they said, 'Draw near so that the Messenger of God might dictate for you.' Others said the same thing that ʿUmar said. When they increased the clamour and disagreement, and the Messenger of God was grieved, he said, 'Leave me.'" Ibn ʿAbbās used to say, "The calamity—the entire calamity—is [a result of] what came between the Messenger of God and his dictating that document for them, i.e., their clamour and disagreement."[6]

The phrase *lammā ḥaḍarat rasūl allāh al-wafāt* signals, even more clearly than *lammā ḥuḍira* in the preceding report, a connection with Q. 2:180 and the preparation of a last will and testament. The present report singles out among the Prophet's attendants ʿUmar b. al-Khaṭṭāb, who intervenes to persuade the others not to allow Muhammad to carry out his stated intention. ʿUmar justifies his position on two grounds: Muhammad's pain might cause him to say something that he did not intend to say, and, further, the Community's possession of the Book of God ought to be sufficient to settle any disagreements that might arise.[7] There is a certain irony to these arguments. We have already seen that ʿUmar continued to be perplexed by the term *kalāla* even after Muhammad referred him to Q. 4:176 for clarification.[8] And as we shall see below, Abū Bakr, when he designates ʿUmar as the next caliph, will be literally out of his senses.

In a third version of this report, Muhammad succeeds in issuing an oral testament:

Sufyān—Sulaymān b. Abī Muslim, the maternal uncle of Ibn Abī Najīḥ—Saʿīd b. Jubayr—Ibn ʿAbbās said, "Thursday, O Thursday." Then he cried until his tears wet the ground. We said, "O [Ibn] ʿAbbās, what about Thursday?" He said, "The Prophet of God's pain became intense and he said, 'Come to me, and I will dictate for you a document so that you will never go astray afterwards.' But they disagreed among themselves, although disagreement in the presence of a Prophet is not permitted. They said, 'What is the matter with him? Is he delirious? Try to understand

6. Ibn Ḥanbal, *Musnad* (Cairo), 4:356 (no. 2992).

7. Nawawī, Khaṭṭābī, and Qāḍī Iyāḍ somehow manage to exonerate ʿUmar for his behavior on this occasion, the latter, for example, seeing in ʿUmar's response "one of the signs of his intelligence, his virtues and his perceptiveness." (Muslim, *Ṣaḥīḥ*, 3:1257–58, note 3).

8. See chap. 1, p. 34.

him.' So they began to come to him in turns. Then he said, 'Leave me, for [the state] that I am in is better than what you are calling me to.' He gave three commands (Sufyān once said: 'he bequeathed three things'): He said, 'Expel the polytheists from the Arabian peninsula, and consider the deputation lawful as I used to do.' And Saᶜīd passed over the third [command] in silence, and I do not know if he omitted it intentionally (He once said, 'or forgot it.')" Sufyān once said, "He either omitted it or forgot it."[9]

That Ibn ᶜAbbās was reduced to tears indicates that the unruly conduct of Muhammad's attendants (ᶜUmar is not mentioned here) was improper. Although Muhammad does not succeed in dictating the document that he refers to at the outset, he does manage to issue an oral testament in which he makes three statements. Curiously, however, the traditionist, Saᶜīd b. Jubayr, does not mention the third item, and Ibn Ḥanbal's immediate informant, Sufyān, indicates that Saᶜīd either forgot it intentionally or omitted it; in either case the omission constitutes a glaring gap in the collective memory of the early Muslim community.[10]

Abū Bakr's Political Testament

Abū Bakr, who was elected to succeed Muhammad, died in A.D. 634, only two years after assuming the leadership of the Muslim community. Shortly before his death he informed his followers of the provisions he had made for a successor:

Ibn Ḥumayd—Yaḥyā b. Wāḍiḥ—Yūnis b. ᶜAmr—Abū al-Safar said: Abū Bakr looked down on the people from his enclosure. Asmā', the daughter of ᶜUmays was holding him, with tattooed hands, while he was saying, "Are you not pleased with the person whom I am going to appoint as your successor (*a-tarḍawna bi-man astakhlifu ᶜalaykum*)? By God, I have spared no pains and I have not appointed a relative. Rather, I have appointed ᶜUmar b. al-Khaṭṭāb as Successor, so listen to him and obey him." They said, "We hear and obey."[11]

9. Ibn Ḥanbal, *Musnad* (Cairo), 3:286–87 (no. 1935).

10. See also Powers, "The Will of Saᶜd b. Abī Waqqāṣ," p. 46, where Muṣᶜab b. Saᶜd b. Abī Waqqāṣ declares that four verses were revealed about his father, Saᶜd, but omits the fourth verse.

11. Ṭabarī, *Kitāb ta'rīkh al-rusul wa'l-mulūk*, 3:428–29. See also Ibn Saᶜd, *al-Ṭabaqāt al-kubrā*, 3:192.

Abū Bakr announces that he has appointed ʿUmar, the Companion whose peculiar behavior had prevented Muhammad from dictating a last will and testament, to be his Successor. This is the first reported instance of the appointment of a political successor in Islam. Now, it stands to reason that if Abū Bakr could appoint a successor, Muhammad—had it not been for the intervention of ʿUmar and the other, unnamed, Companions—might have done the same.

So that there would be no confusion or disagreement (as there had been after Muhammad's death), ʿUmar's appointment was recorded on a document to which the caliph-apparent drew the attention of his fellow Muslims.[12] This document was drawn up in the following, extremely unusual, circumstances:

> Abū Jaʿfar [al-Ṭabarī]—al-Wāqidī—Ibrāhīm b. Abī al-Naḍr—Muhammad b. Ibrāhīm b. al-Ḥārith said: Abū Bakr called ʿUthmān aside and said, "Write: 'In the name of God, the Merciful, the Compassionate. This is what Abū Bakr b. Abī Quḥāfa bequeathed (*ʿahida ilā*) to the Muslims. As for what follows (*Ammā baʿd*).'" [Muhammad b. Ibrāhīm b. al-Ḥārith] said: Then [Abū Bakr] fainted and [ʿUthmān] moved away from him. ʿUthman wrote, "As for what follows, I have appointed ʿUmar b. al-Khaṭṭāb as your caliph, and there is none better for you than him." Then Abū Bakr regained consciousness and said, "Recite to me." So he recited to him. Abū Bakr said: "God is great!" and he said, "I think that you were afraid that the people would disagree had I died suddenly while unconscious." [ʿUthman] said, "Yes." [Abū Bakr] said, "May God reward you well on behalf of Islam and his family." Abū Bakr acknowledged [the testament] from that point [viz., the point when he lost consciousness].[13]

The report opens with Abū Bakr's dictating his last will and testament to ʿUthman b. ʿAffān (who later becomes the third caliph). The verb *ʿahida ilā* in the opening line of the political testament reminds us of the warning uttered by the anonymous woman after Muhammad had called for writing material, "Be-

12. See Ṭabarī, *Ta'rīkh*, 3:429: ʿUthmān b. Yaḥyā—ʿUthmān al-Qirqisānī—Sufyān b. ʿUyayna—Ismāʿīl—Qays said: "I saw ʿUmar b. al-Khaṭṭāb, sitting together with the people, with a palm branch (*jarīda*) in his hand. He was saying, 'O people, listen and obey the word of the Successor of the Messenger of God. He says: I have spared no pains.'" [Qays] said, "A slave belonging to Abū Bakr, by the name of Shadīd, was with him, carrying the sheet (*ṣaḥīfa*) containing ʿUmar's appointment as caliph."

13. Ṭabarī, *Ta'rīkh*, 3:429.

ware the testament (*ʿahd*) of the Messenger of God." Abū Bakr, apparently weakened by his illness, manages to complete the preliminaries but faints just as he arrives at the substantive section of the document. ʿUthmān steps aside and completes the document as if he were an extension of the caliph's consciousness. Ironically, ʿUmar had argued against allowing Muhammad to dictate a political testament on the ground that the Prophet, as a result of the great pain from which he was suffering, was not in his normal state of mind; yet Abū Bakr was, literally, out of his senses when the appointment of ʿUmar took place. The circumstances of the present appointment, however, occasion no objection. Indeed, when Abū Bakr regains consciousness he commends ʿUthmān's behaviour, saying, "I think you were afraid that the people would disagree had I died suddenly while unconscious." These words, which recall Muhammad's statement, "Let me dictate a document for you so that no two men will disagree after me," lend support to my assumption that the Prophet sought to dictate a political testament in which he would nominate a successor.

ʿUmar's Political Testament

The reports that relate the circumstances of ʿUmar's assassination suggest a direct connection between Q. 4:12b, as I propose to reinterpret it, and the issue of political succession. In chapter 1, I cited anecdotes that focus on ʿUmar and *al-kalāla*; these anecdotes can be traced to earlier sources in which they occur in a more detailed historical context. For example, ʿUmar's declaration of intent to issue a decree about *al-kalāla*, so that the Qur'an reciters will not disagree about it,[14] was made in a sermon that he delivered after he had seen a vision presaging his assassination. In this report, the reference to *al-kalāla* follows immediately upon a discussion of the procedure for designating the next caliph:

> ʿAffān—Hammām b. Yaḥyā—Qatāda—Sālim b. Abī al-Jaʿd al-Ghaṭafānī—Maʿdān b. Abī Ṭalḥa al-Yaʿmarī said: ʿUmar b. al-Khaṭṭāb stood on the pulpit on Friday and praised God repeatedly. Then he mentioned the Messenger of God and he mentioned Abū

14. See chap. 1, p. 37.

Bakr. Then he said, "I have seen a vision which I have only seen because my appointed term is at hand. I saw, [it was] as if a cock pecked me twice. (Maᶜdān b. Abī Ṭalḥa said, "He told me it was a red cock"). I told [this] to Asmā' bint ᶜUmays, the wife of Abū Bakr, and she said, 'A foreigner is going to kill you.'"

[ᶜUmar] said, "The people are ordering me to appoint a successor. Verily, God does not exist for the purpose of causing his religion and the succession (*khilāfa*) that he entrusted to his prophet to go astray. Therefore, should anything befall me, the affair (*shūra*) is for these six persons, with whom, at the time of his death, the Messenger of God was well pleased. So listen and obey whichever one of them to whom you swear allegiance. I know there are people who will contest this matter. I have fought them with this hand of mine for the sake of Islam. Those are the enemies of God, the infidels, the errant ones.

"By God, with regard to that which my master entrusted to me (*ᶜahida ilayya*) [when] he appointed me as successor, I leave nothing that is of more concern to me than *al-kalāla*. By God, the Prophet of God did not become cross with me about anything, from the time I became a Companion, as strongly as he did in the matter of *al-kalāla*, until he poked his finger in my chest and said, 'Let the summer verse that was revealed at the end of *Sūrat al-Nisā'* be sufficient for you.' Verily, if I live, I will issue a decree about it that will be known both to those who recite [the Qur'an] and those who do not recite [it].

"Verily, I call God as my witness against the commanders of the garrison towns, I sent them only in order to teach the people their religion, to clarify for them the *sunna* of their Prophet, and to bring before me that which is not clear to them.

"Then you, O people, eat from two plants (*shajaratayn*) which, in my opinion, are nothing but abominations, namely, garlic and onion. By God, I used to see the Prophet of God—[when] he detected their smell on a man, he would issue a command about him, and he would be taken by the hand and expelled from the mosque, until he was brought to [the cemetery of] *al-Baqīᶜ*. Therefore, whoever would eat them must cook them first." He delivered the sermon to the people on Friday and he was killed on Wednesday.[15]

After mentioning his dream or vision, ᶜUmar delivers a long sermon in which he mentions four issues: the question of political succession, his confusion about *al-kalāla*, his reasons for sending the commanders to the garrison towns, and a regulation

15. Ibn Ḥanbal, *Musnad* (Cairo), 1:192–93 (no. 89); ibid., 1:235 (no. 186) and 1:302 (no. 341); and Ibn Saᶜd, 3:335–36.

concerning the use of onion and garlic. Muslim lexicographers and jurists define *al-kalāla* as "a person who dies leaving neither parent nor child," or "all the heirs except for parents and children," and they view Q. 4:12b as awarding a small fractional share of the estate to uterine siblings. But if we accept this explanation of *al-kalāla* and of the legal significance of the verse, it is difficult to see why either would have caused ʿUmar such anguish. I suspect that Q. 4:12b originally referred to the possibility of designating a testamentary heir and that the early Muslim community eliminated this reference by imposing a secondary reading (*qirā'a*) on the consonantal text of the Qur'an and redefining *al-kalāla*. The presence in the Qur'an of a verse referring to a mechanism for designating an heir would have constituted a source of embarrassment for those of Muhammad's Companions who maintained that he had not designated a successor. It would have been in their interest to modify the interpretation of Q. 4:12b so as to eliminate the sole Qur'anic reference to the *possibility of designating an heir.* Seen in this context, ʿUmar's intention to issue a decree regarding the recitation of the verse in which the word *al-kalāla* occurs can be read as an allusion to the reinterpretation of that verse by means of the imposition of a secondary reading.[16]

ʿUmar was assassinated on the Wednesday following the Friday on which he delivered this sermon. Variant versions of his deathbed declaration corroborate the soundness of my attempt to establish a link between the question of political succession and ʿUmar's concern for *al-kalāla*. One version reads as follows:

> Yaḥyā b. Ḥammād and ʿAffān—Abū ʿAwāna—Dā'ūd b. ʿAbd Allāh al-Awdī—Ḥumayd b. ʿAbd al-Raḥmān al-Ḥimyarī—Ibn ʿAbbās informed us, in Basra, "I was the first person to reach ʿUmar when he was stabbed. He said, 'Commit three [things] to memory, for I fear that the people will not reach me: As for me, I did not issue a decree concerning *al-kalāla*; and I did not appoint a suc-

16. See chap. 1. The verb *ṭaʿana,* which occurs several times in the report, may serve as a linguistic bridge linking together the first two parts of the report. After mentioning the *shūra* that would elect the next caliph, ʿUmar says, "I know there are people who will contest (*yaṭʿanūna fī*) this matter." Then, when discussing *al-kalāla,* ʿUmar mentions that Muhammad finally poked (*ṭaʿana*) him in the chest. Is it merely a coincidence, then, that ʿUmar was stabbed to death (*ṭuʿina*) five days after delivering the present sermon? Regarding the stabbing, see Ibn Ḥanbal, *Musnad* (Cairo), 1:295 (no. 322).

> cessor over the people'; and every slave belonging to him [*sic*] is free. The people said to him, 'Appoint a successor.' He said, 'Whatever I do, one who is better than I has done it. If I leave the matter to the people, then the Prophet of God left it [to them]. And if I appoint a successor, then one who is better than I, Abū Bakr, appointed a successor.'"[17]

ʿUmar's denial is here the first of three items that he asks Ibn ʿAbbās to memorize. Note that there seems to be a problem with the third statement issued by the dying caliph. The narrative shifts from the first person to the third person ("and every slave belonging to him is free"), suggesting that these are not the words of ʿUmar, but those of Ibn ʿAbbās, the narrator of the report.[18] This shift or confusion has been eliminated in the following variant, in which ʿUmar asks Ibn ʿAbbās to memorize only two items:

> Hawdha b. Khalīfa—ʿAwf—Muhammad—Ibn ʿAbbās said, "When it was the morning [after the day that] ʿUmar was wounded, I was among those who carried him, until we put him in the house." He said, "He regained consciousness and said, 'Who struck me?'" I said, "Abū Lu'lu', the slave of al-Mughīra b. Shuʿba." ʿUmar replied, "This is the work of your companions. It was my desire that no infidel slave should enter [Medina]. But you prevailed over me. So commit two [things] to memory: I did not appoint a successor and I did not issue any decree concerning *al-kalāla*." (ʿAwf and someone other than Muhammad said that he said, "I did not issue any decree in the matter of the grandfather and the brothers.")[19]

The issue of political succession and the controversy over *al-kalāla* are here directly juxtaposed. It is understandable that there should have been some confusion as to whether or not ʿUmar actually issued a decree about this word. In one text (cited in chapter 1), ʿUmar announced his intention to issue such a decree, but reneged on his promise after the appearance of a snake caused his audience to scatter.[20] Furthermore, only five days previous to his assassination, ʿUmar had stated, "If I live, I shall is-

17. Ibid. But cf. Ibn Saʿd, 3:353, where all three statements are attributed to ʿUmar as direct speech.

18. As was the case regarding the third statement of Muhammad's oral declaration, once again there is a gap in the collective memory of the Muslims.

19. Ibn Saʿd, 3:352; cf. idem, 3:341.

20. See chap. 1, pp. 34–35.

sue a decree about it [viz., *al-kalāla*] that will be known to both those who recite [the Qur'an] and those who do not recite [it]."[21] And in a variant of ᶜUmar's deathbed scene, he called for and erased a document that he had already written about the word.[22] Clearly, it was believed that someone had issued a decree about *al-kalāla*, and the sources portray ᶜUmar as going to great lengths both to suppress the decree and to deny having issued it.

The sources seem to be pointing an accusing finger at ᶜUmar b. al-Khaṭṭāb: ᶜUmar is singled out as the spokesman of the group whose improper behavior prevented Muhammad from dictating a last will and testament. He subsequently assumed the office of caliph by virtue of a last will and testament dictated by Abū Bakr under the most suspicious of circumstances. Then, in a sermon delivered five days before his assassination, he admitted that he would leave no issue of more concern to him than *al-kalāla*, vowing to issue a decree about it in order to prevent disagreement among reciters of the Qur'an. And ᶜUmar, himself, seems to have drawn a connection between the issues of political succession and inheritance; on his deathbed, immediately after insisting that he had not designated a political successor, he denied having issued a decree about *al-kalāla*.

Claims Against Muhammad's Estate

Wives and Daughter

Muhammad's failure to leave a last will and testament threw into confusion the matter of the division of his estate. His relatives' attempts to establish a claim to his estate brought them into conflict with the political leaders of the community, first Abū Bakr and later ᶜUmar, both of whom argued that Muhammad's estate, because of his special status as a Prophet, was not subject to the normal rules of inheritance.

After his death, Muhammad's wives wanted to send ᶜUthmān to ask Abū Bakr for their inheritance, but ᶜĀ'isha persuaded her cowives not to press their claim, saying, "Did not the Messenger of God say, *'lā nūrathu mā taraknā ṣadaqatun*?'" The Arabic phrase quoted by ᶜĀ'isha is generally understood by Sunnī Mus-

21. Ibn Saᶜd, 3:336.
22. Ṭabarī, *Jāmiᶜ*, 6:43 (ll. 14–18).

lims as indicating that no one inherits from a Prophet (*lā nūrathu*) and that whatever a prophet leaves should be used for charity (*mā taraknā ṣadaqatun*). In other words, Muhammad's special status as a Prophet invalidates any claims against his estate based upon laws that apply to normal persons. Muhammad's wives, accordingly, dropped their claim.[23]

Fāṭima, Muhammad's daughter, also pressed a claim against his estate. The following exchange between Fāṭima and Abū Bakr is related on the authority of ʿĀ'isha:

> Ḥajjāj b. Muhammad—Layth—ʿUqayl—Ibn Shihāb—ʿUrwa b. al-Zubayr—ʿĀ'isha, the wife of the Prophet, said to [ʿUrwa]: Fāṭima, the daughter of the Messenger of God, sent to Abū Bakr al-Ṣiddīq, asking him for her inheritance from the Messenger of God, from that which God had given him as booty in Medina and Fadak, and whatever remained of the "fifth" of Khaybar. Abū Bakr said, "The Messenger of God said, '*lā nūrathu mā taraknā ṣadaqatun.*' The family of Muhammad only eats from that. By God, I do not change anything belonging to the estate of the Messenger of God from the state that it was in during the lifetime of the Messenger of God. I treat it in exactly the same manner that the Messenger of God treated it." So Abū Bakr refused to give Fāṭima any part of it, and Fāṭima became angry with Abū Bakr about that. Abū Bakr said, "By him in whose hand is my soul, the relatives of the Messenger of God are dearer to me than my [own] relatives. As for the dispute between us regarding the wealth, I have striven after the truth, and I have not left anything that I saw the Messenger of God doing without doing it myself."[24]

Abū Bakr, like ʿĀ'isha, refutes the claim against Muhammad's estate by invoking a statement attributed to the Prophet indicating that Prophets are not subject to the normal rules of inheritance. Muhammad's family, although entitled to be maintained out of that property, has no rights of ownership in it, for it has become a public trust. Abū Bakr insists that he is merely following the example of Muhammad in this matter and that he bears no enmity towards the Prophet's family.

Al-ʿAbbās, Muhammad's paternal uncle, joined Fāṭima in her attempt to establish a claim against the Prophet's estate. When

23. The Shīʿī's altered the syntax of the phrase in such a manner that it conveys the sense that the Prophet's property *is* subject to the same laws of inheritance as ordinary mortals. See, on this subject, Ignaz Goldziher, *Muslim Studies*, 2:102–103.

24. Ibn Ḥanbal, *Musnad* (Cairo), 1:177 (no. 55); see also Ibn Saʿd, 8:28.

the two of them approached Abū Bakr demanding their inheritance, the caliph rejected their claim, stating, "I heard the Messenger of God saying, *'lā nūrathu mā taraknā ṣadaqatun.* The family of Muhammad only eats from this property.'"[25]

ʿUmar, upon assuming the office of the caliphate, inherited from Abū Bakr the question of the claims against Muhammad's estate. After Fāṭima's death in 11/632, al-ʿAbbās continued to press his claim, and he was joined in this by Fāṭima's husband, ʿAlī (who was also the Prophet's paternal cousin). The two men, who apparently had begun to quarrel about their proximity to the Prophet, appealed to ʿUmar to settle their dispute:

> Yaʿqūb—the son of Ibn Shihāb's brother—his uncle—Muhammad b. Muslim—Mālik b. Aws b. al-Ḥadathānī al-Naṣrī related: While I was sitting with [ʿUmar], his chamberlain, Yarfa', entered and said to ʿUmar, "Do you want to see ʿUthmān, ʿAbd al-Raḥmān, Saʿd, and al-Zubayr, who are asking permission [to enter]?" He said, "Yes, give them permission." So they entered, greeted him, and sat down. Then, soon thereafter, Yarfa' said to ʿUmar, "Do you want to see ʿAlī and al-ʿAbbās?" He said, "Yes," so he gave them permission [to enter]. When the two [men] entered they sat down. Al-ʿAbbās said, "O Commander of the Believers, judge between myself and ʿAlī." The group, i.e., ʿUthmān and his companions, said, "Judge between them and set them at ease with one another." ʿUmar said, "Slowly. I adjure you by God, with whose permission the heavens and earth exist, do you know that the Messenger of God said, *'lā nūrathu mā taraknā ṣadaqatun,'* by which the Messenger of God was referring to himself?" The group said, "Indeed, he said that." ʿUmar approached ʿAlī and al-ʿAbbās and said, "I adjure you by God, do you know that the Messenger of God said that?" They said, "Indeed, he said that." ʿUmar said, "Then, verily, I will tell you about this matter. God singled out the Messenger of God in the matter of this booty with something that he did not give to anyone else. God said, 'And whatever spoils of war God has given unto His Messenger from them' [Q. 59 : 7]. This verse [was revealed] specifically for the Messenger of God. Then, by God, he did not take possession of it [i.e., the booty], or appropriate it exclusively for himself. Rather, he gave it to you and distributed it among you, until this property remained. The Messenger of God used to give his family their yearly maintenance out of this property. Then he would take whatever remained and treat it as 'the property of God.' The Prophet of God acted in that way during his lifetime. I adjure you by God, do you know that?" They said, "Yes." He said to ʿAlī and

25. Ibn Ḥanbal, *Musnad* (Cairo), 1 : 178 (no. 58).

> al-ʿAbbās, "I adjure you by God, do you [know this]?" They said, "Yes." [ʿUmar said], "Then the Messenger of God died, and Abū Bakr said, 'I am the successor (*walī*) of the Messenger of God.' So Abū Bakr took it and treated it in the manner that the Messenger of God had done. And now you two" (and he approached ʿAlī and al-ʿAbbās) "claim that Abū Bakr *fīhā kadhā*. God knows that in this matter he was truthful, pious, righteous, and a follower of the correct path."[26]

This long and undoubtedly late report ostensibly reduces the claim against the caliph to a case of infighting between two members of Muhammad's family. ʿUmar's response, however, reflects his extreme sensitivity regarding his right to administer Muhammad's estate. Like ʿĀ'isha and Abū Bakr before him, ʿUmar rejected the claims against Muhammad's estate by invoking the prophetic statement, *"lā nūrathu mā taraknā ṣadaqatun."* Only after forcing first ʿUthmān and his companions and then ʿAlī and al-ʿAbbās to admit that Muhammad had made such a statement did ʿUmar explain the grounds upon which his decision was based: Muhammad did not acquire any property that would pass, on his death, to his heirs. Rather, God had placed certain property in Muhammad's possession by virtue of his prophetic office, and Muhammad administered this property ("the property of God") on behalf of the entire community. When Muhammad died, the new leader of the community, Abū Bakr, assumed the role of administrator of this property, which he endeavored to distribute in the same manner as he had seen Muhammad do. This argument justified ʿUmar's right, over and against that of ʿAlī and al-ʿAbbās, to administer Muhammad's estate.

The phrase *lā nūrathu mā taraknā ṣadaqatun*, which plays such a crucial role in the rejection of the claims against Muhammad's estate, is problematic. In the report cited immediately above, ʿUmar used the phrase and then glossed it by stating, "the Messenger of God was referring to himself"—as if there were some uncertainty about the referent. Two unusual grammatical features may in fact cause some confusion. First, Muhammad referred to himself in the first-person plural, *lā nūrathu* (we are not inherited from) and *mā taraknā* (that which we leave). Secondly, the phrase *mā taraknā* is a relative clause requiring a pronomi-

26. Ibid., 3:213 (no. 1782). See also ibid., 1:187 (no. 78); 1:306 (no. 349); 1:342 (no. 425); and 3:212 (no. 1781).

nal complement referring back to its object, e.g., *mā taraknāHU.* Numerous versions of the statement gloss or emend the phrase so as to eliminate one or the other of these two problems. For example, Abū Bakr and ᶜUmar reportedly heard the Prophet say, *"Innī lā ūrathu"* (No one inherits from me). Here, the subject of the verb has been changed to the first person singular, making it clear that Muhammad was speaking about himself.[27] In another variant, Abū Bakr maintained that he heard the Prophet say, *"Inna al-nabī lā yūrathu"* (No one inherits from a prophet), transforming the phrase into a general principle of law.[28] In each of the last two variants, the second half of the phrase, *mā taraknā ṣadaqatun*, is omitted entirely. Finally, in one version ᶜUmar asked ᶜUthmān and his companions, "Do you know that the Messenger of God said, *'Innā lā nūrathu mā taraknāHU ṣadaqatun?'"*, adding the missing pronominal complement, *hu*, to the verb.[29]

The confusion over the meaning of the phrase *lā nūrathu mā taraknā ṣadaqatun* may explain a curious feature of the report in which ᶜUmar is asked to arbitrate the dispute between ᶜAlī and al-ᶜAbbās. At the very end of the report, ᶜUmar approached the two men, saying, "And now you two . . . are claiming that Abū Bakr *fihā kadhā*. God knows that in this matter he was truthful, pious, righteous, and a follower of the correct path." The exact meaning of the words *fihā kadhā* (roughly: in it, like that) is not immediately apparent. The text may be corrupt, or an editor might be attempting to indicate a gap in the text (*kadhā*). In either case, the continuation makes it clear that ᶜUmar was defending Abū Bakr against an accusation that had been directed against him by ᶜAlī and al-ᶜAbbās. I suspect that the two men may have accused Abū Bakr of lying, for in another variant, ᶜUmar turns to ᶜAlī and al-ᶜAbbās and says, "Abū Bakr told me, *and he swore he was telling the truth,* that he heard the Prophet say, *'Inna al-nabī lā yūrathu'"* (emphasis added).[30] But if we read *kadhaba* (to lie) instead of *kadhā*, then ᶜUmar would have said to ᶜAlī and al-ᶜAbbās, "And now you two . . . are claiming that Abū Bakr *lied* about this matter. God knows that in this matter

27. Ibid., 1:187 (no. 79).
28. Ibid., 1:179 (no. 60) and 1:187 (no. 78).
29. Ibid., 1:228 (no. 172).
30. Ibid., 1:187 (no. 78).

he was truthful, pious, etc." "*Kadhaba,*" thus, would be appropriate here.[31] Be that as it may, the division of Muhammad's estate was clearly a matter of considerable controversy, and it is possible that this controversy may have contributed, indirectly, to the transformation from proto-Islamic to Islamic law.

Early Inheritance Practices

I have been concerned primarily with a discussion of theory rather than practice, with ideas about systems of inheritance rather than the actual division of property. Inasmuch as I seek to demonstrate that the system of inheritance introduced by Muhammad was transformed, during the years immediately following his death, into the *ʿilm al-farāʾiḍ*, it may be useful to consider the actual manner in which estates were divided up during the first century A.H. However, the evidence for such a study is scattered throughout many different types of sources (e.g., collections of *ḥadīth*, commentaries on the Qur'an, histories, biographical dictionaries, belles lettres), and it will require several years of extensive research to gather the relevant information. In the meantime, however, I have chosen the *Ṭabaqāt* of Ibn Saʿd to serve as the basis of a pilot study designed to indicate the types of information likely to be uncovered by the larger study. The primary virtue of this source and others like it is that it includes an entry for each Muslim known to have belonged to a given gener-

31. I would like to suggest, with due caution, that ʿAlī and al-ʿAbbās may have accused Abū Bakr of lying about the statement *lā nūrathu mā taraknā ṣadaqatun*. If, as I maintain, it was originally possible for a man to designate a wife or female in-law as a testamentary heir (Q. 4:12b) and also to leave a bequest for a wife (see chap. 1), then one would expect Muhammad's wives to enquire as to whether or not Muhammad had followed these procedures. Now, if we read *tarakanā* instead of *taraknā* and take the word *ṣadaqa* to mean a "gift" instead of "charity," then it is possible to interpret the phrase as, "We [viz., Muhammad's wives] are not designated as heirs; that which he left us is a gift [or bequest]." This interpretation, which is consistent with my reconstruction of the system of inheritance introduced by Muhammad, completely resolves the grammatical difficulties associated with the traditional understanding of the phrase. The first-person plural (*nūrathu*) is used because it was originally uttered by Muhammad's wives. And the reading *tarakanā* resolves the problem of the missing pronominal complement by transforming the ending *nā* from a subject morpheme into the object of a verb. But, as Patricia Crone has advised me, the proper way of expressing "he left to us," in Arabic, is *taraka lanā*, not *tarakanā*. God knows best!

ation (*ṭabaqa*), frequently indicates the date on which he/she died, and occasionally provides some information about the division of his/her estate. In an effort to see what, if any, patterns will emerge from this initial survey, I have arranged the data in rough chronological order, broken down into three major periods: the lifetime of Muhammad, the period of the four "righteous caliphs," and the Umayyad period. The evidence to be presented below seems to corroborate my contention that the "science of the shares" was not applied until some years after Muhammad's death.

The Period of Revelation

I shall begin with the first reported instance of inheritance in Islam. ʿAdī b. Naḍla, an early convert to Islam, emigrated to Abyssinia, where he was the first of the Emigrants to die. Ibn Saʿd singles out ʿAdī as "the first person to be inherited from in Islam." At the time of his death, ʿAdī left a wife (Bint Naʿja), two sons (Nuʿmān and Naʿīm), and a daughter (Amīna). Of these four potential heirs, only Nuʿmān is reported to have inherited from his father.[32] Ibn Saʿd does not indicate, however, whether Nuʿmān inherited by virtue of a last will and testament or in accordance with rules of intestacy.

As noted earlier, there is ample evidence in the sources to support my assumption that, during the lifetime of Muhammad, it was common to leave a last will and testament. Muhammad himself is reported to have been named as the recipient of a bequest in a number of early testaments. Al-Barāʾ b. Maʿrūr, who died one month before Muhammad emigrated to Medina, in September 622, bequeathed one-third of his estate to the Prophet to do with as he pleased.[33] Similarly, Saʿd b. Mālik al-Saʿīdī, shortly before he died, wrote a last will and testament in which he stipulated that Muhammad was to receive his saddle-bags, camel, and five loads of barley. Muhammad accepted the bequest but immediately turned the property over to the deceased's (unspecified) heirs.[34] Finally, Abū Umāma Asʿad b. Zurāra (d. 1/622) left a last

32. Ibn Saʿd, 4:140: "*awwal man wuritha fi'l-islām.*"
33. Ibid., 3:619.
34. Ibid., 3:625

will and testament in which he assigned guardianship of his three daughters to Muhammad. The girls went to live with the Prophet's family, taking up residence in his wives' apartments.[35]

As one would expect, Muslim men, before going out to battle, made arrangements for the ultimate devolution of their property. An anecdote told in connection with the ransoming of Muhammad's uncle, al-ʿAbbās, may serve as an example. Al-ʿAbbās is reported to have fought against the Muslims at Badr. When he was captured, Muhammad asked him to redeem himself, but he claimed poverty. Muhammad is then reported to have said, "Then where is the money which you left with [your wife], Umm al-Faḍl bint al-Ḥārith, when you left Mecca? You two were alone when you said to her, 'If I am killed, so much is for al-Faḍl, ʿAbd Allāh, Quthām, and ʿUbayd Allāh.'"[36] This anecdote (the primary purpose of which was to bear witness to Muhammad's prophetic powers) corroborates my assumption that it was customary to leave a last will and testament.

The death of sixty-five Muslims at the Battle of Uḥud (3/625) must have led to numerous disputes over property, especially in those cases in which the deceased did not leave a last will and testament. Such cases seem to have been referred to prominent Muslims for settlement. Upon the death of ʿAbd Allāh b. Jaḥsh, for example, Muhammad assumed control of his estate and bought property in Khaybar for the deceased's son.[37] When Saʿd, the client of Ḥāṭib, died, ʿUmar awarded a share of the estate to the deceased's son, ʿAbd Allāh.[38]

A man who had been wounded in battle sometimes succeeded in issuing an oral testament. Abū ʿĀmir al-Ashʿarī, after killing nine enemy combatants, was mortally wounded by the tenth. Before he died (8/630), however, he appointed Abū Mūsā al-Ashʿarī as the executor of his estate. Abū Mūsā brought the deceased's

35. Ibid., 3:610.

36. Ibn Hishām, *Sīra*, p. 463; Ṭabarī, *Ta'rīkh*, 2:466; cited in I. Lichtenstadter, *Introduction to Classical Arabic Literature*, p. 225.

37. Ibn Saʿd, 3:89.

38. Ibid., 3:115. Islamic tradition maintains that the revelation of the inheritance verses was caused by disputes over the estate of Saʿd b. al-Rabīʿ (and variants). In chap. 6, I shall argue that the reports dealing with this "incident," which belong to the genre of literature known as the *asbāb al-nuzūl*, are demonstrably late and not to be relied upon.

horse, armor, and estate (*tarika*) to the Prophet, who gave everything to Abū ʿĀmir's son.[39]

The sources refer to cases in which a person designates one or more persons as his testamentary heir. Muʿādh b. Jabal (d. 18/640) was sent to the Yemen by the Prophet in the year 9/631 and, while the latter was still alive, prepared a last will and testament in which he designated as heir (*warratha*) a sister and daughter, who were each to receive half of his estate.[40]

The Four Righteous Caliphs

The caliphate of Abū Bakr (11–13/632–34): When Sālim, the client of Abū Ḥudhayfa, was killed at the battle of Yamāma (12/633), ʿUmar sold the deceased's estate for 200 dirhams, which he gave to the latter's mother, with the instruction, "Eat them," i.e., use them to buy food.[41] Thus, ʿUmar seems to have given the entire estate to Sālim's mother, a clear violation of the Islamic law of inheritance, which awards a mother no more than one-third of the estate. This is an important detail, because, like many others, it suggests either that the fractional shares mentioned in the Qur'an had not yet become compulsory or that ʿUmar disposed of the estate in accordance with the terms of a last will and testament.

Perhaps the first explicit reference to fractional shares is made in connection with the estate of Abū Bakr, who died leaving his father, two sons, three daughters, and two wives, all of whom inherited from (*waritha min*) the caliph. It is explicitly stated that the caliph's father, Abū Quḥāfa (who died six months later), inherited one-sixth.[42] Abū Quḥāfa, upon being questioned about his inheritance from his son, reported that he returned his share to Abū Bakr's children. This may represent an effort to circumvent the effects of the Islamic law of inheritance, according to which Abū Bakr's children would not have inherited from their

39. Ibid., 4:357–58.

40. Abū Dā'ūd, *Sunan*, 8:100 (no. 2876); see Ibn Hishām, p. 957.

41. Ibn Saʿd, 3:88.

42. Ibid., 3:210. The text does not specify the entitlement of the other heirs, or the total value of the estate.

grandfather what had originally been their father's property. Further, by returning his share to the children only, rather than distributing it to all of the heirs, proportionally, Abū Quḥāfa seems to have been tampering slightly with the "limits of God."

The caliphate of ʿUmar (13–23/634–44): ʿUmar's involvement in the probating of estates, already documented for the lifetime of the Prophet and for the caliphate of Abū Bakr, continued during his own caliphate. When ʿUtba b. Ghazwāna died in Basra in the year 17/638, his servant, Sulaym, brought his property and estate to ʿUmar.[43] Similarly, it was ʿUmar who worked out an arrangement between the heirs of Usayd b. al-Ḥuḍayr (d. 20/640), who died leaving debts of 4,000 dirhams, and Usayd's creditors. Rather than sell the property to cover the debts, ʿUmar concluded an arrangement whereby the creditors received 1,000 dirhams every year for four years from the revenue produced by the property.[44]

Disputes over property, already numerous because of deaths on the battlefield, increased when the plague of ʿAmwās struck Syria in 18/639–40, killing thousands of people.[45] ʿUmar reportedly traveled to Syria in the aftermath of the plague and, in those cases in which the military commanders were unable to determine who the proper heirs were, portioned out the estates of those who had died.[46] Judging from the evidence of one report, ʿUmar distributed the property as he best saw fit, rather than according to any fixed rules: "He distributed the inheritances, and *designated as heir* some of the heirs to the exclusion of others, and then distributed [the wealth] to each one of the heirs who was alive" (emphasis added).[47]

The Arab conquest of the Near East, which began during the caliphate of ʿUmar, funnelled large quantities of wealth and

43. Ibid., 3:99. The text does not indicate what ʿUmar did with the property.

44. Ibid., 3:606.

45. The Islamic sources quote figures that vary between 20,000 and 30,000. Concerning the use of these sources, see L. Conrad, "Arabic Plague Chronologies and Treatises."

46. Ibn Kathīr, *al-Bidāya wa'l-nihāya* (Cairo, 1351/1932), 7:79; cited in Conrad, "Plague," p. 80.

47. Ṭabarī, *Ta'rīkh*, 4:65: *"Qasama 'l-mawārīth wa-warratha baʿḍa 'l-waratha min baʿḍ thumma akhrajaha ilā 'l-aḥyā' min warathat kulli 'mri'in minhum."*

property into the hands of the Arab elite. The estates mentioned in the sources increase in value beginning in ʿUmar's reign. ʿUmar's estate must have been a fairly large one, for it is reported that he died leaving a debt of 86,000 dirhams (paid off with the proceeds of the sale of his house to Muʿāwiya) and that the share of one of his heirs was equal to 100,000 dirhams.[48]

The caliphate of ʿUthmān (23–35/644–56): Extremely large estates are mentioned with increasing frequency during the caliphate of ʿUthmān. For example, ʿAbd al-Raḥmān b. ʿAwf died in 31 or 32/651 or 652, leaving a considerable fortune. The sources indicate that one-eighth of his estate (a clear application of the "science of the shares") was divided up among his four wives, each of whom took either 80,000 or 100,000 dirhams. The total value of the inheritance can thus be determined by multiplying the share of each wife by a factor of thirty-two, i.e., 2,560,000 or 3,200,000 dirhams. And, inasmuch as ʿAbd al-Raḥmān may have exercised his freedom to bequeath up to one-third of his property, these figures may represent as little as 50 percent of the total value of the estate.[49]

ʿAbd Allāh b. Masʿūd (d. 32 or 33/652 or 653) left an estate valued at 90,000 dirhams, a considerable figure, although minuscule compared to the value of ʿAbd al-Raḥmān b. ʿAwf's estate. When ʿAbd Allāh died, a dispute arose over the status of his stipend from the Dīwān. For two years the caliph apparently refused to turn over the stipend to the deceased's heirs, until the executor of ʿAbd Allāh's estate, al-Zubayr b. al-ʿAwwām, came to ʿUthmān and said, "[ʿAbd Allāh's family] needs [the money] more than the Treasury does." Whereupon ʿUthmān reportedly transferred 15,000, 20,000, or 25,000 dirhams to the deceased's family.[50]

48. M. Shibli, *Omar,* 1:286–87. See Ibn Saʿd, 4:161, where Ibn ʿUmar claims to have inherited from his father the sword, inlaid with silver, used by the latter at Badr.

49. Ibn Saʿd, 3:136. According to one account, ʿAbd al-Raḥmān left only three wives, who inherited 80,000 dirhams each. This discrepancy is related to the status of a woman named Ṭumāḍir who had been divorced by ʿAbd al-Raḥmān during his deathbed sickness, leaving him with only three wives. The divorce was apparently not recognized by the Caliph ʿUthmān, who awarded Ṭumāḍir a share of her late husband's estate. (Ibn Saʿd, 8:299).

50. Ibid., 3:160–61.

It is also in this period that the seizure and confiscation of property became a common occurrence. ʿUthmān, probably the wealthiest of the four righteous caliphs, died leaving an estate valued at "30.5 million dirhams and 100,000 dinars." The property was stolen and "disappeared."[51] These figures, however, do not include 200,000 dinars' worth of real estate that ʿUthmān had previously converted into charitable estates, possibly for the use of his heirs.

The caliphate of ʿAlī (35–40/656–61): The estates of several millionaires who died during the caliphate of ʿAlī suffered the same fate as that of ʿUthmān. Various estimates are given for the value of the estate of Ṭalḥa b. ʿUbayd Allāh (d. 36/656): 2.2 million dirhams and 200,000 dinars, 1 million dirhams and 200,000 dinars, or 32.2 million dirhams. But Ṭalḥa's property was confiscated and "he died a poor man."[52]

The estate of al-Zubayr b. al-ʿAwwām (d. 36/656), which included extensive real-estate holdings in Fustat, Alexandria, Kufa, Basra, and Medina, may have been saved from confiscation by the foresight of his sons, who asked their father to divide up the estate among his heirs before he died. Al-Zubayr refused to do so until he had given his creditors sufficient time to collect their debts. So for four consecutive years, he made a public announcement at the annual pilgrimage festival, calling upon his creditors to come and take payment. At the end of this period he divided up his estate, variously estimated at 35 million, 40 million, 51 million, or 52 million dirhams. According to the lowest of these estimates, each wife inherited 1.2 million dirhams.[53]

ʿAlī, the owner of some of the largest estates in the Hijaz,[54] apparently converted most of his property into charitable endowments, so that he died leaving "neither gold nor silver, except 700 dirhams left over from his stipend with which he had intended to purchase a servant."[55] It is during the period of the four righteous caliphs, then, that the sources begin to refer to the application of the Islamic law of inheritance.

51. Ibid., 3:76
52. Ibid., 3:221–22.
53. Ibid., 3:109–10.
54. S. el-Ali, "Muslim Estates in the Hidjaz in the First Century A.H.," p. 257.
55. Ibn Saʿd, 3:38.

The Umayyad Period

The caliphate of Muʿāwiya (41–60/661–80): The desire of people anticipating death to determine the ultimate devolution of their property continued to find expression in the Umayyad period. Shortly before his death in 42/663, ʿAmr b. al-ʿĀṣ said to ʿAbd Allāh, one of his sons, "I want to make a last will and testament." ʿAbd Allāh initially encouraged his father to carry out his intention. "Make a last will and testament," he said, "for your property is in [i.e., inseparable from] my property." But ʿAbd Allāh had second thoughts after ʿAmr named him as the principal beneficiary of the will, and he pointed out to his father the impropriety of singling out one son as the preferred heir.[56] ʿAbd Allāh's behavior may reflect an increasing acceptance of the trend toward egalitarian distribution of property among the entire nuclear family.

As we have seen, Muhammad's wives did not inherit from the Prophet but did receive annual stipends from the Public Treasury, and several of them managed to accumulate considerable amounts of property. At least three of Muhammad's wives died during the caliphate of Muʿāwiya. When Ḥafṣa died in 45/645, her apartment in the mosque was inherited by her brother ʿAbd Allāh b. ʿUmar.[57] Sawda bint Zamʿa, who died in 54/673, bequeathed her apartment to her cowife, ʿĀ'isha.[58] Of greater interest is the case of Ṣafiyya bint Ḥuyayy, Muhammad's eleventh wife, who died in 52/672, leaving an estate valued at 100,000 dirhams. Ṣafiyya was a Jewess who had converted to Islam, thereby making it impossible for her Jewish relatives to inherit any part of her considerable fortune (difference of religion constitutes a bar to inheritance). But Ṣafiyya was able to circumvent this obstacle by bequeathing one-third of her estate to a Jewish nephew (technically, a legacy is not an inheritance). When certain unnamed authorities refused to honor the terms of Ṣafiyya's will, ʿĀ'isha admonished them, saying, "Fear God and give him his bequest." And they did.[59]

56. Qurṭubī, *Jāmiʿ*, 2:257–58. For further details on ʿAmr, see Ibn Saʿd, 4: 254–61; and *SEI*, p. 42.

57. Ibn Saʿd, 8:164.

58. Ibid., 8:164; for details on Sawda, see *SEI*, pp. 503–04.

59. Ibn Saʿd, 8:128; for details on Ṣafiyya, see *SEI*, pp. 487–88.

The sources are often vague about details pertaining to the division of property, e.g., the identity of the heirs, the size of the estate, and the exact manner of its distribution. It is reported, for example, that when al-Walīd b. ʿUtba wrote to Muʿāwiya informing him about the death of Abū Hurayra (57 or 58/676–78), the caliph wrote back, saying, "See whom he left and give his heirs 10,000 dirhams, deal kindly with his slave girls, and treat them in the customary manner, fôr [Abū Hurayra] was among those who came to the aid of ʿUthmān and was with him in the house [when he was killed.]"[60] The source does not indicate the value of Abū Hurayra's estate, who his heirs were, or how the property was distributed. A similar vagueness characterizes a report about the death of ʿAbd al-Raḥmān b. Abī Bakr, sometime before 58/678. We are told only that the deceased's son, ʿAbd Allāh, distributed his father's estate, giving "something" to everyone in the house.[61] (Because of the limited amount of data available, the remainder of the Umayyad period will be treated as a single unit.)

The remainder of the Umayyad period (60–132/680–750): The *waqf* or family endowment came to be used as a means to circumvent the Islamic law of inheritance.[62] Ibn ʿUmar (d. 73/693 during the caliphate of ʿAbd al-Mālik) converted his house into a family endowment that "may not be sold or given away as a gift," perhaps in order to prevent the division of the house into inconvenient fractional shares. By this (and perhaps other) means, Ibn ʿUmar arranged, already during his lifetime, for the ultimate devolution of his property. It is therefore not surprising that when, shortly before his death, certain unnamed persons urged him to leave a last will and testament, he replied, "What shall I bequeath? God knows best what I did in my life. As for now, I do not think that anyone is more entitled to [the property] than [my children]. I will not add anyone to them in their dwellings."[63] Ibn ʿUmar seems to have rejected the idea of leaving a last will and testament because he did not want to disturb the arrangements that he had already made for his children.

60. Ibn Saʿd, 4:340.
61. Zamakhsharī, *Kashshāf*, 1:477.
62. See A. Layish, "The Mālikī Family *waqf* According to Wills and *Waqfiyyāt*."
63. Ibn Saʿd, 4:184.

Conflict of interest between heirs and legatees seems to have been a concern of Ibrāhīm al-Nakhaʿī (d. 95 or 96/713 or 714, during the caliphate of al-Walīd I). Ibrāhīm's wife had apparently bequeathed him some unspecified property after she had entered her deathbed sickness. Her heirs may have challenged the validity of the will, because, when Ibrāhīm subsequently left a bequest for a certain Abū al-Haytham, he stipulated that the latter must return the woman's property to her original heirs.[64]

The preceding pilot study provides support for my hypothesis regarding the shift from proto-Islamic to Islamic law. The custom of providing for the ultimate devolution of one's property by means of a last will and testament seems to have been common throughout the lifetime of Muhammad and into the caliphates of Abū Bakr and ʿUmar. Conversely, there is no evidence in the sources pointing to the existence of anything resembling the Islamic law of inheritance during the lifetime of the Prophet; the earliest reported instances of the application of the Islamic law of inheritance appear to be the shares awarded to Abū Quḥāfa upon the death of Abū Bakr in 634, to the wives of ʿAbd al-Raḥmān b. ʿAwf (d. 651 or 652), and to the wives of al-Zubayr b. al-ʿAwwām, respectively.

At the outset of this chapter I posed a number of questions regarding the postulated shift from proto-Islamic to Islamic law. My investigation of the dispute over the caliphate, claims against Muhammad's estate, and early inheritance practices prompts some tentative explanations for the primary and secondary causes of the transformation. It may also be possible, at this point, to speculate about the identity of those actors who were involved in the transformation, as well as about the mechanism of change.

(1) The primary and secondary causes of the transformation are to be sought in the political, social, economic, and religious history of the first century A.H. The transformation may have been triggered by the dispute over succession to Muhammad, for it would have been in the interest of Abū Bakr, who did not receive any document of appointment from Muhammad, to eliminate the embarrassing reference in Q. 4:12b to the possibility of designating an heir. The reinterpretation of Q. 4:12b would have set in motion a series of changes in the understanding of several

64. Ibid., 6:283.

other Qur'anic verses and prophetic *ḥadīth*, the cumulative effect of which would have been to yield a system of inheritance that imposed compulsory rules for the division of property. The new direction taken by the law of inheritance would have been reinforced by a host of secondary factors: (a) The severe restrictions placed upon testamentary dispositions, especially upon designating an heir, would have supported the efforts of the first two caliphs to refute claims against Muhammad's estate entered by various members of his family; (b) a shift to compulsory rules might have promoted social cohesion and harmony at a time when large quantities of wealth were being funnelled into a relatively small number of hands, on the one hand, and large numbers of Muslims were dying, either on the battlefield or as victims of the plague, on the other; and (c) the transfer of the institution of inheritance from the realm of human determination to that of divine control can be seen as part of a larger movement to place the regulation of all aspects of human behavior under the control of a law that had come to be perceived as an expression of God's will.

(2) The one name that comes up repeatedly in every area that we have considered is that of ʿUmar b. al-Khaṭṭāb, who is portrayed in the Sunnī sources, uncharacteristically, in a decidedly negative light. With regard to the dispute over the caliphate, ʿUmar is singled out as the spokesman of the group whose unruly behavior prevented Muhammad from dictating a last will and testament. ʿUmar later assumed the office of caliph by virtue of a last will and testament "dictated" under extremely suspicious circumstances. Then, in a sermon delivered five days before his assassination, ʿUmar admitted that he would leave no issue of more concern to him than *al-kalāla*, and vowed to issue a decree about this term in order to prevent disagreements over the recitation of the Qur'an. Finally, on his deathbed, immediately after insisting that he had not designated a political successor, ʿUmar vehemently denied having issued a decree about *al-kalāla*. The sources, then, seem to be pointing an accusing finger at the figure of the second caliph.

ʿUmar's involvement in the probating of estates would have put him in a position to influence early inheritance practices and, ultimately, the shape taken by the Islamic law of inheritance. During the lifetime of Muhammad and the caliphate of Abū Bakr, and when ʿUmar himself became caliph, he was called upon repeatedly to solve inheritance disputes. ʿUmar "inherited" from Abū Bakr the dispute over Muhammad's estate and seems to have been concerned to defend his predecessor's name against the accusation that he had uttered a lie in connection with the alleged prophetic dictum, *lā nūrathu mā taraknā ṣadaqatun.* Finally, the need to probate large numbers of estates in the aftermath of the plague of ʿAmwās, which reportedly killed thousands of Muslims, may have predisposed ʿUmar to a system that imposes standard, compulsory rules for the division of property.

(3) The transformation from proto-Islamic to Islamic law probably began prior to the establishment of the consonantal text of the Qur'an. Three historical personalities who figure prominently in the traditional Islamic account of the collection of the Qur'an can be linked to either the Qur'anic inheritance legislation or the formation of the Islamic law of inheritance.[65]

(a) ʿUmar's concern that the death of large numbers of reciters at the battle of al-Yamāma would result in the loss of the divine revelation prompted him to advise Abū Bakr to authorize the preparation of a complete, written text of the Qur'an.[66]

(b) The second collection was made at the instigation of Ḥudhayfa b. al-Yamān, an Arab general who became concerned when Iraqi and Syrian forces fighting in Armenia and Adherbayjan began to argue over the correct way to recite the Qur'an in communal prayers. This same Ḥudayfa is reported to have clashed with ʿUmar over Q. 4:176, as the following three texts cited by Ṭabarī indicate:[67]

65. For an excellent discussion of both the traditional Islamic and western positions on the collection of the Qur'an, see *EI*², "*Ḳur'ān,*" p. 405.

66. The following three points support our attempt to establish ʿUmar's sensitivity to the problem of Qur'an recitation: (1) ʿUmar is reported to have opposed the interpretation of ambiguous verses (*mutashābihāt al-qur'ān*) and to have punished severely Muslims who attempted to explain such passages. The story is told, for example, of how ʿAbd Allāh b. Ṣabīgh was arrested as a result of his interest in such verses and transferred to Medina, where ʿUmar ordered that he be flogged, tore up his manuscripts, and returned him to Basra with the order that he be ostracized (Abbott, *SALP*, 2:108). (2) ʿUmar's reading of an unspecified verse (could it have been Q. 4:12b?) is reported to have prevailed over the reading of Ibn Masʿūd, the sole Qur'an reciter to reject the ʿUthmānic codex (Ibn Saʿd, 3:371–72). (3) It was ʿUmar who, in the year 14/635, created the official position of the Qur'an reciter who was to lead the recitation during the five daily prayers (Juynboll, "The Position of Qur'an Recitation in Early Islam," p. 245).

67. These texts belong to the genre of literature known as the *asbāb al-nuzūl* about which I shall have more to say in chap. 6.

> Ibn Wakīʿ—Muhammad b. Ḥumayd—Maʿmar—Ayyūb—Ibn Sīrīn. He said: "The verse, 'When they ask you for a decision, say: God decrees for you regarding *al-kalāla*,' was revealed while the Prophet was on one of his journeys, and Ḥudhayfa b. al-Yamān was at his side. The Prophet related it to Ḥudhayfa, and Ḥudhayfa related it to ʿUmar b. al-Khaṭṭāb, who was traveling behind him. When ʿUmar became caliph, he asked Ḥudhayfa about it, in the hope that he would explain it. Ḥudhayfa said to him, 'By God, you are impotent (*ʿājiz*) if you think that your position (*imārataka*) requires me to inform you of something that I did not inform you of on that day.' ʿUmar said, 'I meant no such thing, may God have mercy on you.'"[68]

The second text is identical to the first, except that Ḥudhayfa uses the word "fool" (*aḥmaq*) instead of "impotent" (*ʿājiz*) in his response to ʿUmar's inquiry.[69] The third text tells the same story in slightly different words:

> Yaʿqūb b. Ibrāhīm—Ibn ʿUlayya—Ibn ʿAwn—Muhammad b. Sīrīn. He said: "They were on a journey, and the head of Ḥudhayfa's camel was at the tail of the Messenger of God's camel, and the head of ʿUmar's camel was at the tail of the Ḥudhayfa's camel." [Ibn Sīrīn] said: "And 'When they ask you for a decision, say: God decrees for you regarding *al-kalāla*,' was revealed. The Messenger of God told it to Ḥudhayfa, and Ḥudhayfa told it to ʿUmar. Subsequently, ʿUmar asked Ḥudhayfa about it. [Ḥudhayfa] said, 'By God, you are a fool if you think that is how the Messenger of God taught it to me. I have relayed it to you [exactly] as he dictated it to me. By God, I would never add anything to it for you.'" [Ibn Sīrīn] said, "ʿUmar used to say, 'O God, you may have explained it to him, but it has not been explained to me!'"[70]

Ibn Sīrīn begins on a mundane note, stating that Q. 4:176 was revealed "while the Prophet was on one of his journeys" and stresses the proximity of Ḥudhayfa and ʿUmar to Muhammad, a proximity that facilitates the oral transmission of the verse.[71] The time frame then shifts forward to the caliphate of ʿUmar, who asks Ḥudhayfa to clarify some unspecified aspect of the

68. Ṭabarī, *Jāmiʿ*, 6:42 (ll. 15–19).

69. Ibid., (ll. 20–21).

70. Ibid., (ll. 22–26).

71. This may be a topos. Cf. the report cited in chap. 5, in which the Companion, ʿAmr b. Khārija says, "I was under the upper part of the Messenger of God's camel. It was chewing its cud and saliva was running between my shoulders. . . . [Then] I heard [Muhammad] say," etc.

verse.[72] Ḥudhayfa responds sharply, telling ʿUmar that he is a fool (or impotent) and insinuating that ʿUmar sought to use his authority as caliph to introduce some change into the verse. ʿUmar denies the accusation, at the same time admitting to the Divinity that he still does not understand the verse.

Although one would expect the commentators to clarify the exact nature of ʿUmar's uncertainty, they demonstrate virtually no interest in the subject.[73] We can only speculate, then, as to how a traditional Muslim scholar might have explained ʿUmar's confusion—if he had chosen to address himself to this issue. Q. 4:12b, when read in the traditional manner, appears to award siblings a different share of the estate than does Q. 4:176. The commentators resolve this discrepancy by drawing a distinction between the types of sibling mentioned in the two verses, uterines in the former, and consanguines and/or germanes in the latter.[74] So pehaps Ḥudhayfa understood ʿUmar as wanting to make these interpolations part of the Qur'anic text; this would account for the latter's denial, "By God, I will never add anything to it."

But it is possible to explain ʿUmar's confusion in another, less

72. It may be significant, in this respect, that Ḥudhayfa was known as *ṣāḥib al-sirr*, i.e., the bearer of Muhammad's signet ring, *al-sirr*, but, literally, "the possessor of the secret." See Ibn Ḥajar, *ʿIṣāba*, 2:45 (no. 1249); and Ibn ʿAbd al-Barr, *Istīʿāb*, 1:334–35 (no. 492).

73. Ṭabarī (*Jāmiʿ*, 6:42) makes no attempt to clarify ʿUmar's confusion, noting only that Q. 4:176 was revealed while Muhammad "was on a journey." After Ṭabarī, even this minimal interest disappears. Wāḥidī (*Asbāb*, p. 180) and Suyūṭī (*Lubāb*, p. 116), when discussing the revelation of Q. 4:176, do not mention the Ḥudhayfa text. Ibn Kathīr (*Tafsīr*, 1:594) does quote two versions of the text, but makes no attempt to explain ʿUmar's confusion. Otherwise, the text passed out of general circulation. The Ḥudhayfa text may have been rejected on technical grounds. Ibn Kathīr (1:594) notes a break in the chain of authorities between Ibn Sīrīn (b. 653) and Ḥudhayfa (d. 656) and refers to an alternative *isnād* (cited in the *Musnad* of al-Bazzār), in which the name of Ḥudhayfa's son, Abū ʿUbayda, appears between that of Ḥudhayfa and Ibn Sīrīn, thereby completing the link. But Ibn Kathīr quotes al-Bazzār, himself, as rejecting this report on the ground that it is transmitted by only a single Companion, Ḥudhayfa, and by means of only a single chain of transmission. The text may also have been neglected because it constitutes merely a narrative (*khabar*) about the revelation of Q. 4:176, not a cause (*sabab*) of revelation. (Regarding this distinction, see Suyūṭī, *Lubāb*, pp. 7–8, and Wansbrough, *Quranic Studies*, p. 142.) Finally, Sunnī scholars may have avoided the text because of the clash between the negative manner in which ʿUmar is portrayed and his image as one of the four righteous caliphs.

74. See chap. 1, p. 29.

traditional, manner. Q. 4:176, the ostensible subject of these three texts, is the second of two Qur'anic verses containing the word *kalāla*, a word that seems to have plagued ʿUmar for much of his adult life.[75] And, according to at least one Muslim scholar, it was ʿUmar's confusion about *al-kalāla* which led to the revelation of Q. 4:176: Ibn Mardawayhi reports that Q. 4:176 was revealed to Muhammad after the Prophet had been approached by ʿUmar, asking, "*Kayfa yūrathu al-kalāla?*"—an allusion to the opening line of Q. 4:12b (*Wa-in kāna rajulun yūrathu kalālatan*).[76] Ḥudhayfa's insinuation that ʿUmar sought to add something to the Qur'an can therefore be taken as an allusion to the postulated reinterpretation of Q. 4:12b. But whatever the meaning of ʿUmar's confusion, the preceding texts clearly establish a connection between Ḥudhayfa, at whose instigation the second collection of the Qur'an was made, and the Qur'anic inheritance verses.

(c) Finally, there is the figure of Zayd b. Thābit. It was Zayd who was charged by Abū Bakr with the task of collecting all of the fragments on which the individual revelations had been recorded, so that he could write them out on sheets (*ṣuḥuf*); Zayd was one of four members of the commission appointed by ʿUthmān to establish an official text of the Qur'an; and Zayd is also reported to have been the first person to write a treatise on the Islamic law of inheritance, appropriately entitled the *Kitāb al-farā'iḍ*. This treatise gained early recognition as an irreplaceable source of law; Zuhrī is reported to have said that "knowledge of the law of inheritance would have disappeared had not Zayd fixed it in writing."[77]

75. See chap. 1, pp. 32–37.

76. Suyūṭī, *Lubāb*, p. 116.

77. Sezgin, *GAS*, 1:396: "*Lawlā anna Zayd b. Thābit kataba 'l-farā'iḍ lara'ayta annahā satadhabu min al-nās.*" The *Kitāb al-farā'iḍ*, which was transmitted by Zayd's student, Qabīṣa (d. 86/705) and his son, Khārija, was reportedly used by Mālik and Shāfiʿī as the basis for their writings on this subject. A considerable portion of Zayd's treatise may be preserved in the *Sunan* of Bayhaqī, who devotes a section to the outstanding place of Zayd and his *Kitāb al-farā'iḍ*. Bayhaqī also claims to preserve fragments of Zayd's *Risāla* on inheritance which he addressed to Muʿāwiya. See Sezgin, *GAS*, 1:395–96, 402. For further details on Zayd, see Ibn Saʿd, 2:358–62; Bukhārī, *Ta'rīkh*, 2:380–81; Ibn Ḥajar, *Tahdhīb*, 3:399.

5

On the Abrogation of the Bequest Verses

Islamic tradition teaches that the Qur'an was revealed to Muhammad *seriatim* over the course of twenty-two years and that certain early verses were abrogated or superseded by other, later, ones. By the fourth/tenth century Muslim scholars had identified over 235 instances of abrogation (*naskh*), and that number would eventually double.[1] The doctrine of abrogation poses a difficult theological problem, for it seems to call into question the wisdom of God by attributing a change of mind to the theoretically changeless and eternal divine will. The Muʿtazilīs, for example, challenged the widely held belief in the uncreatedness of the Qur'an by arguing that if the Qur'an is subject to abrogation it cannot be eternal.[2] Orthodox theologians have responded to this problem in one of two ways. Some managed to reduce the number of abrogated verses by harmonizing the apparent contradiction between pairs of abrogated and abrogating verses; Suyūṭī (d. 1505) recognized only 20 instances of abrogation and Shāh Walī Allāh (d. 1762) reduced that number to 5.[3] Others went so far as to reject the doctrine of abrogation in its entirety. Abū Muslim al-Iṣfahānī (d. 1066) maintained that abrogation does not

1. See, for example: Naḥḥās (d. 338/950), *Kitāb al-nāsikh wa'l-mansūkh*; Jaṣṣāṣ (d. 370/981), *Aḥkām al-qur'ān*; Ibn Salāmah (d. 410/1019), *Kitāb al-nāsikh wa'l-mansūkh*; Ibn al-ʿArabī (d. 543/1148), *Aḥkām al-qur'ān*; Ibn Ḥazm [*sic*] [= al-Ḥāzimī (d. 584/1188)], *Fī maʿrifat al-nāsikh wa'l-mansūkh* (on the identification of this text, see Rippin, "Al-Zuhrī, *Naskh al-Qur'ān* and the problem of early *tafsīr* texts," *BSOAS* 47 (1984)); ʿAbd al-Mutāʿal al-Jabarī, *al-Nāsikh fi'l-sharīʿa al-Islāmiyya*, p. 71.

2. Rāzī (d. 606/1210), *al-Tafsīr al-kabīr* (Cairo, 1307/1889), 1:446; Aḥmad Ḥasan, "The Theory of *Naskh*," p. 184.

3. Hahn, "Sir Sayyid Aḥmad Khān's *The Controversy over Abrogation (in the Qur'an)*: An Annotated Translation," p. 124.

occur within the Qur'an itself and that the Qur'anic references to "abrogation" and "replacement" (e.g., 2:106 and 16:101) referred, originally, to the supersession of Jewish and Christian religious practices and their replacement by others designed specifically for the Muslim community.[4] More recently, Sir Sayyid Aḥmad Khān (d. 1898) declared that "no verse of the Qur'an is abrogated"[5] and Aslam Jayrapuri asserted that "God's words are too lofty to be abrogated by human opinion."[6]

The doctrine of abrogation has attracted the attention of numerous Qur'an specialists, most recently J. Burton and J. Wansbrough, both of whom discuss it in connection with the question of the date at which the Qur'an was compiled.[7] Western legal historians, on the other hand, have expressed little serious interest in *naskh* and, to the best of my knowledge, there has been no attempt to study systematically the application of the doctrine to a specific verse or set of verses. I therefore propose to examine Q. 2:180 and 2:240 ("the bequest verses"), which, according to the general consensus of Muslim scholars, were abrogated by Q. 4:11–12 ("the inheritance verses"). Western legal historians, following the general lines of this consensus, have treated the abrogation of the bequest verses uncritically, dismissing the phenomenon as an inevitable occurrence of the early years of Islamic history.[8] An examination of the sources, however, reveals that the status of the two bequest verses was a subject of controversy among Muslim scholars during the first centuries of Islam. Although many early authorities hold for abrogation of the bequest verses, others argue that they were not abrogated and have always remained in force. It was not until approximately the tenth century A.D. that the case for abrogation emerged as the majority position, but the outcome of this controversy was by no means a foregone conclusion. Nevertheless, once the argument for abrogation emerged as the prevailing position, the commentators began to disregard the claims that had been made by

4. Ibid., p. 126; Ḥasan, "*Naskh*," p. 187.

5. Hahn, p. 126; Ḥasan, "*Naskh*," p. 188.

6. Baljon, *Modern Muslim Koran Interpretation*, p. 49; Ḥasan, "*Naskh*," p. 188.

7. Burton, *The Collection of the Qur'ān*, pp. 46–104, 225–40; Wansbrough, *Quranic Studies: Sources and Methods of Scriptural Interpretation*, pp. 192–202.

8. See, for example: Robert Roberts, *The Social Laws of the Qoran*, p. 62, note 2; J. Schacht, "*Mīrāth*," *SEI*, pp. 384–85; Coulson, *A History of Islamic Law*, p. 16; idem, *Succession in the Muslim Family*, pp. 213–14.

the opponents of abrogation, until the very terms of the controversy were eventually forgotten.

At the end of chapter 1, I anticipated the argument of the present chapter, to wit, that the bequest verses remained in force throughout the lifetime of the Prophet, and that it was only a quarter century after his death, at the very earliest, that these verses came to be seen as having been abrogated. I propose to substantiate this claim here by reconstructing the controversy surrounding the abrogation of the bequest verses in its historical fullness. This controversy may be followed during four successive stages of doctrinal development: the period of revelation (610–32); the period of the early authorities (632–799); the period of the collection of *ḥadīth* (ninth century); and the classical period (tenth to fifteenth centuries). By reconstructing the various stages of the controversy, I hope to demonstrate that the abrogation of the bequest verses was not the result of a change in the divine will, as Islamic tradition maintains, but that Muslim authorities applied the doctrine to these verses in the years following the death of Muhammad as a result of changed perceptions of the meaning of the divine word.[9]

Period of Revelation: 610–32

It will be remembered that, according to Islamic tradition, the law of inheritance developed in three distinct stages.[10] First, the bequest verses, which were revealed "at the beginning of Islam," reflect a system of inheritance that leaves the individual rela-

9. Both Burton and Wansbrough have alluded to the possibility that the doctrine of abrogation may have been applied to some verses subsequent to the death of Muhammad. "Playing fast and loose," Burton writes, "with the legal rulings that might be derived from the verses of the revelation to bring them into harmony with the rulings of the *fiqh* was similarly made to sound respectable and legitimate by reference to conscious supersession: *naskh al-ḥukm*, the replacement of the Qur'an ruling, despite the survival in the *muṣḥaf* of the Qur'an's wording." (*Collection*, pp. 46–47). Wansbrough concludes that the modes of abrogation set out in the classical treatises "reflect a concerted effort to identify *naskh* as an originally Qur'anic phenomenon. Once seen to enjoy scriptural sanction, the principle of abrogation could in theory and with impunity be applied across the entire range of source materials for the formulation of Muslim Law." (*Quranic Studies*, p. 197). That abrogation might have occurred after the death of Muhammad is inconceivable in the eyes of Islamic orthodoxy (see, for example, Zarkashī, *Kitāb al-burhān fī ʿulūm al-qur'ān* (Cairo, 1376/1957), 1:235).

10. For a more comprehensive discussion of this evolution, see my introduction.

tively free to determine whom his heirs will be and how much they will inherit. Then, the permissive and discretionary system characteristic of early Islam came to an abrupt end in 625 when, as a result of an inheritance dispute brought before Muhammad, Q. 4:11–12, in which the Divinity specifies whom the heirs will be and how much they will inherit, were revealed. Finally, the relationship between the voluntary and compulsory aspects of the system was clarified by the *sunna* of the Prophet, which imposes two major restrictions on the power of testation. The first restriction ("a bequest may not exceed one-third of the estate")[11] is generally understood as an attempt to strike a balance between the compulsory and voluntary aspects of the law of inheritance: a minimum of two-thirds of any estate is distributed in accordance with the compulsory rules established in the inheritance verses; a maximum of one-third may be used to make discretionary bequests.[12]

The second restriction had as its object the elimination of an apparent overlap between the voluntary and compulsory aspects of the law of inheritance. Q. 2:180 and 2:240 indicate that a person contemplating death must leave a bequest for parents and wives, while Q. 4:11–12 award these same persons specific shares of the estate. Is it possible, then, for a parent or wife to receive a bequest of up to one-third of the estate in addition to the fractional share specified in the inheritance verses? Apparently not, for Muhammad is reported to have declared, on the occasion of his Farewell Pilgrimage (632), "No bequest to an heir" (*lā waṣiyya li-wārith*).[13] Muslim scholars have taken this statement, Muhammad's final pronouncement on the subject of inheritance, to mean that a bequest may not be made in favor of any person who qualifies as an heir, i.e., any person who is awarded a fractional share of the estate. Together these two prophetic dicta, "a bequest may not exceed one-third" and "no bequest to an heir," define the relationship between the voluntary and compulsory aspects of the law of inheritance.[14]

11. The report relating this incident occurs in all of the standard collections of *ḥadīth*. See, for example, Bukhārī, *Ṣaḥīḥ*, 2:186; and Muslim, *Ṣaḥīḥ*, 3:1250–53 (nos. 5–10).

12. For a different explanation of the function of the one-third restriction see chap. 1, pp. 50–51.

13. Ibn Hishām, *Sīra*, p. 970. For further references see notes 63–65 and 67–70.

14. For a fuller account of this relationship, see Coulson, *Succession*, pp. 213–58.

Although most Muslim legists and commentators, since the middle of the first/seventh century, have held that the bequest verses were abrogated, it must be noted that the Qur'an does not contain any explicit reference to their abrogation. Indeed, there can be no better witness to the importance of testamentary dispositions during the lifetime of Muhammad than the Qur'an itself. Of ten verses (Q. 2:180–82, 2:240, 4:8, 4:11–12, 4:176, and 5:105–06) that deal directly with inheritance, all but two (Q. 4:8 and 4:176) refer to testamentary dispositions. Furthermore, the alleged abrogating verses, Q. 4:11–12, mention bequests four times without saying anything about abrogation!

The *ḥadīth* literature, similarly, does not portray Muhammad as having ever referred to the abrogation of the bequest verses. Even the prophetic dictum, "no bequest to an heir," which is traditionally viewed as an indicator of abrogation, does not explicitly mention abrogation and, furthermore, there is reason to believe that this dictum was not put into circulation in the form of a prophetic *ḥadīth* until the first quarter of the third/ninth century (see below). Indeed, there are numerous reports that suggest that Muhammad, far from wanting to restrict testamentary dispositions, attached the utmost importance to the drawing up of a last will and testament. According to one widely circulated report, Muhammad once said, "It is not the right of any man who has property to bequeath to spend three [consecutive] nights unless his testament is written and in his possession."[15] After hearing this pronouncement, ʿAbd Allāh b. ʿUmar (d. 693) is reported to have said, "I have not spent a single night without my last will and testament being written and in my possession."[16] Another report suggests that Muhammad viewed the drawing up of a last will and testament as a meritorious act that would ensure entrance to heaven: "He who dies leaving a last will and testament dies on the path [of God] and the precedent [of the Prophet], and he dies in fear of God, bearing witness [to His oneness], and he dies forgiven."[17] In still another report, Muhammad indicates that he considers the expression of a man's good or bad nature, as reflected in his last will and testament, to be more important

15. ʿAbd al-Razzāq (d. 211/826), *Muṣannaf*, 9:56 (no. 16326); Muslim, *Ṣaḥīḥ*, 3:1250 (no. 4); Ibn Ḥanbal, *Musnad* (Cairo), 6:261 (no. 4469); 7:45 (no. 4902); 8:231 (no. 6100); Nasāʾī, *Sunan*, 6:199–200.

16. Muslim, *Ṣaḥīḥ*, 3:1250 (no. 4); Ibn Ḥanbal, *Musnad* (Cairo), 7:231 (no. 6100).

17. Ibn Māja, *Sunan*, 2:901 (no. 2701).

than the accumulated deeds of an entire lifetime: "A man may do good deeds for seventy years but if he acts unjustly when he leaves his last will and testament, the wickedness of his deed will be sealed upon him, and he will enter the Fire. If, [on the other hand], a man acts wickedly for seventy years but is just in his last will and testament, the goodness of his deed will be sealed upon him, and he will enter the Garden."[18] Finally, in another report Muhammad places a last will and testament on the level of the obligation to pay the alms tax (*zakāt*), one of the five pillars of Islam: "If death approaches a man, and he makes a last will and testament, and his testament is in accordance with the Book of God, it serves as atonement for any alms tax that he omitted during his lifetime."[19] It is difficult to reconcile the great importance attached to the drawing up of a last will and testament, as reflected in these reports, with the alleged abrogation of the bequest verses and the severe restrictions placed upon testamentary dispositions. Whether or not these reports preserve Muhammad's actual words, they were probably put into circulation before the bequest verses had come to be seen as having been abrogated.

The great emphasis placed upon testamentary dispositions in both the Qur'an and *ḥadīth* makes it reasonable to assume that Muhammad himself would have left a last will and testament. As was pointed out in chapter 4, the Sunnī sources indicate that Muhammad did, in fact, attempt to dictate a last will and testament shortly before he died, but was prevented from carrying out his intention by the unruly behavior of several Companions, among whom only ʿUmar is singled out.[20] Furthermore, some of Muhammad's followers reacted with surprise at his failure to leave a last will and testament. Several of the classical collections of *ḥadīth* contain a section, in the chapter on testamentary dispositions (*waṣāya*), entitled "Did the Prophet leave a last will and testament?" (*hal awṣā al-nabī?*).[21] The reports contained in this section fall into two broad categories, those that raise the question of whether the Prophet left a last will and testament,

18. Ibn Ḥanbal, *Musnad* (Cairo), 14:127 (no. 7728); Ibn Māja, 2:902 (no. 2704); Abū D̄a'ūd, *Sunan*, 8:68–69 (no. 2850).

19. Ibn Māja, 2:902 (no. 2705).

20. See chap. 4, pp. 114–17.

21. Nasā'ī, 6:200–201; Ibn Māja, 2:900, *bāb* 1; Tirmidhī, *Sunan*, 3:292–93, *bāb* 3.

and those that deny that he did so. The following report containing an exchange between Ṭalḥa b. Muṣarrif (d. 730) and ʿAbd Allāh b. Abī Awfā (d. 705) may serve as an example of the former category:

> I asked Ibn Abī Awfā, "Did the Messenger of God leave a last will and testament?" He said, "No." I said, "Then how [do you explain] '*kutibat al-waṣiyyatu*,' and how [do you explain] that he commanded the people [to leave a last will and testament]?" He said, "He bequeathed the Book of God."[22]

The reference to *kutibat al-waṣiyyatu* may be taken as an allusion to the phrase *kutiba ʿalaykum . . . al-waṣiyyatu* in Q. 2:180, and the statement that Muhammad "commanded the people [to leave a last will and testament]" may be seen as an allusion to the report cited above in which Muhammad refers to the drawing up of a last will and testament as an obligation incumbent upon every Muslim. Ṭalḥa apparently sensed a discrepancy between Muhammad's failure to leave a last will and testament, on the one hand, and the emphasis placed upon testamentary dispositions in both the Qur'an and *ḥadīth*, on the other. Thus, there seems to have been an expectation among certain Companions that Muhammad would leave a last will and testament, and this expectation is linked to the Qur'anic and prophetic pronouncements on testamentary dispositions. What is perhaps most significant in the context of the present investigation is that neither Ṭalḥa nor Ibn Abī Awfā refers to the abrogation of the bequest verses. This may be taken as an indication that the doctrine of abrogation was not applied to the bequest verses until after this report was first put into circulation.

Early Doctrine: ca. 650–799

Q. 2:180

Full Abrogation. Neither the Qur'an nor the prophetic *ḥadīth* contains any explicit reference to the abrogation of the bequest verses. To my knowledge, the first explicit reference to the abrogation of Q. 2:180 occurs in a statement attributed to Ibn ʿAbbās (d. 687) who, in a sermon delivered in Basra, sought to clarify

22. Tirmidhī, 3:292–93 (no. 2202); Bukhārī, *Ṣaḥīḥ*, 2:185; Muslim, *Ṣaḥīḥ*, 3:1256 (nos. 16–17); Ibn Saʿd, *Ṭabaqāt*, 3:183.

parts of *Sūrat al-Baqara.* When he came to Q. 2:180 he said, "This was abrogated."[23] This statement could not have been made prior to A.D. 656, when Ibn ʿAbbās was appointed governor of Basra.[24] Other statements attributed to Ibn ʿAbbās specify the verses that are believed to have resulted in the abrogation of Q. 2:180: "The bequest was like that [viz., as in Q. 2:180] until the inheritance verse abrogated it;"[25] or, "the shares to which parents and relatives are entitled abrogated the bequest."[26] Similar statements are attributed to other seventh- and eighth-century authorities. Ibn ʿUmar (d. 683) is reported to have said, "the inheritance verse abrogated it [viz., Q. 2:180]."[27] According to ʿAbd al-Raḥmān b. Zayd (d. 798), "God abrogated that [viz., Q. 2:180] entirely and imposed the shares."[28] Mujāhid (d. 722) once explained that "the child was entitled to the inheritance, and parents and relatives were entitled to a bequest . . . , but the bequest was abrogated by a verse in *Sūrat al-Nisā'*."[29] A similar opinion is attributed jointly to ʿIkrima (d. 723) and al-Ḥasan al-Baṣrī (d. 728): "The bequest was like that until the inheritance verse abrogated it."[30] Qatāda (d. 736) maintained that the two inheritance verses in *Sūrat al-Nisā'* abrogated Q. 2:180[31] and the same opinion is attributed to al-Suddī (d. 745).[32] Thus, by the middle of the seventh century A.D. the early authorities had come to view Q. 2:180 as being incompatible with the inheritance verses and they resolved this incompatibility by asserting that the inheritance verses, which were revealed after Q. 2:180, abrogated that verse in its entirety.

Partial Abrogation. The argument for full abrogation of Q. 2:180, although endorsed by a large number of early authorities, suffers from at least two shortcomings. First, it fails to account for the repeated references to bequests in the abrogating verses, Q. 4:11–

23. Ṭabarī, *Jāmiʿ*, 2:118 (ll. 26–28); Bayhaqī, *al-Sunan al-Kubrā* 6:265.
24. *EI*[2], vol. 1, s.v. "Ibn ʿAbbās."
25. Abū Dā'ūd, 8:71 (no. 2852).
26. Ṭabarī, *Jāmiʿ*, 2:119 (ll. 1–2).
27. Ibid., 2:119 (ll. 3–5).
28. Ibid., 2:118 (ll. 24–25).
29. Ibid., 2:119 (ll. 17–19).
30. Ibid., 2:119 (ll. 7–8).
31. Ibid., 2:119 (ll. 12–13).
32. Ibid., 2:119 (ll. 20–23).

12. Second, the argument for abrogation is difficult to reconcile with the language of Q. 2:180 (i.e., "prescribed for you" and "an obligation upon those who fear"). These discrepancies may account for the development of a second position on the status of Q. 2:180 according to which only part of that verse was abrogated. The logic of this argument, which depends upon the ambiguity inherent in the word "relatives" (*aqrabīna*) in Q. 2:180, proceeds as follows: Q. 2:180 prescribes a bequest for parents and relatives, whereas the inheritance verses award shares of the estate to parents, daughters and siblings, but not to any relative more distant than a sibling. Thus, there are a number of relatives of the deceased (such as uncles and cousins) who are not awarded a fractional share of the estate by the inheritance verses. It is therefore possible to interpret the word "relatives" in Q. 2:180 as referring specifically to "relatives who are not awarded a share of the estate by the inheritance verses," or "noninheriting relatives." If so, then it can be argued that abrogation took effect upon the bequest prescribed for parents, and also upon the bequest prescribed for relatives who inherit (i.e., children and siblings), but not upon the bequest prescribed for noninheriting relatives (e.g., uncles, cousins, and the like). This approach has the advantage of eliminating the need to abrogate Q. 2:180 in its entirety.

We find such an argument attributed to a number of early authorities. Ibn ʿAbbās, who has already been mentioned as having held for full abrogation of Q. 2:180, is also reported to have made statements supporting only partial abrogation: "[A bequest] for those who inherit was abrogated, but [a bequest] for relatives who do not inherit was not abrogated";[33] or, "[God] abrogated the bequest for parents and confirmed the bequest for relatives who do not inherit."[34] Rabīʿ (d. 682) argued that parents were entitled to a bequest until the revelation of Q. 4:11, when God added them to the list of persons automatically entitled to a share of the estate; as a result, that part of Q. 2:180 prescribing a bequest for parents was abrogated, and from that time on, bequests came to be used exclusively for noninheriting relatives.[35] The following statement is attributed to Qatāda who, as we have

33. Ibid., 2:117 (ll. 23–25).
34. Ibid., 2:118 (ll. 10–12).
35. Ibid., 2:118 (ll. 13–16).

seen, is also reported to have held for full abrogation: "The bequest was assigned [at first] to parents and relatives. This was later abrogated and a compulsory share was assigned to them [i.e., the parents], while the bequest came to be used for noninheriting relatives. The parents were assigned a specific share, and a bequest to an heir is not permitted (*wa-lā tajūz waṣiyya li-wārith*)."[36] A similar opinion is attributed to Ṭā'ūs (d. 720): "The bequest preceded inheritance for parents and relatives. When the inheritance verse was revealed it abrogated [the bequest] for those who inherit, while a bequest in favor of those who do not inherit remained. Therefore, a bequest for a relative [who inherits] is invalid."[37] Yet a third authority to advocate both full and partial abrogation of Q. 2:180 was al-Ḥasan al-Baṣrī: "Parents and children were entitled to a bequest. Then [a bequest for parents] was abrogated and He gave them their share in *Sūrat al-Nisā'*. [A bequest] for any relative who is an heir was abrogated, whereas a bequest for relatives who do not inherit was not abrogated."[38]

The contention that Q. 2:180 was only partially abrogated resolves both of the aforementioned shortcomings of the full-abrogation position. First, it explains the presence in the abrogating verses of four unqualified references to bequests; if Q. 2:180 was only partially abrogated, then the phrase "after any bequest he bequeaths" repeated four times in Q. 4:11–12 may be taken as a reference to bequests in favor of noninheriting relatives. Secondly, the partial-abrogation position relieves some of the tension between the claim for abrogation and the prescriptive language of Q. 2:180; if this verse was only partially abrogated, then the obligation to leave a bequest remains in effect, at least with respect to noninheriting relatives.

At least two considerations suggest that Muhammad himself was not aware of these subtle hermeneutical distinctions. First, there is no evidence that Muhammad recognized any conflict between Q. 2:180 and the inheritance verses, and it may be significant that when the problem was finally recognized, its resolution was attributed, not to Muhammad, but to his Companions and Successors. Secondly, Ibn ʿAbbās, al-Ḥasan, and Qatāda are

36. Ibid., 2:117 (ll. 17–20).
37. Ibid., 2:117 (ll. 26–28); Bayhaqī, 6:265.
38. Bayhaqī, 6:265; Ṭabarī, *Jāmiʿ*, 2:118 (ll. 1–5).

all reported to have held for *both* full and partial abrogation of Q. 2:180. Although it is possible that these men were undecided between two opinions or perhaps changed their minds, it seems more likely that the multiplication of attribution represents an attempt to lend greater credence to a secondary position by linking it to the same highly respected authorities to whom an earlier position was attributed. Further, as we shall soon see, al-Ḥasan is even reported to have held *against* the abrogation of Q. 2:180.

Specification (takhṣīṣ). Certain scholars appear to have been dissatisfied with the argument for even partial abrogation of Q. 2:180. This dissatisfaction may have resulted either from a general uneasiness with the doctrine of abrogation or from the discrepancy that was perceived between the claim for abrogation and the emphasis placed upon testamentary dispositions by both the Qur'an and the *ḥadīth*, an emphasis that is echoed in statements attributed to a number of early authorities. Ḍaḥḥāk (d. 723), for example, is reported to have said that "he who dies without leaving a bequest for his relatives has sealed his actions with rebelliousness."[39] Similarly, when ʿImrān b. Jarīr asked Abū Mijlaz (d. 725) if a *waṣiyya* is incumbent upon every Muslim, the latter replied, "upon [all] those who leave property."[40] The discrepancy between such statements and the claim for abrogation, combined with a general discomfort with the doctrine of abrogation itself, seems to have resulted in the development of yet a third position regarding the status of Q. 2:180 according to which no part whatsoever of that verse was abrogated. This position was justified with the aid of the hermeneutical device of *takhṣīṣ* or "specification"; it was argued that the inheritance verses did not abrogate Q. 2:180 but merely specified aspects of that verse that had been worded in a general manner.[41] Specifically, it was argued that the words "parents and relatives" in Q. 2:180 did not refer to all parents and relatives, but only to those parents and relatives who do not inherit. By restricting the meaning of the verse in this manner, the scholars eliminated the need to invoke the

39. Ṭabarī, *Jāmiʿ*, 2:116 (ll. 12–13).

40. Ibid., 2:116 (ll. 25–28).

41. For a discussion of *takhṣīṣ* and its relationship to *naskh*, see Wansbrough, *Quranic Studies*, p. 191.

doctrine of abrogation. The *takhṣīṣ* or no-abrogation position is attributed to a number of early authorities, including: Ḥasan al-Baṣrī, Ṭā'ūs, ʿAlā' b. Zayd, Muslim b. Yasār (d. 718), and Ḍaḥḥāk.[42]

There is a subtle but important distinction between the arguments for partial abrogation and those for specification. The proponents of the former position maintain that the obligation to leave a bequest for parents was abrogated, whereas the obligation to leave a bequest for noninheriting relatives was not. The proponents of the latter position argue that Q. 2:180 imposes an obligation to leave a bequest for noninheriting parents *and* relatives. Thus, a parent is not entitled to a bequest within the framework of the argument for partial abrogation, but may receive one within the framework of the *takhṣīṣ* position, provided that he or she does not inherit. Under what circumstances, it may be asked, would a parent not inherit from a child? The answer to this question may provide a clue to the underlying socioreligious factors that contributed to the development of the *takhṣīṣ* position. In Islamic law, a difference of religion acts as a barrier to inheritance, so that a non-Muslim parent may not inherit from a Muslim child, and vice versa. Inheritance, however, is not identical with testamentary succession, and the *takhṣīṣ* position makes it possible to circumvent this restriction by enabling a Muslim testator to make a bequest to a parent or relative who has not converted to Islam.[43]

Once again we must ask whether or not this particular understanding of Q. 2:180 was recognized during the lifetime of Muhammad. Although we cannot rule out the possibility that Q. 2:180 was revealed to Muhammad in connection with the problem of the barrier to inheritance between Muslims and non-Muslims, it is highly unlikely that this was the original understanding of the verse. There is no evidence, for example, that either Muhammad or any of his contemporaries understood the verse in this manner. Furthermore, the first references to specification are attributed to a number of eighth-century authorities who lived at a time when the problem of inheritance between Muslims and non-Muslims would have been especially acute. These two fac-

42. Ṭabarī, *Jāmiʿ*, 2:117 (ll. 1–13); Ibn Salāmah, p. 16; Naḥḥās, pp. 20–21.
43. Mālik, *Muwaṭṭa'*, 2:519–20; Muslim, *Ṣaḥīḥ*, 3:1233; Nasafī, *Tafsīr*, 1:88.

tors, combined with the hermeneutical sophistication of the arguments and the growing discomfort with the doctrine of abrogation in general, combine to suggest that the *takhṣīṣ* position is best viewed as a secondary or perhaps even tertiary stage in the development of legal doctrine.

Q. 2:240

Abrogation. Statements referring to the abrogation of Q. 2:240 begin to appear at approximately the same time, and are attributed to many of the same authorities, as statements referring to the abrogation of Q. 2:180. There are only two positions regarding the status of Q. 2:240: for and against abrogation. There can be no question here of partial abrogation, since the word "wives" in this verse is not susceptible to the same hermeneutical distinctions as the word "relatives" in Q. 2:180.

The authorities who hold for the abrogation of Q. 2:240 make a distinction between two different aspects of the verse, each of which is held to have been abrogated by a different Qur'anic verse. Besides referring to the testator's obligation to leave a bequest for his wife, Q. 2:240 also mentions a one-year time period. The former aspect of the verse is held to have been abrogated by the fractional share of the estate awarded to the widow in Q. 4:12, and the latter aspect is held to have been abrogated by the reference to "four months and ten [nights]" in Q. 2:234; this verse opens with the same words as Q. 2:240 ("And those of you who die leaving wives"), but then fixes the waiting period of the widow at four months and ten nights. The verbal similarity between the opening lines of the two verses made it possible for the commentators to conclude that they deal with the same subject, and they accordingly argued that Q. 2:234 abrogated 2:240 by reducing the waiting period of the widow from one year to four months and ten nights. The following statement, attributed to ʿIkrima and Ḥasan al-Baṣrī (again!), exemplifies the arguments adduced in support of the abrogation of Q. 2:240: "[Q. 2:240] was abrogated by the inheritance verse and the [shares of] one-fourth and one-eighth that were awarded to them [viz., widows]; the one-year term was abrogated by 'four months and ten [nights].'"[44]

44. Ṭabarī, *Jāmiʿ*, 2:581 (ll. 17–20).

Statements similar to this are attributed to Rabīᶜ, Ibn ᶜAbbās, Qatāda, Suddī, Ḍaḥḥāk, ᶜAṭā', and Ibrāhīm.[45]

Against Abrogation. At least one early authority, Mujāhid, insisted that Q. 2:240 had not been abrogated, and in supporting his assertions he exposed the exaggerated literalism of the proponents of abrogation. It is true that both Q. 2:234 and 2:240 open with the phrase "Those of you who die leaving wives," and that the continuation of both verses contains a reference to a period of time—four months and ten nights, and one year, respectively. Even a superficial reading of the two verses, however, reveals that they treat two separate legal phenomena: the former fixes the waiting period of a widow at four months and ten nights, whereas the latter encourages testators to provide maintenance for their wives for at least one year. It is only the confusion of these two issues in such a manner that the one-year period mentioned in Q. 2:240 is erroneously equated with the waiting period of the widow that makes it possible to argue that Q. 2:234 abrogated (part of) Q. 2:240. As the following statement demonstrates, Mujāhid, unlike the proponents of abrogation, realized that the two verses deal with entirely different subjects: "[Four months and ten nights] refers to the woman who is observing the waiting period among her husband's family. This is incumbent upon her. Then God revealed Q. 2:240. God awarded to [widows] the rest of the year, seven months and twenty nights, as a bequest. If she wishes, she may reside [in her husband's house] by virtue of her bequest. But, if she wishes, she may leave. This is [the meaning of] God's Word, 'without expulsion. But if they leave . . .'"[46] Mujāhid, therefore, viewed Q. 2:240 as a supplement to Q. 2:234, rather than Q. 2:234 as abrogating 2:240, thereby eliminating the need to invoke the doctrine of abrogation.

Islamic tradition teaches that all instances of Qur'anic abrogation occurred before Muhammad's death and that a single authorized version of the Qur'an was not established until the caliphate of ᶜUthmān (r. 644–56).[47] The abrogated verses should therefore have been known to the persons entrusted with the task of collecting the Qur'an, and one might have expected them

45. Ibid., 2:579 (l. 17)–580 (l. 25).

46. Ibid., 2:581–82.

47. See *EI*², "Ḳur'ān."

to have omitted these verses from the authorized version; yet numerous abrogated verses are found in the text of the Qur'an and continue to be recited, although they have no legal value whatsoever. The inclusion of Q. 2:240 in the Qur'an was the subject of the following exchange that is reported to have taken place between Ibn al-Zubayr (d. 692) and the Caliph ʿUthmān:

> ʿAbd Allāh b. Abī al-Aswad—Ḥumayd b. al-Aswad and Yazīd b. Zurayʿ—Ḥabīb b. al-Shadīd—Ibn Abī Mulayka—Ibn al-Zubayr. He said: I said to ʿUthmān, "This verse [Q. 2:240] which is in [*Sūrat*] *al-Baqara* was abrogated by the other one [viz., Q. 2:234], so why do you write it?" He replied, "Leave it alone, my nephew. I do not move any part of it from its place."[48]

Islamic tradition accounts for the inclusion of abrogated verses in the Qur'an by means of the concept of *naskh al-ḥukm dūna al-tilāwa* ("the suppression of the ruling without [suppressing] the recitation").[49] The confusion reflected in the above anecdote may also be explained, however, by the assumption that the doctrine of abrogation was applied to Q. 2:240 (and also to Q. 2:180) only after the authorized version of the Qur'an had already been established, so that it was no longer possible to remove a verse that had allegedly been abrogated.

Several points should be kept in mind as we proceed with our reconstruction of subsequent stages of the arguments for and against the abrogation of the bequest verses. First, once the fractional shares mentioned in Q. 4:11–12 came to be viewed as compulsory rules applicable to all cases, the early authorities were forced to regard the bequest and inheritance verses as being in essential conflict with one another, a conflict that was resolved by invoking the doctrine of abrogation. None of these authorities considers the possibility that the two sets of verses might complement one another, the former regulating testate succession and the latter cases of intestacy. Second, both the proponents and the opponents of abrogation appear to have arrived at their respective conclusions based upon their own personal opinions of the relationship between the bequest and inheri-

48. Bukhārī, *Ṣaḥīḥ*, 3:209–10, *bāb* 45; Qurṭubī, *Jāmiʿ*, 3:226; Ibn Kathīr, *Tafsīr*, 1:296; Burton, "Those are the High-Flying Cranes," pp. 251–52; idem, *Collection*, p. 162.

49. For a discussion of this mode of abrogation, see Burton, *Collection*, pp. 49–67.

tance verses. Third, the subtlety of the hermeneutical distinctions invoked, the multiplication of attribution and the inclusion of abrogated verses in the Qur'an combine to suggest that the doctrine of abrogation was applied to the bequest verses after Muhammad's death but before it had become customary to justify legal doctrine on the basis of the *sunna* of the Prophet.

"No Bequest to an Heir"—From Legal Maxim to Prophetic *Ḥadīth* (Ninth Century)

Shāfiʿī (d. 820)

Neither the Qur'an nor the *ḥadīth* contains any evidence to suggest that, during the lifetime of Muhammad, the bequest verses were considered to have been abrogated. The first explicit reference to the abrogation of these verses occurs ca. 650. During the next century and a half, legal authorities were divided among themselves regarding the status of the bequest verses. Some considered these two verses to have been entirely abrogated, others held that they had been only partially abrogated, and a third group maintained that they had not been abrogated at all. Those authorities who held for either full or partial abrogation routinely state, with no further explanation, "the bequest verses were abrogated by the inheritance verses."

Perhaps the most interesting aspect of the early doctrine on the status of the bequest verses is the absence of any reference to the prophetic dictum "no bequest to an heir" (*lā waṣiyya li-wārith*), alleged to have been uttered by Muhammad towards the end of his life. This statement, as we shall see, plays a key role in what would become the classical doctrine on the abrogation of the bequest verses. Yet, of the eighteen authorities cited by Ṭabarī who hold for either full or partial abrogation of the bequest verses, not a single one mentions this prophetic dictum in support of these positions. Furthermore, in the one instance in which the phrase "a bequest to an heir is not permitted" is mentioned, it is quoted in the form of a legal maxim uttered by Qatāda, not in the form of a prophetic dictum.[50] If the phrase had

50. See above, pp. 151–52.

been in circulation in the form of a prophetic dictum, it stands to reason that at least some of these authorities would have referred to it. The fact that they do not suggests that we may be dealing with a legal maxim that began to circulate in the first quarter of the eighth century and was subsequently put in the form of a prophetic *ḥadīth*. A plausible explanation for this assumption is provided by developments in legal doctrine during the ninth century.

The phrase "a bequest to an heir is not permitted" circulated in the form of a general legal maxim between the first quarter of the eighth century, when it is mentioned by Qatāda, and the last quarter of that century, when it is mentioned by Mālik (d. 795), still in the form of a general legal maxim. Section 5 of the chapter on testamentary dispositions in Mālik's *Muwaṭṭa'* reads as follows:

> Yaḥyā said: "I heard Mālik say regarding this verse [Q. 2:180] that it is abrogated. The word of God, blessed and exalted, 'if he leaves wealth, a bequest for parents and relatives' was abrogated by that which was revealed, namely, the award of shares in the Book of God, the powerful and exalted."
>
> He said: "And I heard Mālik say, 'The established precedent among us (*al-sunna al-thābita ʿindanā*) upon which there is no disagreement is that a bequest to an heir is not permitted (*lā tajūz waṣiyya li-wārith*) without the consent of the [other] heirs of the deceased.'"[51]

The phrase "a bequest to an heir is not permitted" is identical in wording to the statement attributed to Qatāda half a century earlier and, like that statement, is invoked in connection with the status of the bequest verses. Indeed, to the best of my knowledge, this is the only connection in which this phrase is ever mentioned in the sources. Mālik gives no indication whatsoever that the phrase "a bequest to an heir is not permitted" was ever uttered by Muhammad. To the contrary, by referring to it as "the established precedent among us upon which there is no disagreement," he suggests that there was no *sunna* of the prophet on this subject.

The phrase "no bequest to an heir" appears in the form of a

51. Mālik, 2:765.

prophetic dictum for perhaps the first time in the *Risāla* of Shāfiʿī (d. 820), a student of Mālik.[52] Like Qatāda and Mālik, Shāfiʿī cites the phrase in connection with the abrogation of the bequest verses. But his treatment of this question differs from that of either Qatāda or Mālik in that he attempts to justify the abrogation of these verses on theoretical grounds. An examination of Shāfiʿī's discussion of this issue may shed light on the process whereby the phrase "no bequest to an heir" was transformed from a general legal maxim into a prophetic dictum.

The *Risāla* contains one of the earliest systematic treatments of the doctrine of abrogation.[53] By the beginning of the ninth century, it was no longer sufficient merely to assert that one verse had been abrogated by another; rather it was incumbent upon the scholar who held for abrogation of a particular verse to support his case with a specific indicator (*dalīl*) found in either the Qur'an or *ḥadīth*. Shāfiʿī himself conceded that the Qur'an contains very few such indicators, so that "most of the abrogating [communications] can be known only by [indications provided in] the *sunna* of the Apostle."[54] This statement indicates one reason why the prophetic *ḥadīth* were of such great importance to Shāfiʿī.

Thus, by Shāfiʿī's time, the simple assertion that "the bequest verses were abrogated by the inheritance verses" was not sufficient to demonstrate that abrogation had occurred. To be acceptable, the assertion had to be supported by a Qur'anic or prophetic indicator. The inheritance verses, however, contain no explicit references to the abrogation of the bequest verses; indeed, the fourfold repetition in Q. 4:11–12 of the phrase "after any bequest he bequeaths" can be taken as an indication of the continuing permissibility of bequests. If so, then a mother or father might receive a bequest of up to one-third of the estate, in

52. Shāfiʿī, *Risāla*; English translation by Majīd Khaddūrī, *Islamic Jurisprudence: Shāfiʿī's Risāla*. The phrase is also cited in the form of a prophetic dictum in Ibn Hishām (d. 833), *Sīra*, p. 970. Inasmuch as Ibn Hishām's text is, essentially, an edition of the *Sīra* of Ibn Isḥāq (d. 768), it may be possible to push back the *terminus a quo* of this report to the middle of the eighth century A.D. But then why is it that none of the eighteen authorities cited by Ṭabarī (see above, pp. 149–58) seems to be aware of the prophetic dictum?

53. Wansbrough, *Quranic Studies*, p. 193. For a list of early treatises on abrogation see al-Nadīm, *Fihrist*, 1:81–82.

54. Khaddūrī, p. 184, par. 189; Shāfiʿī, *Risāla*, p. 103, par. 608.

addition to the fractional share specified in Q. 4:11. This, of course, would have the effect of upsetting the relative balance of entitlement of the various Qur'anic heirs as defined by the inheritance verses.

The doctrine of abrogation may have been applied to the bequest verses in order to prevent any one of the Qur'anic heirs from receiving a supplement to the share that he or she was awarded by God. By ca. 650, the fractional shares mentioned in the inheritance verses had come to be understood by the legists as compulsory rules which, since they had been revealed by God, must be strictly obeyed. So long as the inheritance verses were viewed in this manner there could be no escaping the inevitable conflict between the bequest verses and the inheritance verses. The legists, who first became aware of this conflict in the years immediately following the death of Muhammad, resolved it by invoking the doctrine of abrogation. But a systematic justification for this position was apparently not developed until the time of Shāfiʿī.

Shāfiʿī begins the last section of his chapter on abrogation by quoting the bequest verses.[55] Then, after mentioning the subsequent revelation of the inheritance verses, he formulates the theoretical problem confronting him in the following terms:

> The two verses [Q. 4:11–12] may be interpreted as confirming the bequest for parents and relatives [prescribed in Q. 2:180], and the bequest for the wife [prescribed in Q. 2:240], and inheritance together with bequests, so that one may take by means of both inheritance and bequests. [But] it may also be interpreted as inheritance abrogating bequests. Since both interpretations are possible, as we have indicated, it is incumbent upon the learned to find an indication (*dalāla*) in the Book of God [as to which of the two is correct;] if no text is found in the Book of God, they should seek it in the *sunna* of the Apostle. If such evidence is found, whatever is on the authority of the Apostle is as [if] received from God, by virtue of God's command to obey His [Apostle].[56]

Shāfiʿī can conceive of only two ways in which the bequest and inheritance verses may be related to one another: they are either mutually compatible (bequests and inheritance) or mutually exclusive (bequests abrogated by inheritance). The correct choice

55. Shāfiʿī, *Risāla*, p. 68, pars. 393–94; Khaddūrī, p. 141, par. 128.
56. Shāfiʿī, *Risāla*, p. 69, pars. 396–97; Khaddūrī, p. 141, par. 128.

must be based upon evidence found in either the Qur'an or the prophetic *ḥadīth*. The assertion that the *sunna* of the Prophet is an authoritative source of legislation, on a level with the Qur'an, is one of Shāfiʿī's greatest contributions to Islamic jurisprudence.[57]

Next, Shāfiʿī attempts to determine which of the two abovementioned possibilities is the correct one. He apparently could find no statement in the Qur'an that might serve as an indicator of abrogation, so that justification of the case for abrogation depended on the discovery of an indicator in the *sunna* of the Prophet. In other words, Shāfiʿī needed such a *sunna* if the case for abrogation was to prevail, and it is at this point in the argument that he makes the following decisive statement:

> We have found that those learned in legal interpretation and the authorities in the campaigns, whether from Quraysh or other [tribes], are agreed that in the year of the conquest [of Mecca], the Prophet said, "No bequest to an heir (*lā waṣiyya li-wārith*), and a believer shall not be slain for the blood of an unbeliever."[58]

This statement, which contains what may be the earliest reference to the phrase "no bequest to an heir" in the form of a prophetic dictum, is significant for two additional reasons. First, it contains an "historical" detail not mentioned in the earlier statements attributed to Mālik and Qatāda, namely, that the phrase "no bequest to an heir" was uttered by Muhammad in the year of the conquest of Mecca, i.e., 630. Secondly, although Shāfiʿī asserts that the prophetic dictum had met the general acceptance of the relevant authorities, he does not, as yet, provide an *isnād*; this is curious inasmuch as, elsewhere in the *Risāla*, Shāfiʿī insists that only an authentic *sunna* of the Prophet, transmitted by reliable authorities, constitutes a valid source of law. We turn now to a consideration of these two phenomena.

The exigencies of Shāfiʿī's theory of sources (*uṣūl*) may account for his assertion that the prophetic dictum was uttered during the year of the conquest of Mecca. The primary function of the *sunna* of the Prophet, Shāfiʿī argued, was to specify the meaning of general communications established in the Qur'an.

57. Schacht, *The Origins of Muhammadan Jurisprudence*, pp. 11–20.
58. Shāfiʿī, *Risāla*, p. 69, par. 398; Khaddūrī, pp. 141–42.

It is therefore essential for Shāfiʿī that a given explanatory *sunna* be seen to have been established after the date at which the verse requiring explanation had been revealed. Otherwise, "it would be possible to reject all the traditions of the Apostle"[59] that were found to be at variance with the Qur'an. In the present case, if the prophetic dictum "no bequest to an heir" were held to have been established prior to the revelation of the bequest verses, then it could be argued that those verses had abrogated the *sunna* of the Prophet. This, of course, is the very opposite of the result sought by Shāfiʿī. It is thus no coincidence that by the ninth century the bequest verses, inheritance verses, and prophetic dictum "no bequest to an heir" had been placed in a chronological continuum corresponding to the logical progression required to demonstrate abrogation: God had prescribed a bequest for parents and wives "in the beginning of Islam." Then, shortly after the battle of Uḥud (625), God revealed the inheritance verses, which award a specific share of the estate to these same persons. Finally, in the year of the conquest of Mecca (630), Muhammad indicated that no "heir," that is to say, no person who receives a fractional share of the estate, may receive a bequest. The prophetic dictum thus provides a clear indication of the abrogation of the bequest verses.

Shāfiʿī's citation of the *matn* (text) of the *ḥadīth* without, at first, providing the *isnād* may be related to his sensitivity to possible objections to the *isnād* itself. After first citing the prophetic dictum, Shāfiʿī makes the following statement, which seems to have been intended to silence any such objections:

> This report has been transmitted from those who have heard it from the authorities on the life of Muhammad (*ahl al-ʿilm bi'l-maghāzī*).
>
> So this is a transmission of the public from the public and it is therefore of greater authority, in part, than the transmission of one [individual] from another. Furthermore, we have found that the scholars are agreed on it (*ʿalayhi mujmaʿīn*).
>
> He said: Some of the Syrian [transmitters] have related a report which is not confirmed by the traditionists, because some of the transmitters are unknown. So we have transmitted it from the Prophet as an interrupted [report].
>
> We have accepted it, as I indicated, on the basis of the transmis-

59. Khaddūrī, p. 127, par. 109; Shāfiʿī, *Risāla*, p. 58, par. 333.

sion of the authorities on the campaigns and the consensus (*ijmāʿ*) of the public, even if we have already mentioned the report. We rely, in general, on the transmission of the authorities on the campaigns and the consensus of the people.

Sufyān informed us, on the authority of Sulaymān al-Aḥwal, on the authority of Mujāhid, that the Messenger of God said, "No bequest to an heir."[60]

In this statement, Shāfiʿī appeals repeatedly to the authority of the experts on Muhammad's campaigns and to the consensus of the public in order to lend credence to the prophetic dictum. These appeals, however, cannot disguise a serious defect in the *isnād* known to Shāfiʿī (Sufyān—Sulaymān al-Aḥwal—Mujāhid—Muhammad), for Mujāhid, who was born after Muhammad died, could not possibly have been in direct contact with the Prophet. Indeed, Shāfiʿī admits that the *isnād* is "broken" (*munqaṭiʿ*). This is curious because elsewhere in the *Risāla*, Shāfiʿī rejects reports on the grounds that their *isnād*s are defective.[61] In the present instance, Shāfiʿī appears to have lowered his standards and attempted to offset the formal defect in the chain of authorities by appealing to the doctrine of consensus. As the title of this section of the *Risāla* indicates, it is not the *ḥadīth* itself, but the *ḥadīth* as confirmed by the doctrine of consensus, that serves as the indicator of abrogation: "The Abrogating and Abrogated [communications] which are indicated by the *sunna* and consensus."[62]

We may sum up the argument to this point as follows: At some point during the first quarter of the eighth century, the proponents of abrogation began to circulate the legal maxim, "no bequest to an heir." But, because the argument for abrogation of the bequest verses required the production of a suitable prophetic *sunna*, this maxim was subsequently put into the form of a prophetic dictum that was supposedly uttered by Muhammad towards the end of his life. As a prophetic dictum, the report circulated, at first, with a defective *isnād*, but, as we shall now see, this defect was corrected during the second half of the ninth century.

60. Shāfiʿī, *Risāla*, p. 69, pars. 398–402; Khaddūrī, p. 142.

61. Shāfiʿī, *Risāla*, p. 105, par. 619; Khaddūrī, p. 189, par. 197.

62. Shāfiʿī, *Risāla*, p. 68; Khaddūrī, p. 141.

The Ḥadīth *Collections*

Shāfiʿī provided the theoretical arguments necessary to ensure the ultimate success of the proponents of abrogation, for the prophetic dictum "no bequest to an heir" removes all doubt regarding the status of the bequest verses. Although the *isnād* of the report containing this dictum was defective, it did not remain so for long. Within a century after Shāfiʿī's death the *isnād* was improved and the *matn*, too, was substantially modified. It is possible to trace the growth of this report by examining the different forms in which it appears in the collections compiled during the ninth century.

Several versions of the report had been put into circulation by the first half of the ninth century. One of the earliest versions is found in the *Muṣannaf* of ʿAbd al-Razzāq (d. 826), where it occurs in the following form:

> ʿAbd al-Razzāq—Maʿmar—Maṭar al-Warrāq—Shahr b. Ḥawshab—ʿAmr b. Khārija. He said, "I heard the Apostle of God saying, 'No bequest to an heir.'"[63]

Although the *matn* of this report is identical to the one known to Shāfiʿī, the *isnād*s of the two reports differ considerably. The *isnād* cited by ʿAbd al-Razzāq passes through an entirely different chain of authorities and, more important, includes a Companion of the Prophet, ʿAmr b. Khārija.

The *Sunan* of Ibn Shuʿbah (d. 842) contains five different versions of the report, three of which resemble the version known to Shāfiʿī (they have defective *isnād*s and short *matn*s that do not indicate the date upon which the prophetic dictum was uttered).[64] The other two versions, however, are quite different from the version known to Shāfiʿī; not only are their *isnād*s complete but their *matn*s are long and refer to the date upon which the prophetic dictum was uttered. The fourth version reads as follows:

> Saʿīd—Ismāʿīl b. ʿAyyāsh—Shuraḥbīl b. Muslim al-Khawlānī—Abū Umāma al-Bāhilī. He said, "I heard the Apostle of God saying, during the year of the Farewell Pilgrimage, 'Verily, God gave a

63. ʿAbd al-Razzāq, 9:70 (no. 16376).

64. Ibn Shuʿbah, *Sunan*, vol. 3, pt. i, p. 107 (nos. 425, 426, and 429).

share to every person who is entitled to one, so no bequest to an heir. The child belongs to the [marriage] bed, and the fornicator is stoned. Your account is with God until the Day of Resurrection: the curse of God is upon him who claims [paternity] from someone who is not his father or claims to be affiliated with those who are not his patrons—no compensatory atonement may be accepted from him. A wife may not spend anything from her house without the permission of her husband.' Someone said, 'O Apostle of God, not even [for] food?' He said, 'That is the most desirable part of our wealth.' Then he said, 'A loan of nonfungible items is carried out, a gift is returnable, a debt is executed and a claimant pays [damages].'"[65]

This version of the report is considerably more developed than any of the others we have examined so far: (1) The *isnād*, which is complete, rests upon the ultimate authority of a Companion of the Prophet, Abū Umāma al-Bāhilī. (2) The year in which the dictum was uttered is, for the first time, specifically mentioned in the *matn* of the report: "the year of the Farewell Pilgrimage," i.e., 632. Although this is two years after the date mentioned by Shāfiʿī, the discrepancy does not affect the question of abrogation, both dates being subsequent to the revelation of the bequest and inheritance verses. We may then be dealing with what R. M. Speight has referred to, while tracing the development of another *ḥadīth*, as "a form in search of a natural setting."[66] That is to say, once the legal maxim "no bequest to an heir" was put in the form of a prophetic dictum, an appropriate occasion for the utterance of the dictum was sought. Any date after the revelation of the bequest and inheritance verses was acceptable: although Shāfiʿī placed it in the year of the conquest of Mecca, 630, others seem to have found the year of the Farewell Pilgrimage, 632, more appropriate. (3) The prophetic dictum has been expanded to include a rationalization for the proscription of bequests, namely, the fact that "God gave a share to every person who is entitled to one," an oblique reference to the inheritance verses. (4) Finally, the proscription of bequests is here only the first of a series of legal pronouncements allegedly made by Muhammad on this occasion.

The fifth version cited by Ibn Shuʿbah reads as follows:

65. Ibid., pp. 107–8 (no. 427).

66. Speight, "The Will of Saʿd b. a. Waqqāṣ," p. 254.

Saᶜīd—Hushaym—Ṭalḥa Abū Muḥammad, *mawlā* of Bāhila—Qatāda—Shahr b. Ḥawshab—ᶜAmr b. Khārija. He said, "I was present with the Apostle of God during his pilgrimage." He said, "I was underneath the upper part of the neck of the Apostle of God's camel, and it was chewing its food, and its saliva was flowing between my shoulders." He said, "I heard him say, 'Verily, God gave a share to every person who is entitled to one, so a bequest to an heir is not permitted. Verily, the child belongs to the bed and the fornicator is stoned. The curse of God, the angels, and all the people is upon him who claims [paternity] from someone who is not his father or claims affiliation with those who are not his patrons; no compensatory atonement may be accepted from him.'"[67]

This report appears to be a composite of three separate statements attributed to ᶜAmr b. Khārija. In the first statement, ᶜAmr specifies that the prophetic dictum was uttered, not merely during the year of the Farewell Pilgrimage, but during the course of the Pilgrimage itself. In the second statement, ᶜAmr introduces a vivid detail that serves to highlight the fact that he was in a position to hear anything that the Prophet might say, for on this particular occasion he was standing directly under the prophet's camel, and the camel's saliva was dripping on his shoulders, thereby establishing a direct physical link between the two men. Finally, the third statement contains the prohibition of bequests which, as in the version attributed to Abū Umāma, is once again the first of a series of legal pronouncements. The composite nature of this text, which would subsequently be eliminated, points to an intermediate stage in the development of the *ḥadīth*.

The five versions cited by Ibn Shuᶜbah appear to reflect successive stages in the growth of the tradition. Versions one through three all have defective *isnād*s and relatively short *matn*s in which there is no indication of the year in which the prophetic dictum was uttered; these represent the earliest stage of development. Versions four and five, with their complete *isnād*s and relatively long *matn*s that do refer to the year in which the prophetic dictum was allegedly uttered, seem to represent a secondary stage of development.

Ḥadīth specialists were, of course, aware of the tendency of partisan groups to disguise their doctrines in the form of prophetic dicta and, by means of a rigorous scrutiny of *isnād*s, they

67. Ibn Shuᶜbah, vol. 3, pt. i, p. 108 (no. 428); see also Ibn Hishām, p. 970.

attempted to eliminate such texts. Judging from the response of several of the most famous compilers of traditions, the report containing the prophetic dictum "no bequest to an heir" was, at first, viewed with considerable suspicion. Of the five versions cited by Ibn Shuᶜbah, only the fifth is found in the *Musnad* of Aḥmad b. Ḥanbal (d. 855).[68] Furthermore, not a single version of this report is found in either the *Ṣaḥīḥ* of Bukhārī (d. 869) or the *Ṣaḥīḥ* of Muslim (d. 874), the two most highly regarded collections of *ḥadīth*. In his chapter on testamentary dispositions, Muslim makes no reference whatsoever to the phrase, "no bequest to an heir," either as a legal maxim or a prophetic dictum.[69] Bukhārī, who also does not cite this phrase in the form of a prophetic dictum, does refer to it in the form of a general legal maxim. The sixth section of his chapter on testamentary dispositions reads as follows:

> *Section 6:* "No bequest to an heir." Muḥammad b. Yūsuf—Warqā'—Ibn Abī Najīḥ—ᶜAṭā'—Ibn ᶜAbbās. He said, "The child was entitled to the property and the parents were entitled to a bequest. Then God abrogated as much of that [Q. 2:180] as He wanted: He gave the male the share of two females and He gave each of the parents one-sixth; He gave the wife one-eighth and one-fourth, and the husband one-half and one-fourth."[70]

The title of this section suggests that Bukhārī is about to refer to a version of the report containing the prophetic dictum "no bequest to an heir." This expectation is disappointed, however, as Bukhārī cites a report in which Ibn ᶜAbbās refers to the abrogation of Q. 2:180.

Thus, although several versions of the prophetic dictum "no bequest to an heir" had been in circulation for at least half a century prior to the compilation of the two *Ṣaḥīḥ*s, not one of these texts is included in either of these collections. An examination of the *isnād*s of these texts may provide an explanation for this phenomenon. The rejection of the first three versions cited by Ibn Shuᶜbah may be explained by the fact that the *isnād* of each of these texts is broken. Versions four and five, on the other hand, may have been rejected on account of doubts regarding the trust-

68. Ibn Ḥanbal, *Musnad* (Beirut), 4:186–87, 238–39 (eleven versions of *isnād* passing through ᶜAmr b. Khārija).

69. Muslim, *Ṣaḥīḥ*, 3:1249–59.

70. Bukhārī, *Ṣaḥīḥ*, 2:187.

worthiness of several of the traditionists in their respective chains of authorities.

The *isnād* of version four (Saʿīd—Ismāʿīl b. ʿAyyāsh—Shuraḥbīl b. Muslim—Abū Umāma—Muhammad) is doubly weak. First, the trustworthiness of Ismāʿīl b. ʿAyyāsh (d. 797) seems to have been in doubt. Although certain authorities maintained that Ismāʿīl committed thirty thousand *ḥadīth* to memory during his lifetime, others charged that his memory "changed" when he became older, that he became confused about both *isnād*s and *matn*s, and that he made frequent mistakes.[71] And although some authorities considered him to be trustworthy, others did not. Abū Isḥāq al-Fazārī, for example, warned against the acceptance of reports transmitted by Ismāʿīl: "Take from al-Baqiyya that which is related on the authority of trustworthy [transmitters], but do not take anything from Ismāʿīl b. ʿAyyāsh."[72] Bukhārī expressed concern (*wa-fīhi naẓarun*) regarding reports that Ismāʿīl, a Syrian, transmitted from non-Syrians.[73] Nasā'ī classified him as "weak" (*ḍaʿīf*)[74] and Ibn Ḥibbān included him among the weak traditionists in his *Kitāb al-majrūḥīn*.[75] Secondly, there also seem to have been doubts about the trustworthiness of Abū Umāma,[76] the Companion who allegedly heard Muhammad utter the statement "no bequest to an heir." On the basis of estimates of his age when he died, Abū Umāma could have been zero, 15, or 20 years old in the year 10/632.[77] The possibility that he might not have been alive in the year of the Farewell Pilgrimage, or was only a young boy, aroused the suspicion of a certain Sulaym b. ʿĀmir, who asked Abū Umāma, "How old were you on the day of the Farewell Pilgrimage?" To this Abū

71. 30,000 *ḥadīth*: Ibn Ḥajar al-ʿAsqalānī, *Tahdhīb al-tahdhīb*, 1:321–23; Dhahabī, *al-ʿIbar fī khabar man ghabar*, 1:278–79 (20,000 *ḥadīth*). Confusion: Ibn Ḥibbān, *Kitāb al-majrūḥīn*, 1:113; Ibn Ḥajar, *Tahdhīb*, 1:323.

72. Tirmidhī, 3:293–94; see also Dhahabī, *Mīzān al-iʿtidāl fī naqd al-rijāl*, 1:244.

73. Dhahabī, *Tadhkirat al-ḥuffāẓ*, 1:253; see also Bukhārī, *Kitāb al-ta'rīkh al-kabīr*, 1:369–70.

74. Dhahabī, *Tadhkira*, 1:253.

75. 1:113.

76. Abū Umāma's full name is Ṣudayya b. ʿAjlān b. Wahb, Abū Umāma al-Bāhilī (for references see following note).

77. Ibn Ḥajar, *Tahdhīb*, 4:420–21; Dhahabī, *al-Kāshif fī maʿrifat man lahu riwāya fi'l-kutub al-sitta*, 2:28; Ibn Ḥibbān, *Kitāb mashāhīr ʿulamā' al-amṣār*, p. 50; Ibn ʿAbd al-Barr, *al-Istīʿāb fī maʿrifat al-aṣḥāb*, 2:737 (no. 1237).

Umāma replied, "On that day I was 30 years old."[78] This answer complicates matters further for, as Ibn Ḥajar al-ʿAsqalānī notes, if Abū Umāma had been 30 years old at the time, as he claimed, then he would have been at least 106 years old when he died.[79] Yet, according to the most generous estimate, he died at the age of 91![80] Thus, even if Abū Umāma had been alive in the year of the Farewell Pilgrimage, his attempt to make it appear as if he had been a fully grown man at the time would constitute grounds for rejection of reports that he transmitted. This, combined with the doubts concerning the trustworthiness of Ismāʿīl b. ʿAyyāsh, provides a reasonable explanation for the rejection of this version of the *ḥadīth* by Muslim and Bukhārī.

The rejection of version five (Saʿīd—Ṭalḥa—Qatāda—Shahr b. Ḥawshab—ʿAmr b. Khārija—the Prophet) may be related to the personage of Shahr b. Ḥawshab (d. 729).[81] Several authorities give Shahr very low ratings for trustworthiness: Nasā'ī, Ibn ʿAdī, and al-Ḥākim Abū Muḥammad classify him as "not strong";[82] Mūsā b. Hārūn, Sājī, and Bayhaqī classify him as "weak";[83] Ibn Ḥibbān and Ibn ʿAdī charge that he is "not to be cited as evidence";[84] and Ibn Ḥazm labels him as "disreputable."[85] Muslim relates that Ibn ʿAwn, in response to an inquiry regarding the status of a *ḥadīth* transmitted by Shahr, exclaimed: "Verily, Shahr, they abandoned him. Verily, Shahr, they abandoned him."[86] But doubts concerning Shahr's trustworthiness can be linked directly to the report containing the prophetic dictum, "no bequest to an heir." This report, which is a composite of three separate statements, contains the detail that ʿAmr b. Khārija "was underneath the upper part of the neck of the Apostle of God's camel." The presence of this detail in several reports transmitted by Shahr ap-

78. Ibn Ḥajar, *Tahdhīb*, 4:420–21; Bukhārī, *Ta'rīkh*, vol. 2, pt. ii, pp. 326–27.

79. Ibn Ḥajar, *Tahdhīb*, 4:420–21.

80. See note 77. Lying about one's age seems to have been a common practice among traditionists. See, on this phenomenon, Juynboll, *Muslim Tradition*, pp. 46–48.

81. Shahr b. Ḥawshab al-Ashʿarī, Abū Saʿīd al-Shāmī, *mawlā* of Asmā' bint Yazīd b. al-Sakan (Ibn Ḥajar, *Tahdhīb*, 4:369).

82. Dhahabī, *Mīzān*, 2:283 (no. 3756); Ibn Ḥajar, *Tahdhīb*, 4:369–72.

83. Ibn Ḥajar, *Tahdhīb*, 4:369–72.

84. Dhahabī, *Mīzān*, 2:283–84.

85. Ibn Ḥajar, *Tahdhīb*, 4:371–72.

86. Dhahabī, *Kāshif*, 2:16 (no. 2333), note 2; Dhahabī, *Mīzān*, 2:283–85; Ibn Ḥajar, *Tahdhīb*, 4:369–70; Ibn Ḥibbān, *Majrūḥīn*, 1:358.

pears to have aroused the suspicion of the *isnād* critics. Dawlābī, for example, asserted that "Shahr's reports do not resemble the reports of [normal] people; it is as if he were infatuated (*muwallaᶜ*) with the reins of the Prophet's camel."[87] This statement suggests that the detail involving the Prophet's camel may have been added to the report in order to lend greater credence to it. This, combined with the general doubts regarding Shahr's trustworthiness, would explain why this version of the report was rejected by Muslim and Bukhārī.

The rejection of the prophetic dictum, "no bequest to an heir," threatened to undermine Shāfiᶜī's justification for the abrogation of the bequest verses. Muslim scholars living in the final quarter of the ninth century responded to this challenge in at least two ways. The first response, exemplified by Ibn Qutayba (d. 889), was to develop a justification for abrogation that did not depend on the prophetic dictum.[88] Where previous scholars had failed in locating a Qur'anic indicator of abrogation, Ibn Qutayba succeeded by arguing that such an indicator is contained in Q. 4: 13–14, the two verses that immediately follow the inheritance verses.[89] Ibn Qutayba understood the "limits" (*ḥudūd*) mentioned in Q. 4:13–14 as a reference to the fractional shares specified in the inheritance verses. Any attempt to supplement these limits by leaving a bequest for one or more of the heirs is, according to Ibn Qutayba, a transgression of the divine command. Thus, unlike Shāfiᶜī, Ibn Qutayba was able to locate an indicator of abrogation in the Qur'an itself.

The second response was to ignore or overlook the doubts regarding the trustworthiness of Ismāᶜīl b. ᶜAyyāsh, Abū Umāma, and Shahr b. Ḥawshab. This attitude may account for the inclusion of several versions of the report in the collections compiled during the final quarter of the ninth century. Ibn Māja (d. 886) includes three different versions of the report, all with complete *isnād*s, in his *Sunan*: one passes through ᶜAmr b. Khārija, a second through Abū Umāma, and the third through Anas b. Mālik.[90] Tirmidhī (d. 892) cites two versions of the report, with *isnād*s

87. Dhahabī, *Mīzān*, 2:283–85.

88. Ibn Qutayba, *Ta'wīl mukhtalif al-ḥadīth*, pp. 193–94; translated by Gérald Lecomte as *Le traité des Divergences du Ḥadīth d'Ibn Qutayba*, pp. 214–15, sec. 45, pars. 213–14.

89. A translation of these two verses will be found in my introduction, p. 13.

90. Ibn Māja, *Sunan*, 2:905 (nos. 2712–14).

passing through Abū Umāma and ʿAmr b. Khārija, respectively; apparently, he preferred the latter version, which he refers to as "*ḥasan ṣaḥīḥ*."[91] Finally, Nasāʾī quotes three different examples of the version with the *isnād* passing through ʿAmr b. Khārija.[92] Thus, by the beginning of the tenth century the report containing the prophetic dictum "no bequest to an heir" was returned to circulation after having initially been rejected by Muslim and Bukhārī. The inclusion of this report in the collections of Ibn Māja, Tirmidhī, and Nasāʾī may be related to the central role that it plays in the theoretical justification advanced by Shāfiʿī for the abrogation of the bequest verses.

To summarize, during the course of the ninth century the legal maxim, "no bequest to an heir," was put in the form of a prophetic dictum. The *isnād* of this report, which was at first incomplete, was gradually improved and eventually won admission to most, if not all, of the classical collections. Even these developments, however, did not eliminate all of the stumbling blocks that lay in the way of those scholars who sought to develop a satisfactory theoretical justification for the abrogation of the bequest verses. This is because the prophetic dictum "no bequest to an heir" was transmitted by at most three Companions and therefore qualified as one of the *āḥād* or isolated reports; such a report yields only probable knowledge and therefore may not be used as an indicator of abrogation, for which purpose only widely circulated (*mutawātir*) reports may be used.[93] This posed yet another problem for the proponents of abrogation and, to see how they attempted to resolve it, we turn now to the final stage in the development of the arguments for and against the abrogation of the bequest verses.

The Classical Doctrine (Tenth to Fifteenth Centuries)

Q. 2:180

Although the classical commentators discuss four different positions regarding the status of Q. 2:180—full abrogation, partial

91. Tirmidhī, *Sunan*, 3:293–94 (nos. 2203–04).

92. Nasāʾī, *Sunan*, 6:207.

93. J. Robson, "*Ḥadīth*," in *EI*², 3:25.

abrogation, specification, and no abrogation—it will be sufficient for our purposes to focus on the first and last of these four positions.

Full Abrogation. The following statement by Zamakhsharī (d. 1144), a typical example of the classical argument for the abrogation of Q. 2:180, reflects the developments that had taken place since the end of the ninth century.

> The bequest for an heir was in the beginning of Islam. Then it was abrogated by the inheritance verse, and by his word, "God gave a share to every person who is entitled to one, so no bequest to an heir," and by the fact that the Community has accepted it [viz., the *ḥadīth*], to the point that it was treated as a widely circulated report, despite its being one of the *āḥād*. This is because they do not accept anything unless it is an established [report] the transmission of which is sound.[94]

In this statement, Zamakhsharī first combines the argument of the seventh- and eighth-century authorities with that of Shāfiʿī and then adds a further twist of his own. The early authorities had routinely referred to the abrogation of Q. 2:180 by the inheritance verses without mentioning the prophetic dictum "no bequest to an heir." Shāfiʿī subsequently invoked the prophetic dictum as an indicator of partial abrogation, taking care not to confuse the indicator with the abrogating verse itself.[95] In Zamakhsharī's statement, the distinction between the indicator and the abrogating verse is blurred and the prophetic dictum appears to be invoked in support of full abrogation of Q. 2:180. Zamakhsharī asserts that Q. 2:180 was abrogated by *both* the Qur'an and the *ḥadīth* and then mentions a third source of abrogation, the consensus of the community. Although the classification of a report as "*mutawātir*" is normally determined by the number of Companions who transmitted it, Zamakhsharī states that in the present instance the general acceptance of an isolated report by the Community had the effect of raising it to the level of *tawātur* (widespread circulation). We thus see how the appeal to consensus was used to overcome successive defects in the *is-*

94. *Kashshāf*, 1:224.

95. The distinction is essential because, according to Shāfiʿī, the *ḥadīth* cannot abrogate the Qur'an. See Khaddūrī, pp. 123–28, 184–85; Shāfiʿī, *Risāla*, pp. 54–58.

nād of the report containing the prophetic dictum "no bequest to an heir." Shāfiʿī invoked the doctrine of consensus in order to offset the fact that the *isnād* of the report known to him was interrupted. This *isnād* was subsequently improved, but the *ḥadīth* never acquired the formal status of *tawātur*. Three hundred years after Shāfiʿī, Zamakhsharī invoked the doctrine of consensus in order to overcome this defect. Thus, the ultimate justification for the abrogation of Q. 2:180 rests upon the consensus of Muslim scholars, which, in view of the prophetic dictum, "My community will never agree on an error," is probably the best possible justification.

Although the argument that the general acceptance of the report by the Community raises it to the level of widespread circulation is repeated by a number of later commentators, one notices a tendency to downplay the significance of the formal status of the report. Bayḍāwī, for example, in his treatment of Q. 2:180, makes a statement very similar to that of Zamakhsharī, except that he does not mention that the report is one of the *āḥād*: "This ruling occurred at the beginning of Islam. Then it was abrogated by the inheritance verse and the prophetic dictum, 'God gave a share to every person who is entitled to one, so no bequest to an heir.'"[96] Nasafī (d. 1310), who also favored abrogation of Q. 2:180, appears to have been sufficiently uncomfortable with the prophetic dictum not to mention it when discussing the abrogation of that verse.[97]

The argument for full abrogation nevertheless emerged as the majority position. Nīsābūrī (d. 1328/9) and Ibn Kathīr (d. 1372) explicitly state that "the majority of the commentators and respected legists" held for full abrogation of Q. 2:180.[98] Similarly, Ibn Juzayy (d. 1340), after stating the cases for and against abrogation, indicates that "the former is the more widespread opinion."[99]

Against Abrogation. The emergence of full abrogation as the majority position did not prevent a small number of commentators from either pointing out the shortcomings of this position or

96. *Anwār al-tanzīl,* 1:100–101.

97. *Tafsīr,* 1:88.

98. Nīsābūrī, *Gharā'ib,* 2:95; Ibn Kathīr, 1:211.

99. Ibn Juzayy, *Tashīl,* 1:125.

articulating an alternative to it. One of the earliest and perhaps the outstanding representative of this group was Abū Muslim al-Iṣfahānī (d. 1066), a Muʿtazilī grammarian and author of a twenty-volume commentary on the Qur'an.[100] Abū Muslim's position on Q. 2:180, as preserved by Fakhr al-Dīn al-Rāzī, appears to have been as follows:

> 1. This verse [Q. 2:180] does not contradict the inheritance verses. Its meaning is, "Prescribed for you is that which God commanded, namely, the award of inheritance to parents and relatives as mentioned in the verse 'God commands you concerning your children.'" Or, [it means], "It is prescribed for the person approaching death to bequeath to parents and relatives the full amount commanded by God for them and not to decrease their shares."
>
> 2. The establishment of inheritance for relatives is not inconsistent with the establishment of a bequest. [Inheritance] is a gift from God while a bequest is a gift from the person approaching death. Therefore, an heir may receive both a bequest and an inheritance, by virtue of the two verses.
>
> 3. Even if we were of the opinion that [the two verses were] contradictory, it would be possible to construe the inheritance verse as specifying [Q. 2:180]. This is because [Q. 2:180] makes a bequest to relatives obligatory. Then, the inheritance verse excludes the inheriting relative [from entitlement to a bequest], leaving the noninheriting relative within [the scope of] this verse. The reason for this is that some parents inherit, while others, on account of a difference of religion, slavery, or homicide, [which are all barriers to inheritance], do not inherit. . . . [Similarly,] any relative who qualifies as an heir is not entitled to a bequest, while those who do not qualify as an heir are entitled to a bequest, because of the tie of blood.[101]

In this statement, Abū Muslim develops three different ways of conceptualizing the relationship between Q. 2:180 and the inheritance verses. First, he argues that there is no need to view Q. 2:180 and the inheritance verses as being mutually exclusive. Rather, the inheritance verses can be seen as establishing, not compulsory rules that take effect in all circumstances, but

100. Abū Muslim Muḥammad b. ʿAlī b. Muḥammad b. al-Ḥusayn b. Mihrayazd (Mahrabzud) al-Naḥwī al-Muʿallim al-Iṣbahānī al-Adīb. See Muḥammad b. ʿAlī al-Dāwūdī, *Ṭabaqāt al-mufassirīn*, 2:211 (no. 543); Suyūṭī, *Bughyat al-wuʿāt fī ṭabaqāt al-lughawiyyīn wa'l-nuḥāt*, 1:188 (no. 313); Ṣafadī, *al-Wāfī bi'l-wafayāt*, 4:130 (no. 1639); Dhahabī, *Mīzān*, 3:655 (no. 7973); Jomier, *Le Commentaire Coranique du Manâr*, pp. 194–95.

101. Rāzī, *al-Tafsīr al-Kabīr*, 5:67.

guidelines for *testate* succession. The inheritance verses may be understood as specifying the ideal, or perhaps the minimum, size of the bequest that had been prescribed, if only in general terms, in Q. 2:180. Viewed in this manner, both Q. 2:180 and the inheritance verses regulate testate succession. Alternatively, it is possible to view Q. 2:180 and the inheritance verses as being mutually compatible. Bequests and inheritance are two different types of gift, the former emanating from man, the latter from God, and there is no reason why an heir should not receive both. Finally, Abū Muslim states that even if one were to admit, for the sake of argument, that Q. 2:180 and the inheritance verses were mutually exclusive, this contradiction can be resolved by applying the concept of specification. According to all three of these alternatives, there is no need to abrogate Q. 2:180!

A century and a half later, Rāzī himself came out against the abrogation of Q. 2:180. Rāzī opens his discussion of the verse by referring to the dispute over its status and he then indicates that there are three objections that can be made to the arguments offered by the proponents of abrogation. Of these, we are concerned here only with the first objection, in which Rāzī examines each of the indicators adduced by the proponents of abrogation and demonstrates that they are all invalid:

> 1. That it became abrogated by the fact that God gave to the heirs, to every person who is entitled, his share and no more. This is improbable (*baʿīd*), because the obligation [to award] a certain amount by means of a bequest is not rendered forbidden by the amount [awarded] to those who were added to the heirs (*ahl al-mīrāth*). This necessitates, at the most, specification, not abrogation. Someone may object, "There is no escape from the fact that [Q. 2:180] is abrogated with regard to those who are survived only by parents, because [in that case] the parents inherit all of the property, so that nothing remains to bequeath." This, however, constitutes specification, not abrogation.
>
> 2. That it became abrogated by virtue of his word, "no bequest to an heir." This would be more likely (*aqrab*), except for the difficulty with it, namely, that it is an isolated report, and it is not permitted to abrogate the Qur'an with [such a report]. Someone may object to this point by arguing that, despite its being isolated, this report was willingly accepted by the *imāms*, so that it was attached to the widespread reports. One should respond to this [as follows]: "Is it asserted that the *imāms* accepted it on the basis of probable knowledge (*ẓann*) or apodictic knowledge (*qaṭʿ*)?" The first point is conceded (*muslam*), except that this constitutes a

consensus among them, despite its being an isolated report, and abrogation of the Qur'an by [consensus] is not permitted. The second point is forbidden because, had they declared apodictically that it is sound, when it is one of the isolated reports, then they would have agreed upon an error, which is not permitted.

3. That it became abrogated by means of consensus. It is not permitted to invoke the doctrine of consensus to abrogate the Qur'an, because the doctrine of consensus indicates that the abrogating indicator is present. But in invoking consensus, they fail to mention the indicator. [Furthermore], one may object: "Since it is established that there exists within the Islamic Community those who deny the validity of this [instance of] abrogation, how can it be maintained that a general consensus has been established regarding abrogation?"

4. That it was abrogated by means of an analogical indication, i.e., that we say, "Had this bequest been obligatory, then in the absence of a bequest it follows by necessity that the entitlement of those relatives continues, by analogy to debts which are not covered by a bequest [yet must still be paid]." However, in the absence of a bequest to those relatives, they do not have a claim to anything, because of the indicator of His Word in the inheritance verses "after any bequest he bequeaths or debt." The plain meaning of the verse requires that, if there is no debt or bequest, then all of the property is distributed among the heirs [rather than to the relatives mentioned in Q. 2:180]. Furthermore, one may object that the abrogation of the Qur'an by means of an analogy is not permitted. God knows best![102]

Rāzī demonstrates that none of the four "sources" invoked by the proponents of abrogation—Qur'an, *ḥadīth*, *ijmāʿ*, and *qiyās*—constitutes an acceptable indicator of abrogation. As for Q. 4:11–12, there is no reason why an heir should not receive both a bequest and a share of the estate and, furthermore, the shares mentioned in the inheritance verses can be seen as merely specifying, rather than abrogating, Q. 2:180. The prophetic dictum, "no bequest to an heir," is disqualified because it occurs in an isolated report, which cannot serve as an indicator of abrogation. Furthermore, those *imāms* who claim that the general acceptance of this report raises it to the level of widespread circulation have either relied upon probable knowledge or agreed upon an error! The doctrine of consensus may not, in the absence of a valid Qur'anic or prophetic indicator, be relied upon as an indicator of abrogation. It is not clear, moreover, that any such consen-

102. Ibid., 5:68.

sus exists with regard to the abrogation of Q. 2:180, inasmuch as a number of scholars are known to have held against abrogation! Finally, analogy, like consensus, cannot by itself serve as an indicator of abrogation and, furthermore, the analogy cited by the proponents of abrogation is a weak one. In this manner, Rāzī demonstrates that there is absolutely no basis for the contention that Q. 2:180 was abrogated.

Abū Muslim and Rāzī were ultimately unsuccessful in their attempt to discredit the majority position, incurring the derision of some of their colleagues in the process.[103] Still, the intellectual rigor of their arguments seems to have troubled many of the proponents of abrogation. For example, after stating the majority position, Zamakhsharī quotes the arguments of Abū Muslim without, however, indicating their source.[104] Bayḍāwī, too, after stating the majority position, adds what appear to be his personal reservations on the matter:

> This is an open question (*wa-fīhi naẓarun*) because the inheritance verse does not contradict [Q. 2:180]; indeed, it confirms it because it indicates the absolute precedence of a bequest. [Furthermore], the *ḥadīth* ["no bequest to an heir"] is one of the isolated reports and its acceptance by the community does not raise it to the level of widespread circulation. It is possible that this [objection] is avoided by the person who explains the bequest as that which God commanded, namely the award of shares of the estate to parents and relatives in His Word, "God commands you," or as the person anticipating death bequeathing them the full amount awarded by God.[105]

Q. 2:240

We arrive, finally, at the classical doctrine regarding the status of Q. 2:240. It will be remembered that of all the early authorities who discussed the status of this verse, only Mujāhid held against abrogation. The proponents of abrogation contended that Q. 2: 240 contains two separate legal provisions, each of which was subsequently abrogated by a different Qur'anic verse: the one-

103. Ibn Kathīr (1:211) expresses surprise at Rāzī's support for this position ("*Wa'l-ʿajab min* Abī ʿAbd Allāh al-Rāzī").

104. *Kashshāf*, 1:224.

105. *Anwār*, 1:101 (ll. 1–4).

year "waiting period" was reduced to four months and ten nights by Q. 2:234, and the testator's obligation to make provisions for his wife's maintenance was abrogated by Q. 4:12, which awards a fractional share of the estate to the widow. During the classical period, as previously, there are only two positions regarding the status of Q. 2:240—for and against abrogation.

For Abrogation. Although the general framework of the classical doctrine is identical to that of previous stages, there are one or two differences that seem to reflect an increase in the sophistication of legal doctrine. First, there is general agreement among both the proponents and opponents of abrogation that there are one or more words missing from the opening line of Q. 2:240 (*wa'lladhīna yutawaffawna minkum wa-yadharūna azwājan waṣiyyatan li-azwājihim*). The omission is held to have occurred between the words *azwājan* and *waṣiyyatan*, and the various emendations proposed appear to be determined by doctrinal considerations. The proponents of abrogation, who prefer to see the bequest as an obligation imposed by God and later removed by Him, emend the verse as follows: [*li-yūṣū*] *waṣiyyatan li-azwājihim*, or [*kataba allāhu ʿalayhim*] *waṣiyyatan*, i.e., "[Let them leave] a bequest for their wives" or "[God obligated them to leave] a bequest for their wives."[106] The opponents of abrogation, who prefer to see the making of a bequest as a nonobligatory option available to the testator, propose a different emendation which will be dealt with below.

The second difference between the early and classical doctrine is an increased sensitivity to the arrangement of the abrogating and abrogated verses. The specialists in abrogation maintain that in any given pair of abrogated and abrogating verses, the former must precede the latter, not only in order of revelation (*nuzūl*) but also in order of recitation (*tilāwa*).[107] For example, the verse enjoining a bequest for parents was not only revealed prior to the verse awarding parents a fractional share of the estate, but is also recited before that verse; the abrogated verse, Q. 2:180, precedes

106. Ṭabarī, *Jāmiʿ*, 2:578–79; Zamakhsharī, 1:289; Bayḍāwī, 1:125–26. These emendations (*taqdīrāt*) are cited by the commentators for purposes of explanation only, and should not be confused with variant readings (*qirā'āt*) cited by specialists in Qur'an-recitation. See also Ibn Khālawayh, *Mukhtaṣar*, p. 15; idem, *Ḥujja*, p. 74.

107. Ibn Salāmah, p. 26.

the abrogating verse, Q. 4:11. Now, the authorities who hold for abrogation of Q. 2:240 routinely assert that the widow's obligation to wait in her deceased husband's house for one year was reduced to four months and ten nights by Q. 2:234; this, however, contradicts the rule, inasmuch as Q. 2:234 is recited before Q. 2:240. This discrepancy did not escape the attention of the classical commentators, most of whom attempt to explain it away. Zamakhsharī, for example, maintains that the recitation of Q. 2:234 prior to that of Q. 2:240 should not be taken as indicating that the former verse was revealed prior to the latter, and he provides an example of another exception to the rule.[108] Bayḍāwī makes the same claim as Zamakhsharī, and Nasafī and Jalālān also refer to the issue.[109] The exception to the rule admitted in this case may be taken as support for our contention that the doctrine of abrogation was applied to Q. 2:240 *after* the death of Muhammad and in all likelihood after the establishment of a standard version of the Qur'an. It will be remembered in this connection that in an anecdote set during the caliphate of ʿUthmān, Ibn al-Zubayr asked the caliph why he included Q. 2:240 in the Qur'an when the verse was known to have been abrogated.

The classical doctrine is otherwise identical to that of the seventh- and eighth-century authorities. Zamakhsharī, for example, discusses the abrogation of Q. 2:240 in the following terms: "This [Q. 2:240] was at the beginning of Islam. Then the waiting period was abrogated by His Word, 'four months and ten [nights],' and maintenance was abrogated by inheritance, which is one-fourth and one-eighth."[110] Qurṭubī summarizes the case for abrogation as follows:

> The widow used to sit in the house of the deceased for one year, and she would be maintained out of his wealth, as long as she did not leave the dwelling; however, if she left, then the heirs are not held responsible for cutting off her maintenance. Then, the one year [waiting period] was abrogated by "four months and ten [nights]" and maintenance was abrogated by "one-fourth and one-eighth" in *Sūrat al-Nisāʾ*. This opinion was held by Ibn ʿAbbās, Ḍaḥḥāk, Ibn Zayd, and Rabīʿ.[111]

108. *Kashshāf*, 1:289.
109. Bayḍāwī, *Anwār*, 1:126; Nasafī, *Tafsīr*, 1:117; Maḥallī, *Tafsīr*, 1:44.
110. *Kashshāf*, 1:289.
111. Qurṭubī, *Jāmiʿ*, 3:226.

Statements similar to these are found in the other classical commentaries.[112]

The argument for the abrogation of Q. 2:240 had emerged as the majority position by the tenth century. After documenting the arguments for and against abrogation, Ṭabarī indicates that the former is the correct opinion (*awlā bi'l-ṣawāb*).[113] Nīsābūrī remarks that "most of the commentators" hold for abrogation, and Ibn Kathīr states that "the majority" hold this position.[114] The ultimate success of this position may explain why, beginning in the eleventh century, many of the commentators do not even refer to the existence of an alternative position.[115]

The classical doctrine on the status of Q. 2:240 differs from the classical position on Q. 2:180 in one important respect: whereas most of the commentators mention the prophetic dictum, "no bequest to an heir," in their discussions of Q. 2:180, any reference to this dictum is conspicuously absent from their treatment of Q. 2:240. This is curious, inasmuch as this dictum was invoked by Shāfiʿī in connection with the abrogation of *both* of the bequest verses. Of the classical commentators who hold for the abrogation of Q. 2:240, only Nīsābūrī mentions the dictum, without, however, referring to its status as an isolated report.[116] The general silence of the commentators may be taken as a measure of their discomfort with the dictum; they apparently preferred silence to the task of having to account for the abrogation of a Qur'anic verse by an isolated report. Thus, for the classical commentators, the husband's obligation to leave a bequest for his wife was abrogated solely by Q. 4:12; neither *ḥadīth* nor *ijmāʿ* is mentioned as an indicator of abrogation.

Against Abrogation. Abū Muslim al-Iṣfahānī attempted to challenge the majority position on the status of Q. 2:240, arguing that the verse was not abrogated but effective (*muḥkama*). He

112. Ṭabarī, *Jāmiʿ*, 2:582 (ll. 11–16); Bayḍāwī, 1:126; Nasafī, 1:117; Nīsābūrī, *Gharā'ib*, 2:300; Ibn Juzayy, 1:153; Ibn Kathīr, 1:296–97; Maḥallī, *Tafsīr*, 44.

113. Ṭabarī, *Jāmiʿ*, 2:582 (l. 11).

114. Nīsābūrī, *Gharā'ib*, 2:300; Ibn Kathīr, 1:296.

115. Zamakhsharī, 1:289; Bayḍāwī, 1:125–26; Nasafī, 1:117; Ibn Juzayy, 1:153; Maḥallī, *Tafsīr*, 1:44.

116. Nīsābūrī, *Gharā'ib*, 2:300.

suggested that in order to be properly understood, Q. 2:240 must be seen against the background of the social situation in pre-Islamic Arabia. Prior to Islam, a widow was *obligated* to remain in her deceased husband's dwelling for one year. Islam not only reduced the waiting period to four months and ten nights (Q. 2:234), but also offered the widow who had observed the waiting period the *choice* of either remaining in that dwelling for the remainder of the year, or leaving. Her entitlement to maintenance continued so long as she chose to remain. Thus, Abū Muslim viewed the bequest mentioned in Q. 2:240, not as an obligation imposed by God, but as an option available to the prospective testator; Q. 2:240 defines the rights of widows whose husbands had availed themselves of this option. This interpretation is reflected in Abū Muslim's emendation of the aforementioned gap in the opening line of the verse: [*wa-qad waṣṣaw*] *waṣiyyatan li-azwājihim*, i.e., "[having bequeathed] a bequest to their wives."[117] Abū Muslim glosses Q. 2:240 in the following manner:

> If one of you dies and leaves a wife, having [previously] left a bequest for his wife of one year's maintenance and lodging, then, if they leave prior to that and go against the [provisions of] the husband's bequest, after having observed the time period established by God [i.e., four months and ten nights], "there is no sin (*ḥaraj*) with respect to anything reasonable that they do with themselves," i.e., a valid marriage, because their remaining [in his dwelling] in accordance with the bequest is not binding.[118]

Thus, the "four months and ten [nights]" mentioned in Q. 2:234 refer to an obligatory waiting period, whereas the "one year" mentioned in Q. 2:240 refers to the widow's right to be maintained out of her husband's estate for up to a year, if she agrees to remain in his dwelling and not to remarry. The two time periods are connected with quite different issues and it is only the blurring of the above-mentioned distinction that necessitates the abrogation of Q. 2:240.[119]

Rāzī developed this challenge to the majority position even further. After providing a full and objective account of the argu-

117. Rāzī, 6:169.

118. Ibid., 6:169–70.

119. That the two verses, Q. 2:234 and 2:240, deal with an entirely different subject was noted by Burton (*Collection*, p. 61).

ments adduced by the proponents of abrogation, which he acknowledges as the majority position, Rāzī cites the arguments of Mujāhid and Abū Muslim al-Iṣfahānī.[120] He then gives three reasons why he himself prefers the unsuccessful minority position:

> (1) Abrogation is a contradiction of the "source" (*aṣl*). Therefore, nonabrogation is required to the extent possible.
>
> (2) The abrogating verse [should] be revealed after the abrogated one. If it was revealed subsequently, then it is preferable that it should also be read subsequently, because this arrangement is better. As for the abrogating verse being read before the abrogated one, even if this were permissible in general, still, it is considered to be a poor arrangement, and the Word of God must be free from such defects to the extent possible. Since this verse [Q. 2:240] is recited after that one [Q. 2:234] it is preferable that it not be considered to have been abrogated by it.
>
> (3) It is established in the science of jurisprudence (*uṣūl al-fiqh*) that when one is confronted with abrogation and specification, specification is preferred. In the present case, if we specify these two verses by two situations, in conformity with the opinion of Mujāhid, then abrogation is eliminated. Therefore, adoption of Mujāhid's position is preferable to adhering to abrogation without a clear indicator (*dalīl*). The same is true with regard to the opinion of Abū Muslim, because you [i.e., the proponents of abrogation] say, "The emendation (*taqdīr*) of the verse is, 'a bequest to their wives [is incumbent upon them],' or '[Let them bequeath] a bequest,'" so that you attribute this ordinance (*ḥukm*) to God. [But] Abū Muslim says, "The emendation of the verse is, 'And those of you who die [leaving] a bequest for their wives,' or '[having bequeathed] a bequest to their wives,'" so that he attributes these words to the husband. If we must [postulate] an ellipsis (*iḍmār*), then your suggestion is inferior to his, because your suggestion necessitates bringing abrogation close to the verse. Therefore, every sound mind will testify that Abū Muslim's emendation is better than yours and that there is no indicator of abrogation in this case, not to mention the poor arrangement that is implicit in the argument for abrogation, from which the Word of God must be kept free. This is clear speech.[121]

Rāzī's contention that Q. 2:240 was not abrogated by Q. 4:12 and Q. 2:234 is based upon three considerations. First, the doctrine of abrogation is to be avoided whenever possible. Secondly, the order in which the two verses are recited suggests that Q. 2:240 did not abrogate Q. 2:234. Finally, the policy of avoiding

120. Rāzī, 6:169.
121. Ibid., 6:170.

abrogation suggests that the arguments of Mujāhid and Abū Muslim, which require specification, are *ipso facto* superior to those of the proponents of abrogation. Thus, as was the case with Q. 2:180, Rāzī demonstrates that there are no acceptable grounds upon which to base an argument for the abrogation of Q. 2:240.

Summary and Conclusions

There exists a substantial body of evidence suggesting that the bequest verses remained in force until at least 632 and perhaps for ten or twenty years thereafter. Both the Qur'an and the *ḥadīth* place considerable emphasis upon testamentary dispositions and neither source contains an explicit reference to the abrogation of the bequest verses. The repeated occurrence in Q. 4: 11–12 of the phrase, "after any bequest he bequeaths," casts doubt upon the contention that the inheritance verses abrogated the bequest verses. Similarly, the prophetic dictum, "no bequest to an heir," even if it were authentic, does not explicitly refer to the abrogation of the bequest verses. Finally, there is the fact that the sources portray Muhammad as attempting, albeit unsuccessfully, to dictate a last will and testament shortly before he died, and that Ṭalḥa b. Muṣarrif perceived a discrepancy between Muhammad's failure to leave a will and the various Qur'anic and prophetic decrees on that subject.

Conversely, there is evidence pointing to the possibility that the doctrine of abrogation was not applied to the bequest verses for at least a quarter of a century after Muhammad's death. Explicit references to the abrogation of the bequest verses, which only begin to be made after 656, are attributed, not to Muhammad, but to Companions, Followers, and Successors. The alleged exchange between Ibn al-Zubayr and the Caliph ʿUthmān on the subject of Q. 2:240 suggests that the inclusion of abrogated verses in the standard text of the Qur'an, a phenomenon that would subsequently be rationalized by the concept of *naskh al-ḥukm dūna al-tilāwa,* was initially cause for surprise, and it supports the assumption that Q. 2:240 was not abrogated until the authorized version of the Qur'an had been established. This assumption is corroborated by the order in which Q. 2:234 and Q. 2:240 are recited; the exception to the rule that the abrogating verse must be recited after the verse it abrogates is difficult to explain if abrogation had actually occurred during the period of revelation.

The three components of the classical justification for the abrogation of the bequest verses—Qur'an, *ḥadīth*, and *ijmāᶜ*—are the product of an historical process that unfolded over the course of many centuries. The seventh- and eighth-century authorities routinely assert that the bequest verses were abrogated by the inheritance verses, without referring to either the prophetic dictum, "no bequest to an heir," or to consensus. The legal maxim, "a bequest to an heir is not permitted," began to circulate in the eighth century in connection with the debate over the status of the bequest verses, but was only put in the form of a prophetic dictum during the first quarter of the ninth century. The dictum provided Shāfiᶜī with the authoritative indicator needed to account for the abrogation of the bequest verses; indeed, without it, it is doubtful whether the case for abrogation would have prevailed. Shāfiᶜī compensated for a defect in the *isnād* by appealing to the consensus of the scholars. Although the defect was soon corrected, the report was rejected by both Muslim and Bukhārī, probably as a result of doubts regarding the trustworthiness of several transmitters in the *isnād*s. The report eventually found its way into the collections compiled by Ibn Māja, Tirmidhī, Abū Dā'ūd, and others, but still only qualified as an isolated report which, according to Islamic legal theory, does not possess the force to serve as an indicator of abrogation. This secondary defect was overcome by again appealing to the doctrine of consensus which, it is argued, had the effect of raising the report to the level of widespread transmission. The peculiar history of this report may explain why the classical commentators, after citing the prophetic dictum in their discussion of Q. 2:180, curiously omit any reference to it in their treatment of Q. 2:240.

Numerous Muslim scholars have challenged the alleged abrogation of the bequest verses. Opposition to the abrogation of Q. 2:180 is attributed to eighth-century authorities such as al-Ḥasan al-Baṣrī, Ṭā'ūs, ᶜAlā' b. Zayd, Muslim b. Yasār, and Ḍaḥḥāk, and opposition to the abrogation of Q. 2:240 is attributed to Mujāhid. Among the classical commentators, Abū Muslim al-Iṣfahānī and Fakhr al-Dīn al-Rāzī stand out among the opponents of abrogation. Rāzī argued (convincingly, to my mind) that all of the indicators adduced by the proponents of abrogation are unacceptable; the force of his argument seems to have caused at least some of the ostensible proponents of abrogation to reconsider the validity of their position. Although the argument for abrogation came to be recognized as the majority position, individual scholars have continued to challenge this conclusion, the most recent example being the Egyptian reformer Muhammad Abduh.[122] Clearly there was no unanimity on this issue.

Orthodoxy, by definition, imposes limits upon belief and thought, and Islamic orthodoxy is no exception. The fractional shares mentioned in the inheritance verses came to be seen as compulsory rules to be applied in all circumstances; these shares are literally the "limits of God" which must be strictly obeyed; to ignore or disregard them is to disobey the divine command and to invite divine retribution in the Hereafter; the rules established in the inheritance verses are a reflection of God's infallible wisdom and were revealed in order to compensate for man's inevitable ignorance. This conception of the inheritance verses as compulsory rules reflecting the divine will may explain why so few Muslim scholars have ever attempted to suggest an alternative explanation of the relationship between the bequest and inheritance verses; even the opponents of abrogation are, for the most part, working within this same conceptual framework. In view of this tendency, the following statement by Qurṭubī, made with reference to the prophetic dictum, "no bequest to an heir," is especially noteworthy:

> If it had not been for that *ḥadīth*, then it would have been possible to have both of these verses [Q. 2:180 and 4:11], so that [the heirs] would take property from the testator either in accordance with a last will and testament, or by inheritance if he did not leave a will or if something remained after the will. However, this possibility is prevented by the *ḥadīth* and *ijmāᶜ*.[123]

Qurṭubī momentarily entertains the possibility that the bequest verses and inheritance verses complement one another, the former dealing with testate succession, the latter with cases of intestacy. To the best of my knowledge, no other Muslim scholar has ever made this distinction. Even Qurṭubī, however, is

122. Jomier, *Manâr*, p. 198; Rashīd Riḍā, *al-Manâr*, 2:135–36.

123. Qurṭubī, 2:263: *Wa-lawlā hādhā al-ḥadīth la-amkana al-jamᶜu bayna al-āyatayni bi-an ya'khudhū al-māl ᶜan al-muwarrith bi'l-waṣiyya wa bi'l-mīrāth in lam yūṣi aw mā baqiya baᶜda al-waṣiyya.*

compelled to dismiss his hypothesis immediately, for there is no way for him to dispose of either the prophetic dictum or the doctrine of consensus.

The historian, and especially the non-Muslim historian, is not bound by the same constraints as was Qurṭubī. On the preceding pages, I have attempted to demonstrate that both of the obstacles confronted by Qurṭubī are the product of historical processes: the legal maxim, "no bequest to an heir," was put in the form of a prophetic dictum at the beginning of the ninth century in order to provide an authoritative indicator of abrogation; the doctrine of consensus was invoked, beginning in the ninth century, first in order to compensate for the fact that the *isnād* of the earliest versions of the *ḥadīth* was interrupted, and subsequently in order to overcome the status of the improved *ḥadīth* as an isolated report. Thus, from the standpoint of the historian, the *ḥadīth* and *ijmāʿ* do not necessarily preclude the possibility alluded to by Qurṭubī.

Indeed, it is conceivable that Qurṭubī's hypothetical distinction between testate and intestate succession has roots in early Islamic history. I maintain that, during the lifetime of Muhammad, the importance of testate succession was much greater than is generally believed. In chapter 1, I argued that Q. 4:12b can be read in such a manner that it explicitly refers to the possibility of designating a testamentary heir, the presence of certain close blood relatives notwithstanding, and further, that the restriction of bequests to one-third of the estate originally functioned as a means to strike a balance between the recipients of bequests, on the one hand, and the testamentary heir on the other. There is therefore reason to believe that the power of testation, which is severely restricted within the framework of what became the Islamic law of inheritance, was virtually unlimited during the lifetime of Muhammad and remained so for at least a short period after his death. This raises the possibility that Qurṭubī's distinction between testate succession and intestacy may reflect the original relationship between the bequest and inheritance verses.

Indeed, within the terms of the proto-Islamic law of inheritance, the intergenerational transmission of property by means of a last will and testament was a normal and accepted procedure. The testator was free to determine whom his heir(s) would be and to specify the property that the heir(s) would inherit; the testator had the power to disinherit close blood relatives, although they might claim a small fractional share of the estate as compensation (Q. 4:12b). The testator might also, in addition to designating an heir, leave bequests for parents, relatives and wives (Q. 2:180 and 2:240); indeed, he was encouraged to do so provided that the bequests did not exceed one-third of the estate's net value. The importance of testate succession during the lifetime of Muhammad is reflected in numerous other Qur'anic verses and prophetic *ḥadīth*. Only in the absence of a will did the fractional shares mentioned in the inheritance verses become operative.

This system was radically transformed in the period immediately following Muhammad's death. First, Q. 4:12b was reinterpreted in such a manner as to obscure the reference to the possibility of designating an heir, the only such reference in the Qur'an. The fractional shares mentioned in the inheritance verses soon came to be treated, not as rules of intestacy, but as compulsory rules to be applied in all cases. These two changes make it appear as if the bequest verses are incompatible with the inheritance verses, and the apparent conflict was resolved, no sooner than the middle of the first/seventh century, by invoking the doctrine of abrogation. Muslim authorities attempted to find an indicator of abrogation in the Qur'an and *ḥadīth*, but without much success, so that justification for the abrogation of the bequest verses came to rest, ultimately, upon the infallible consensus of the Community. The abrogation of these verses, then, was the result, not of any change in the divine will, but of changed perceptions of the meaning of the divine word. The application of the doctrine of abrogation to the bequest verses was, in its time, a dynamic measure intended to bring the law into harmony with contemporary political, social, and theological developments. An understanding of when and why the doctrine was applied to these verses may make it possible to restore to Islamic law a measure of the dynamism that was characteristic of its formative period.

6

The *Asbāb al-Nuzūl* and the Inheritance Verses

The genre of literature known in Arabic as the *asbāb al-nuzūl* (occasions of the revelation) developed in connection with attempts, during the first centuries A.H., to reconstruct the life of the Prophet Muhammad.[1] The *asbāb al-nuzūl*, which consist of reports indicating where, when, and under what circumstances certain Qur'anic verses were revealed, have attracted the attention of western specialists on the Qur'an and Islamic law. Although the former group has adopted a cautious, critical approach to the corpus,[2] the latter tend to treat the *asbāb al-nuzūl* in an uncritical manner, accepting such reports more or less at their face value. This is especially apparent in studies of the Islamic law of inheritance, for much of the evidence upon which the superimposition theory is based is derived from the corpus of *asbāb al-nuzūl*.[3] Coulson, for example, begins his discussion of this theory by quoting a report in which the wife of Saʿd b. al-Rabīʿ appeals to Muhammad on behalf of herself and her daughters, who had been deprived of their inheritance by her late

1. A. T. Welch, "*al-Ḳur'ān*," *EI*², 5:415.

2. See, for example, Richard Bell, *Introduction to the Quran*, p. 100 (the stories are "imagined from the passages themselves"); W. Montgomery Watt, *Bell's Introduction to the Qur'ān*, p. 108; J. Wansbrough, *Quranic Studies*, pp. 178–79 ("the historical value of such material is restricted"); J. Burton, *The Collection of the Qur'ān*, p. 185 ("One must bear in mind the essentially narrative (*haggada*) nature of *tafsīr* and *asbāb al-nuzūl*"); A. T. Welch, "*al-Ḳur'ān*," 5:415 (the stories "probably have some historical validity, but there is often good reason to suspect elaborate embellishment"); and Andrew L. Rippin, "The Quranic *Asbāb al-Nuzūl* Material," p. 3 (the primary function of the *asbāb al-nuzūl* was "to create an edifying narrative in which the interpretation of a given Quranic verse may be embodied").

3. Concerning this theory, see my introduction, pp. 14–17.

husband's paternal cousins; then, we are told, God revealed Q. 4:11–12, which award shares of the estate, *inter alia*, to wives and daughters.[4] Without pausing to assess the reliability of this report, Coulson remarks that "Saʿd's case embodies the essence of the changes introduced under Islam into the customary Arabian law of inheritance."[5]

Such uncritical reliance upon the *asbāb al-nuzūl* is, in my opinion, unfounded and calls into question the validity of the superimposition theory. To demonstrate this, I shall present and analyze the *asbāb al-nuzūl* associated with four Qur'anic inheritance verses (4:8, 4:11–12, and 4:176), paying attention to the date at which these reports were put into circulation, to the exegetical function of details, and to the problem of variants. I maintain that the "occasions of the revelation" were first put into circulation towards the end of the first century A.H. for the purposes of Qur'anic exegesis, i.e., to provide an appropriate narrative background for the revelation of Qur'anic verses, and that they do not preserve authentic historical events. My attitude towards these reports thus does not differ from that of the Qur'an specialists mentioned above. But my purpose here is to bring this conclusion to the attention of legal historians and to argue that the *asbāb al-nuzūl* do not constitute a reliable source for reconstructing the formation of Islamic law.

Q. 4:8

Umm Kuḥḥa: The Wife of Thaʿlaba

The *ḥadīth* collections, to the best of my knowledge, do not contain any *asbāb al-nuzūl* relating to Q. 4:8. Ṭabarī (d. 923) preserves three *sabab* (sing. of *asbāb*) reports: Qatāda (d. 735) is reputed to have said, "It was their custom not to award the inheritance to females. Then 'To women a share of what parents and kindred leave' was revealed."[6] A similar statement is attributed

4. I shall discuss this report at greater length below.

5. Coulson, *Succession in the Muslim Family*, pp. 29–30; see also idem, *Conflicts and Tensions in Islamic Jurisprudence*, pp. 10–12, and Bousquet and Peltier, *Les successions agnatiques mitigées*, pp. 86, 116.

6. Ṭabarī, *Jāmiʿ*, 4:262, ll. 12–13 (*isnād*: al-Ḥasan b. Yaḥyā—ʿAbd al-Razzāq—Maʿmar—Qatāda). For details on Qatāda, an early Qur'an commentator, see Fuat Sezgin, *GAS*, 1:31–32.

to Ibn Zayd (d. 798): "During the *jāhiliyya*, women did not inherit from their fathers; an adult male would inherit, but a minor, even if a male, would not. So God, may He be exalted, said [Q. 4:8]."[7] In a third, longer report, ʿIkrima (d. 723) mentions the exact occasion on which Q. 4:8 was revealed:

> Al-Qāsim—al-Ḥusayn—Ḥajjāj—Ibn Jurayj—ʿIkrima. He said: "[Q. 4:8] was revealed regarding Umm Kuḥḥa, Bint Kuḥḥa, Thaʿlaba, and Aws b. Suwayd, who are Helpers. One of them [viz., Thaʿlaba] was her husband and the other was the paternal uncle of her child. She said, 'O Messenger of God, my husband died, leaving me and his daughter, but we have not been given any part of the inheritance (*fa-lam nuwarrath*).' Her child's paternal uncle said, 'O Messenger of God, she does not ride a horse, manage a family, or wound an enemy. She is acquired but does not acquire.' Then [Q. 4:8] was revealed."[8]

It is unlikely that Q. 4:8 was revealed for the reasons suggested by Qatāda and Ibn Zayd, or that the encounter between Umm Kuḥḥa and Muhammad ever took place. The *isnād*s of these reports take us back only to the beginning of the second/eighth century, the generation of the Successors and, further, their contents reflect the type of exegetical concerns that would have been characteristic of the late first-century commentators. For example, the customs of the pre-Islamic Arabs, as presented by Qatāda, Ibn Zayd, and ʿIkrima, evidence the *jāhilī* background against which the commentators sought to juxtapose the Qur'anic legislation.[9] The Qur'an, by extending the right to inherit to the weaker members of society, such as females and minor males, repudiated the tribal ethos of the *jāhiliyya*, which supposedly limited the right to inherit to the active, male members of the tribe. These reports thus provide a religio-ethical explanation for the Qur'anic inheritance legislation. Also, the report attributed to ʿIkrima serves a further exegetical interest by exemplifying the manner in which justice was dispensed by the Prophet, who is shown settling a dispute by consulting with the Divinity. The relatively late date at which these reports were first put into circulation, combined with the

7. Ṭabarī, *Jāmiʿ*, 4:262, ll. 20–23 (*isnād*: Yūnis—Ibn Wahb—Ibn Zayd).

8. Ibid., 4:262 (ll. 14–19).

9. For further details on this function of the *asbāb al-nuzūl*, see Rippin, "The Exegetical Function of the *Asbāb al-Nuzūl*," p. 441.

exegetical concerns reflected in them, suggests that they do not preserve actual historical events.

A further argument against the historicity of the report attributed to ʿIkrima has to do with the way in which the details of this report change from one version to the next. Its basic outline or narrative structure ("NS," for short) may be summarized as follows: A man dies, leaving a wife and daughter; his paternal cousin seizes his estate and refusés to share it with the women; the widow complains to the Prophet; and God reveals a verse of the Qur'an which serves as the basis for settling the dispute. While this narrative structure (hereafter "NS1") remains remarkably stable in variant versions of the report, the details of the narrative change with dizzying rapidity, as will immediately become apparent.

Umm Kujja: The Wife of Aws b. Thābit

Wāḥidī (d. 1075 or 6) cites the following report in which the revelation of Q. 4:8 is linked to the wife of Aws b. Thābit al-Anṣārī:[10]

> The commentators said, "Aws b. Thābit al-Anṣārī died leaving a wife named Umm Kujja, and three daughters. Two men, the paternal cousins of the deceased and executors [of his estate], Suwayd and ʿArfaja, arose, seized his property, and did not give anything to his wife or daughters. It was their custom, during the *jāhiliyya*, not to award the inheritance to females, or to minors—even if they were males; only adult males were given the inheritance. They used to say, 'Only those who fight on horseback and seize booty are given [the inheritance].' So Umm Kujja came to the Messenger of God and said, 'O Messenger of God, Aws b. Thābit died leaving me—his wife—with his three daughters. But I have nothing to spend on them, even though their father left property, which is in the possession of Suwayd and ʿArfaja, who will not give me or his daughters anything. [The daughters] are under my authority, but [the two uncles] do not give me anything to eat or drink, and do not pay any attention to [the daughters].'
>
> The Messenger of God called the two [men], and they said, 'O

10. Aws b. Thābit b. al-Mundhir b. Ḥaram b. ʿAmr b. Zayd Manāt b. ʿAdī b. ʿAmr b. Mālik b. al-Najjār al-Anṣārī. The biographers differ over the date on which Aws died, some putting it in 625, others during the caliphate of ʿUthmān (r. 644–56). For further information, see Ibn ʿAbd al-Barr, *Istīʿāb*, 1:117 (no. 103); Ibn Ḥajar, *ʿIṣāba*, 1:144–45 (no. 318); Bukhārī, *Ta'rīkh*, vol. 1, pt. ii, p. 19 (no. 1550).

> Messenger of God, her children do not ride a horse, manage a family, or wound an enemy.' The Messenger of God said, 'Go away so that I might see what God will introduce.' They left, and then God, may He be exalted, revealed this verse [Q. 4:8]."[11]

Wāḥidī, who generally insists that reports about occasions of revelation must be based upon eyewitness accounts,[12] prefaces this particular report with the uncharacteristically vague statement, "The commentators said." Wāḥidī is probably referring to Qatāda, Ibn Zayd, and ʿIkrima, for he seems to have taken the three independent reports cited above and woven them into a single narrative. But his failure to identify the transmitters may well result from his sensitivity to the relatively late date at which those reports were put into circulation.[13]

The narrative structure of the present report is identical to that of the preceding one (when a man dies leaving a wife and daughters, his relatives seize his estate and refuse to share it with the women; the widow complains to the Prophet, and God reveals a verse of the Qur'an). Several internal details, however, have been changed: the name of the deceased (Thaʿlaba becomes Aws b. Thābit), the name of his wife (Umm Kuḥḥa becomes Umm Kujja), the number of daughters (one, named, becomes three, unnamed), and the number of paternal cousins (one becomes two).

The text of this particular report became the classical *sabab al-nuzūl* for Q. 4:8, finding its way—without a proper *isnād* —into numerous later commentaries.[14] The narrative structure

11. Wāḥidī, *Asbāb*, pp. 137–38.

12. E.g., *Asbāb*, p. 5: "*lā yaḥillu 'l-qawl fī asbāb nuzūl al-kitāb illā bi'l-riwāya wa'l-samāʿ mimman shāhadū al-tanzīl.*" See also Suyūṭī, *Lubāb al-nuqūl fī asbāb al-nuzūl*, p. 6 (margin); Wansbrough, *Quranic Studies*, pp. 178–79.

13. The demands of legal theory resulted, ultimately, in the creation of a proper chain of authorities for this report. In *Lubāb*, p. 82 (margin), Suyūṭī cites a variant of the Aws report with the following *isnād*: Abū al-Shaykh and Ibn Ḥibbān—al-Kalbī—Abū al-Ṣāliḥ—Ibn ʿAbbās. Ibn Kathīr (*Tafsīr*, 1:454–55) cites a short variant with the *isnād*: Ibn Mardawayhi—Ibn Harāsh—Sufyān al-Thawrī—ʿAbd Allāh b. Muhammad b. ʿAqīl—Jābir. Most of the commentators, however, cite the report without mentioning an *isnād*. See the following note for references.

14. Zamakhsharī, *Kashshāf*, 1:476 (no *isnād*); Rāzī, *al-Tafsīr al-kabīr*, 9:194 (on the authority of Ibn ʿAbbās, without an *isnād*); Qurṭubī, *Jāmiʿ*, 5:46 (no *isnād*); Bayḍāwī, *Anwār al-tanzīl*, 1:196 (no *isnād*); Nasafī, *Tafsīr*, 1:206 (no *isnād*); Nīsābūrī, *Gharā'ib*, 4:182 (on the authority of Ibn ʿAbbās, without an *isnād*).

remains the same, although some versions introduce subtle changes which emphasize the contrast between the *jāhiliyya* and Islam. Indeed, Alūsī notes that Q. 4:8 was revealed "in order to highlight the cancellation of *Jāhilī* law,"[15] and Qurṭubī cites a version which concludes with a rebuke to the two men who appealed to tribal values in order to justify seizure of the estate in question.[16]

Q. 4:11–12

Ta'khīr al-Bayān ʿan Waqt al-Khiṭāb

The incident involving Umm Kujja and her daughters led to the revelation of Q. 4:8, which establishes the right of females to inherit. But since it is Q. 4:11–12 (the inheritance verses) that determine the exact entitlement of females, the commentators were obliged to explain why that incident did not lead immediately to the revelation of the inheritance verses. Some authorities maintained that Q. 4:11–12 actually abrogated Q. 4:8,[17] but this opinion was overshadowed by the argument that God revealed Q. 4:11–12, subsequently, in order to clarify the principle established in Q. 4:8 (*"ta'khīr al-bayān ʿan waqt al-khiṭāb"*). Rāzī (d. 1209) cites a version of the Umm Kujja report which concludes with the following explanation of the mechanics of revelation:

> The Prophet said, "Return to your house until I determine what God will introduce." Then [Q. 4:8] was revealed to the Prophet, indicating that both males and females are entitled to a share. But God, may He be exalted, did not specify, in this verse, the amount [of their shares]. So the Messenger of God sent to the two executors [of the estate], saying, "Do not touch any of the property belonging to Aws." *Then "God commands you concerning your children" [Q. 4:11] was revealed, and the share of the*

15. Alūsī, *Rūḥ*, 4:320 (l. 16).

16. Qurṭubī, 5:46: ". . . so God revealed this verse [Q. 4:8] in order to rebuke them and in order to nullify their statement [viz., that only adult males are entitled to inherit] and their ignorant conduct, for minor heirs should have a greater right to property than adults, because of their inability to deal for themselves and watch out for their own interests. But they [viz., the two paternal cousins] inverted this rule, cancelled the rationale, were led astray by their passions, and were mistaken in their conduct."

17. E.g., Ibn Salāmah, *al-Nāsikh wa'l-mansūkh*, p. 31.

husband and wife [Q. 4:12] was revealed. The Messenger of God ordered the two executors to give the wife one-eighth, but to hold on to the daughters' share. Later, he sent to them saying, "Give the daughters their share." And they did.[18] [Emphasis added.]

The Wife of Saᶜd b. al-Rabīᶜ

Another way to deal with the discrepancy between the incident involving Umm Kujja and the revelation of Q. 4:11–12 was to modify the "historical" record so that the incident in question leads directly to the revelation of the inheritance verses. This is exactly what happens in variant versions of the preceding report in which different principals staff the narrative. Consider, for example, the version cited by Coulson (referred to at the beginning of this chapter) in which the revelation of Q. 4:11–12 is linked to an incident involving the (unnamed) wife of Saᶜd b. al-Rabīᶜ:[19]

> Muhammad b. Abī ᶜUmar al-ᶜAdanī—Sufyān b. ᶜUyayna—ᶜAbd Allāh b. Muhammad b. ᶜAqīl—Jābir b. ᶜAbd Allāh. He said, "The wife of Saᶜd b. al-Rabīᶜ brought Saᶜd's two daughters to the Prophet and said, 'O Messenger of God, these are the two daughters of Saᶜd, who was killed [while] with you on the day of *Uḥud.* Their paternal uncle took everything that their father left. Verily, a woman cannot marry without her property.' The Messenger of God was silent until the inheritance verse (*āyat al-farḍ*) was revealed.[20] Then the Messenger of God called Saᶜd b. al-Rabīᶜ's brother and said, 'Give Saᶜd's two daughters two-thirds of his property, give his wife one-eighth, and you take whatever remains.'"[21]

This report, unlike the previous ones, contains a complete *isnād* going back to the Companion, Jābir b. ᶜAbd Allāh. The presence of Jābir is problematic (see below), and his name may have been inserted into the *isnād* in order to remedy some defect. (His sta-

18. Rāzī, 9:194. See also Zamakhsharī, 1:476–77; Bayḍāwī, 1:196; Nasafī, 1:206; Nīsābūrī, *Gharā'ib*, 4:182; Alūsī, 4:320.

19. Saᶜd's full name is Saᶜd b. al-Rabīᶜ b. ᶜAmr b. Abī Zuhayr b. Mālik b. Imrū'l Qays b. Mālik al-Agharr b. Thaᶜlaba b. Kaᶜb al-Khazrajī al-Anṣārī al-Khazrajī. Biographical details may be found in Ibn Saᶜd, *Ṭabaqāt*, 2:43; Ibn ᶜAbd al-Barr, 2:589–91; Ibn Ḥajar, *ᶜIṣāba*, 3:58–59 (no. 3155).

20. The continuation of the report makes it clear that the "*āyat al-farḍ*," here, refers to Q. 4:11–12.

21. Ibn Māja, *Sunan*, 2:908 (no. 2720); see also Tirmidhī, *Sunan*, 3:280 (no. 2172); Abū Dā'ūd, *Sunan*, 8:99–100 (no. 2875); Wāḥidī, p. 139; Ibn al-ᶜArabī, *Aḥkām*, 1:333 (top).

tus as a Companion who died in 697 at the age of ninety-four would have made him an especially attractive choice.[22])

The first part of this report, up to the words, "Verily, a woman cannot marry without her property," repeats the same narrative structure as the reports associated with Q. 4:8: a man dies leaving a wife and daughters; his paternal cousin seizes the estate and refuses to share it with the women; the widow complains to the prophet; and a Qur'anic verse is revealed. But here the incident leads directly to the revelation of Q. 4:11–12 and, perhaps in order to create the sense of an independent historical event, the traditionists have modified the details of the narrative, e.g., the name of the deceased, and the number of daughters and paternal cousins.

Some of these changes, in addition to creating a fresh historical setting, respond to specific exegetical concerns. For instance, the commentators had been greatly vexed by the fact that Q. 4:11 awards an only daughter half of the estate, and awards two-thirds of the estate to "females above two," but does not specify the entitlement of two daughters. They sometimes solved this problem by drawing an analogy to Q. 4:176, which awards two-thirds of the estate to two sisters ("If they are two [sisters], then they are entitled to two-thirds of what he leaves"), but this solution may have been open to criticism. Having a prophetic *sunna* which lends credence to this solution, however, would have been of considerable effect, and this may well have prompted the detail that Saʿd is said to be the father of two daughters.[23]

Further changes in the text of the Saʿd incident facilitated the understanding of other aspects of Q. 4:11–12. These two verses award shares of the estate to various members of the deceased's family, but do not indicate who—if anybody—inherits what remains after the distribution of these shares. The Saʿd report, as a *sunna* of the Prophet, by mentioning the award to Saʿd's brother,

22. M. J. Kister, "Djābir b. ʿAbd Allāh," *EI*[2], supplement, fascicule 3–4, pp. 230–32. See below for a report in which Jābir claims that Q. 4:11–12 were revealed about himself! On the "age trick," see Juynboll, *Muslim Tradition*, pp. 46–48.

23. Ibn ʿAbd al-Barr (2:591) explicitly refers to the exegetical function of this detail: "Saʿd b. al-Rabīʿ left two daughters, and the Messenger of God gave them two-thirds. This constituted [Muhammad's] first clarification of the sign in His Word, 'If they are females above two, then they are entitled to two-thirds of what he leaves.' This verse [viz., 4:11] was revealed regarding [Saʿd's two daughters] and in that manner God's intention became known, and it became known that by His Word 'above two' He meant 'two or more.'"

creates a precedent for the practice of awarding this residue to the closest surviving male agnate (the Prophet awards him "whatever remains" after the distribution of the shares).[24] Thus, a problem of designation is solved.

The report indicates that the Saʿd incident occurred sometime after the battle of Uḥud (625), and it seems to me that this detail, too, serves a purpose in facilitating the understanding of Q. 4:11–12. Muslims, during the seventh century A.D., had come to view these two verses as having abrogated Q. 2:180 and 2:240,[25] a view which requires that the revelation of the inheritance verses follow that of the bequest verses. The commentators had identified the time of the latter's revelation as at "the beginning of Islam."[26] Thus, the detail that Q. 4:11–12 were revealed after A.D. 625 facilitated the application of the abrogation doctrine. Another difficulty is remedied.

The Wife of Thābit b. Qays

In another variant, Jābir b. ʿAbd Allāh relates that the inheritance verses were revealed in connection with an incident involving the wife of Thābit b. Qays:[27] This report is virtually identical to the previous one, except that the woman who appeals to Muhammad on behalf of her two daughters indicates that she is the widow of Thābit b. Qays, rather than Saʿd b. al-Rabīʿ. But the biographical dictionaries indicate that Thābit b. Qays was killed at the battle of Yamāma (633), eight years after the battle of Uḥud—if not later![28] This calls for some explanation. Abū Dā'ūd

24. See Coulson, *Conflicts*, pp. 10–11, where the author refers to this function of the Saʿd report. Note, however, that Coulson treats the *asbāb al-nuzūl* as if they represent authentic seventh-century events.

25. I have discussed the abrogation of these verses in chap. 5.

26. See, for example, Zamakhsharī, 1:289.

27. Abū Dā'ūd, 8:98 (no. 2874) (*isnād*: Musaddad—Bishr b. al-Mufaḍḍal—ʿAbd Allāh b. Muhammad b. ʿAqīl—Jābir b. ʿAbd Allāh). Thābit's full name is Thābit b. Qays b. Shammāsh al-Anṣārī. For biographical details, see Ibn Ḥajar, *ʿIṣāba*, 1:422 (no. 990); idem, *Tahdhīb al-tahdhīb*, 2:12–13; Bukhārī, *Ta'rīkh*, vol. 1, pt. ii, p. 167 (no. 2081); Dhahabī, *Kāshif*, 1:171 (no. 700).

28. Dhahabī, *Kāshif*, 1:171 (no. 700). See also Bukhārī, *Ta'rīkh*, vol. 1, pt. ii, p. 167 (no. 2081): Thābit died "during the caliphate of Abū Bakr." Ibn ʿAbd al-Barr (1:206, no. 261) indicates that Thābit died "during the caliphate of Muʿāwiya" (r. 661–80).

attributes the mistake to Bishr b. al-Mufaḍḍal, the transmitter directly above ᶜAbd Allāh b. ᶜAqīl in the *isnād*: "Bishr erred, for the two girls are the daughters of Saᶜd b. al-Rabīᶜ, whereas Thābit b. Qays was killed on the day of al-Yamāma."[29] But later Qur'an commentators, ignoring Abū Dā'ūd, routinely assert that Q. 4: 11–12 were revealed about either Saᶜd b. al-Rabīᶜ or Thābit b. Qays, thereby demonstrating that once an error entered the tradition, it took on a life of its own.[30] This tendency, I submit, is characteristic, and it has caused—rather than solved—problems of misreading.

Umm Kuḥḥa: The Wife of ᶜAbd al-Raḥmān b. Thābit

In a report attributed to Suddī (d. 745),[31] the revelation of the inheritance verses is linked to the wife of ᶜAbd al-Raḥmān b. Thābit:

> Muhammad b. al-Ḥusayn—Aḥmad b. Mufaḍḍal—Asbāt—al-Suddī ("God commands you concerning your children: a male is entitled to the share of two females"): "The people of the *jāhiliyya* would not give the inheritance to minor girls or boys, and an adult man would not inherit from his child, unless [the latter] was able to engage in combat. ᶜAbd al-Raḥmān, the brother of Ḥassān, the poet, died leaving a wife named Umm Kuḥḥa and five sisters. The heirs came and took his property. Umm Kuḥḥa complained to the Prophet about this. Then God, may He be exalted, revealed this verse, 'If they are females above two, they are entitled to two-thirds of what he leaves; but if she is one, she is entitled to half.' Then He said, regarding Umm Kuḥḥa, 'They are entitled to one-fourth of what you leave, if you do not have a child; but if you have a child, they are entitled to one-eighth.'"[32]

This report, which introduces several changes into NS1,[33] is obviously corrupt. Umm Kuḥḥa appeals to the Prophet on behalf of herself and the deceased's five *sisters*; then, we are told, "If

29. Abū Dā'ūd, 8:99 (no. 2874); see also Ibn Ḥajar, *ᶜIṣāba*, 1:422 (no. 990).

30. Wāḥidī, pp. 138–39; Nīsābūrī, *Gharā'ib*, 4:192; Qurṭubī, 5:58.

31. See Sezgin, *GAS*, 1:32–33 (no. 11).

32. Ṭabarī, *Jāmiᶜ*, 4:275 (ll. 10–17).

33. Deceased becomes ᶜAbd al-Raḥmān b. Thābit; daughter(s) becomes four sisters; paternal cousin(s) becomes unidentified heirs.

they are females above two" was revealed. But the "females" here can only refer to daughters, as the commentators confirm.[34] Thus, there is a discrepancy between the specific details of the case, on the one hand, and the verse that was revealed, on the other. The literature puzzlingly suggests that an incident involving sisters has led to the revelation of a verse awarding shares of the estate to daughters; the discrepancy was resolved by an evolving modification of the details in the narrative. Ibn Ḥajar al-ʿAsqalānī, quoting from the *Tafsīr* of Suddī, cites a variant in which the sisters are transformed into brothers: "[ʿAbd al-Raḥmān] died during the period of the Prophet, leaving a wife and five brothers. [The brothers] took his property and did not give his wife anything. She complained to the Messenger of God. Then the inheritance verse was revealed."[35] Here, the sisters on whose behalf Umm Kuḥḥa had appealed to the Prophet are transformed into brothers who become her antagonists. The report does not specify how the estate was divided, but we may assume that Umm Kuḥḥa took one-quarter (there are no children), and that the brothers took the rest. Suyūṭī and Ṭabāṭabā'ī cite reports in which the problem is resolved in a different manner: "ʿAbd al-Raḥmān . . . died leaving a wife and five daughters."[36] This version at last brings the case into harmony with Q. 4:11; an incident involving daughters leads to the revelation of a verse awarding shares to the same.[37]

Jābir b. ʿAbd Allāh

The incident most closely associated with the revelation of Q. 4:11–12 is one in the life of the Companion, Jābir b. ʿAbd Allāh:[38]

34. E.g., Ṭabarī, *Jāmiʿ*, 4:276; Zamakhsharī, 1:481–82; Ṭabarsī, *Majmaʿ al-bayān*, 3:32–33; Rāzī, 9:205.

35. Ibn Ḥajar, *ʿIṣāba*, 4:293 (no. 5095).

36. Suyūṭī, *Lubāb*, pp. 83–84 (margin); Ṭabāṭabā'ī, *Mīzān*, 4:218.

37. I shall take up later in this chapter another problem with this report, the very existence of ʿAbd al-Raḥmān b. Thābit.

38. Jābir b. ʿAbd Allāh b. ʿAmr al-Anṣārī al-Sulamī (d. 697). For further details, see Ibn ʿAbd al-Barr, 1:219–20 (no. 286); Ibn Ḥajar, *ʿIṣāba*, 1:434–35 (no. 1027); idem, *Tahdhīb*, 2:42–43; Bukhārī, *Ta'rīkh*, vol. 1, pt. ii, p. 207 (no. 2208); Dhahabī, *Tadhkirat al-ḥuffāẓ*, 1:43 (no. 21).

> ʿAbd Allāh—My father—Muhammad b. Jaʿfar—Shuʿba and Ḥajjāj—Shuʿba—Muhammad b. al-Munkadir said: I heard Jābir b. ʿAbd Allāh say, "The Messenger of God came to me while I was in pain, unconscious." He said, "He performed the ritual ablution and then poured [the water] on me. (Or he said, "They poured [the water] on me.") I regained consciousness and said, 'Verily, nobody except *kalāla*[39] will inherit from me, so how should the inheritance [be divided]?'" He said, "Then the inheritance verse (*āyat al-farḍ*) was revealed."[40]

Jābir's presence in this report (hereafter "NS2") poses a problem. I have already presented two reports in which Jābir, himself, asserted that the inheritance verse was revealed as a result of an incident involving the widow of either Saʿd b. al-Rabīʿ or Thābit b. Qays.[41] It is unlikely that Jābir would have transmitted these reports and at the same time claimed that the inheritance verse was revealed about himself. Clearly, Jābir's name was inserted after the fact into either the *isnād* of the Saʿd and Thābit reports or else into the *matn* of the present report (NS2). Two considerations favor the former. The *asbāb al-nuzūl* associated with Q. 4:8 circulated initially without a complete *isnād*, and the chain of authorities in which Jābir appears as a transmitter may have been created to correct that defect. Moreover, substantive considerations suggest that NS2 was put into circulation prior to NS1, in any of its variations. Although the encounter between Muhammad and Jābir does create an appropriate circumstance for the revelation of an inheritance verse, NS2, otherwise, does not serve any legal or exegetical function. It specifies for Jābir no exact familial situation; manifests no concern with the mechanics of dividing up property; provides no date on which the incident occurred; and evidences no religio-ethical justification for introducing the Qur'anic inheritance laws. The report most probably circulated, at first, in order to demonstrate the therapeutic powers of prayer and Prophecy. NS2, thus, seems to reflect an early, relatively unsophisticated, stage of legal and exegetical development.

Muslim scholars were, at first, unable to identify the exact

39. The commentators and lexicographers understand the term *kalāla*, here, as "heirs more distant than a parent or child." See Muslim, *Ṣaḥīḥ*, 3:1234–35, note 3. For a different interpretation of the meaning of this word see chap. 1.

40. Ibn Ḥanbal, *Musnad* (Beirut), 3:298. See also Bukhārī, *Ṣaḥīḥ*, 3:224; Muslim, *Ṣaḥīḥ*, 3:1234–36 (nos. 5–8); Ibn Māja, 2:911 (no. 2728); Abū Dā'ūd, 8:93–95; Tirmidhī, 3:282 (nos. 2177–78) and 4:301 (nos. 5003–04).

41. See above, pp. 195 and 197.

verse that was revealed on this occasion. The phrase *āyat al-farḍ* at the end of the report could refer to Q. 4:11, 4:12, and/or 4:176 (see below), all of which award shares to various members of the family. Identification of the verse was made possible by modifying the internal details of the narrative. Muslim authorities came to associate Q. 4:11–12 ("God commands you concerning your children") with the inheritance rights of children,[42] and Q. 4:176 (which focuses exclusively on brothers and sisters) with that of siblings. The traditionists were able to identify the verse that was revealed by circulating reports in which Jābir specifies his familial situation. In some versions, Jābir indicates that he will leave an unspecified number of children;[43] in others, seven or nine sisters;[44] in yet others he makes no reference whatsoever to his potential heirs.[45] In those versions in which Jābir indicates that he will be survived by children or in which he makes no reference to his heirs, his question to the Prophet induces the revelation of Q. 4:11–12.[46] But in those versions in which Jābir indicates that he will be inherited by *al-kalāla* or by sisters, his question is followed by the revelation of Q. 4:176, which opens with the words, "When they ask you for a decision, say, 'God decrees for you regarding *al-kalāla*,'" and awards shares of the estate to siblings.[47] So by the end of the ninth century the report had branched out in two directions leading variously to the revelation of Q. 4:11–12 or of 4:176.

42. This identification is misleading. In addition to awarding shares to children, Q. 4:11–12 award shares to mothers, husbands, wives, and (uterine) siblings.

43. Tirmidhī, 3:282 (no. 2177).

44. Abū Dā'ūd, 8:93–95 (nos. 2869–70); Tirmidhī, 3:282, no. 2177 ("He had nine sisters"). The biographical dictionaries confirm the fact that Jābir had sisters at the time. In Dhahabī, *Tadhkira*, 1:43, we read that Jābir was unable to participate in the battles of Badr and Uḥud because his father made him stay home and take care of his sisters. See Kister, "Djābir," p. 230.

45. Bukhārī, *Ṣaḥīḥ*, 3:224; Muslim, *Ṣaḥīḥ*, 3:1234 (nos. 5–7); Ibn Māja, 2:911 (no. 2728); Tirmidhī, 4:301 (nos. 5003–04).

46. Tirmidhī (3:282, no. 2177) cites the following version of the report: ʿAbd b. Ḥumayd—ʿAbd al-Raḥmān b. Saʿd—ʿAmr b. Abī Qays—Muhammad b. al-Munkadir—Jābir b. ʿAbd Allāh. He said, "The Messenger of God came to me, when I was sick among the Banū Salāmah. I said, 'O Prophet of God, how shall I divide my property among my children?' But he did not answer me. Then 'God commands you concerning your children: a male is entitled to the share of two females' was revealed." See also, Bukhārī, *Ṣaḥīḥ*, 3:224; Muslim, *Ṣaḥīḥ*, 3:1234 (no. 6); Tirmidhī, 4:301 (no. 5004).

47. Muslim, *Ṣaḥīḥ*, 3:1234 (nos. 5 and 8); Abū Dā'ūd, 8:93–95 (nos. 2869–70); Tirmidhī, 3:282 (no. 2178).

Q. 4:176

The sources link the revelation of Q. 4:176, reportedly the last verse of the Qur'an to have been revealed to Muhammad,[48] to two different incidents: in one (NS2), the Prophet, while out walking with Abū Bakr, stops to visit Jābir b. ʿAbd Allāh; in the other (NS3), the Prophet is out riding his camel, accompanied by Ḥudhayfa b. al-Yamān and ʿUmar b. al-Khaṭṭāb. Having dealt with NS3 in chapter 4,[49] I shall attend here to NS2.

Jābir b. ʿAbd Allāh

Q. 4:176 opens with a reference to certain unnamed persons who ask Muhammad an unspecified question ("When they ask you for a decision, say . . ."). A primary function of the *asbāb al-nuzūl* was to provide an appropriate context for such unspecified details. The second branch of NS2, in which Jābir asks Muhammad a question about his [viz., Jābir's] sisters, provides an excellent illustration of this function:[50]

> Aḥmad b. Ḥanbal—Sufyān—Ibn al-Munkadir—Jābir: "I was sick, and the Prophet came to visit me when he was walking with Abū Bakr. I was unconscious and did not say anything to him. He performed the ritual ablution and poured [the water] on me. I regained consciousness and said, 'O Messenger of God, what shall I do with my property, since I have sisters?'" [Jābir] said, "Then the inheritance verse, 'When they ask you for a decision, say: God decrees for you regarding the person who dies leaving neither parent nor child,' was revealed."[51]

This report (which, incidentally, highlights the therapeutic

48. Bukhārī, *Ṣaḥīḥ*, 3:231; Tirmidhī, 4:315 (no. 5032); Qurṭubī, 6:28; Bayḍāwī, 1:245.

49. See chap. 4, pp. 139–42.

50. Note, however, that Ṭabarsī (3:296) quotes Qatāda as saying, "The Companions were concerned about *al-kalāla*, so God revealed [Q. 4:176]."

51. Abū Dā'ūd, 8:93–94 (no. 2869); see also Muslim, *Ṣaḥīḥ*, 3:1234 (nos. 5 and 8); Tirmidhī, 3:282 (no. 2178). This tradition is also widely quoted by the commentators: Ṭabarī, *Jāmiʿ*, 6:41 (ll. 12–25); Wāḥidī, p. 180; Zamakhsharī, 1:588–89; Ṭabarsī, 3:296; Qurṭubī, 6:28; Bayḍāwī, 1:245; Nasafī, 1:265; Nīsābūrī, *Gharā'ib*, 6:25–26; Ibn Kathīr, 1:596; and Suyūṭī, *Lubāb*, 116 (margin).

powers of prayer and prophecy) seems to have had as its primary function the creation of a narrative that anticipates the revelation of Q. 4:176 by making Jābir ask a question about sisters; Q. 4:176, then, constitutes the response.

The Problem of "Multiple Occasions"

In analyzing the corpus of *asbāb al-nuzūl* associated with Q. 4:8, 4:11–12, and 4:176, I have considered three different narratives, NS1 and NS2, which exhibit numerous internal variations, and NS3 (the Ḥudhayfa report), which is relatively stable from one version to the next. The information contained in these reports may be organized in many different ways, of which I shall consider two. Consolidation of the specific details mentioned in NS1 and NS2, respectively, yields the following "facts": NS1: A man (Thaᶜlaba, Aws b. Thābit, Aws b. al-Ṣāmit, ᶜAbd al-Raḥmān b. Thābit, or Saᶜd b. al-Rabīᶜ) died leaving a wife (Umm Kuḥḥa, Umm Kujja, or Umm Kuḥla), daughters (one, two, three, or five), or sisters (five), and either one paternal cousin (Aws b. Suwayd) or two paternal cousins (Suwayd and ᶜArfaja, Suwayd and ᶜUrfuṭa, Qatāda and ᶜArfaja, or Khālid and ᶜUrfuṭa). The paternal cousin(s) seized the estate and refused to share it with the women; the widow complained to the Prophet; then one or more verses of the Qur'an (4:8; 4:8, followed shortly thereafter by 4:11–12; or 4:11–12 only) were revealed.

NS2: Jābir b. ᶜAbd Allāh, believing himself to be on the point of death, indicated that he will be survived by children, by *kalāla*, or by sisters (seven or nine); Jābir asked the Prophet about the division of his estate; God revealed a verse of the Qur'an (4:11–12 or 4:176).

If the information is organized around the specific verses that were revealed, the following, different set of "facts" takes shape: Q. 4:8 was revealed about the wife of Thaᶜlaba or about the wife of Aws b. Thābit; the incident involving the latter may also have resulted, after a short delay, in the revelation of Q. 4:11–12. Q. 4:11–12 were revealed about the wife of Saᶜd b. al-Rabīᶜ, Thābit b. Qays, or ᶜAbd al-Raḥmān b. Thābit; or they were revealed about Jābir b. ᶜAbd Allāh. Finally, Q. 4:176 was revealed about Jābir b. ᶜAbd Allāh, while the Prophet was out for a walk, or it was revealed while the Prophet was out for a ride, accompanied by Ḥudhayfa b. al-Yamān and ʿUmar b. al-Khaṭṭāb.

The preceding corpus manifests numerous internal contradictions and discrepancies, a problem that the critical western scholar might dismiss as having been produced by the vagaries of oral and written transmission. Traditional Muslim scholars, with their literalist approach to the sources, could not dismiss the problem so easily. These scholars were faced with the phenomenon of *asbāb mutaʿaddida* (multiple occasions), a term which refers to a single verse's having apparently been revealed as a result of two or more different incidents.[52] Let us consider, for example, how Muslim scholars account for the fact that Q. 4:11–12 are reported to have been revealed: (a) about the wife and daughters of Saʿd b. al-Rabīʿ (and variants), or (b) about Jābir b. ʿAbd Allāh and his children.

One approach, favored by Ibn Ḥajar al-ʿAsqalānī, was to "correct" the tradition by arguing, on historical grounds, that Q. 4:11–12 could not have been revealed about Jābir: "Take it from the one who said that [Q. 4:11–12] were revealed regarding the story of Saʿd's two daughters; it was not revealed in connection with Jābir, because on that day Jābir did not have a child."[53]

The fact that Jābir had sisters, but no daughters, still does not solve the problem. Q. 4:11–12, in addition to awarding shares of the estate to daughters, mothers, and wives, also award a share to uterine brothers and sisters.[54] So an incident in which Jābir is survived by sisters might still have led to the revelation of Q. 4:11–12. Suyūṭī, in an effort to counter this objection, suggests that Q. 4:11–12 were revealed on two separate occasions:

> [Q. 4:11–12] were revealed about both cases. It can be argued that the revelation of the first part of the verse relates to the two daughters, and that the last part of the verse, i.e., "if a man dies leaving neither parent nor child" (*yūrathu kalālatan*), was re-

52. For a general discussion of this phenomenon, see Suyūṭī, *Lubāb*, pp. 8–10 (margin); see also Wansbrough, *Quranic Studies*, p. 177.

53. Suyūṭī, *Lubāb*, p. 83 (margin), ll. 18–20. Ibn Kathīr (1:457, ll. 26–28) makes a similar argument: "It is evident that it is only the last verse of the *Sūra* [viz., Q. 4:176] that was revealed on account of the Jābir report, because he had only sisters at that time and he had no daughters: '*wa-innamā kāna yūrathu kalālatan*' ('he died leaving neither parent nor child'). But we have mentioned the report here, following Bukhārī, because he mentioned it at this point. The second report, on the authority of Jābir [viz., the Saʿd report], is more likely to be related to the revelation of [Q. 4:11–12]. But God knows best."

54. See appendix A.

> vealed about the Jābir report; Jābir's statement, "God commands you concerning your children," means the mention of *al-kalāla* which is attached to this verse.[55]

Suyūṭī argues that the incident involving the daughters of Saᶜd b. al-Rabīᶜ led to the revelation of Q. 4: 11, whereas the incident involving Jābir's sisters resulted in the revelation of Q. 4: 12. But even this explanation is not entirely satisfactory. The Saᶜd report portrays Muhammad as awarding two-thirds of the estate to the two daughters, and one-eighth to the wife. But the latter award derives, not from Q. 4: 11, but from Q. 4: 12. Furthermore, the biographical dictionaries do not indicate that Jābir had uterine sisters, the type of sister awarded a share of the estate in Q. 4: 12.[56]

Some traditionists circulated a report in which the incident involving Saᶜd's wife led to the revelation of a verse other than Q. 4: 11–12, thereby eliminating the conflict between the Saᶜd and Jābir reports. Suyūṭī cites a variant of the Saᶜd report in which Q. 4: 126 is revealed after Saᶜd's wife (here, ᶜAmra bint Ḥazzām) complains to the Prophet on behalf of her daughters. This verse opens with the phrase, "If they ask you for a pronouncement concerning women, say," and proceeds to discuss conduct towards orphaned females.[57] This leaves the Jābir report as the sole *sabab* for Q. 4: 11–12.

Ibn Ḥajar al-ᶜAsqalānī managed to eliminate the incident involving the wife of ᶜAbd al-Raḥmān b. Thābit by exposing the latter as an historical nonentity. The existence of an ᶜAbd al-Raḥmān b. Thābit, brother of the poet, Ḥassān, cannot be confirmed independently of the report quoted earlier. Ibn Ḥajar, the only biographer consulted who includes an entry for this person, admits that the "genealogists do not mention that Ḥassān [b. Thābit] had a brother named ᶜAbd al-Raḥmān."[58]

Ultimately, the Muslim authorities transformed a defect into a virtue by arguing that several different *asbāb al-nuzūl* may be

55. Suyūṭī, *Lubāb*, p. 83 (margin), ll. 21–30.

56. See note 38 for references to the biographical dictionaries.

57. Suyūṭī, *Lubāb*, p. 84 (margin).

58. Ibn Ḥajar, *ᶜIṣāba*, 4: 293 (no. 5095). I suspect that Umm Kujja (and variants), as well as Suwayd and ᶜArfaja (and variants) are also nothing more than historical fictions or literary creations. Ibn Ḥajar, the only biographer consulted who includes an entry for Umm Kuḥḥa, knows her exclusively from the *asbāb* reports. I have not been able to locate Suwayd and ᶜArfaja (or variants) in any of the biographical dictionaries. See *ᶜIṣāba*, 1: 144–45, where Ibn Ḥajar

associated with the revelation of a single verse.[59] After rehearsing all of the reports associated with Q. 4:11–12, Qurṭubī states, "It is not far [from the truth] that the verses were revealed in response to all of these incidents. For that reason the revelation was delayed. God knows best."[60] Ṭabāṭabā'ī, after citing the Jābir and Saᶜd reports, says: "It has been repeatedly mentioned that there is nothing wrong with the fact that several different *asbāb al-nuzūl* are transmitted, and that several of them may be brought together in a single verse."[61]

Conclusion

My analysis of the *asbāb al-nuzūl* associated with Q. 4:8, 4:11–12, and 4:176 is now complete. The reports that I have examined do not, on the whole, inspire much confidence in their historical accuracy. NS1 (the wife-of-a-martyr report) does address itself to issues that would be of interest to the legal historian (e.g., the *raison d'être* of the Qur'anic inheritance laws and the relationship between this legislation and tribal customary law)—if its authenticity could be established. But this is not the case, for the relatively late date at which the different versions of NS1 were put into circulation casts doubt upon their reliability. The earliest report is attributed to ᶜIkrima (d. 723); more than three centuries later, Wāḥidī (d. 1075) expressed his doubts concerning this report by prefacing it with the uncharacteristically vague statement, "The commentators say." NS1 was eventually provided with a complete *isnād*, but this only confirms the tendency—first noted by Schacht—of *isnād*s to grow backwards. As for the contents of these reports, the details of the narrative change so frequently and in such an arbitrary manner that it would be hazardous to single out any one as being authentic.

Although it might be possible to make a case for the historical reliability of NS2 (the Jābir report) and NS3 (the Ḥudhayfa report)—both occur in early sources with complete *isnād*s—neither narrative sheds any light whatsoever on issues of interest to

provides two entries for Aws b. Thābit al-Anṣārī in order to distinguish between the historical figure and the literary creation. On this phenomenon, see Juynboll, *Muslim Tradition*, chap. 4.

59. See Suyūṭī, *Lubāb*, pp. 8–10 (margin).

60. Qurṭubī, 5:57–58.

61. Ṭabāṭabā'ī, *Mīzān*, 4:217.

legal historians. Rather they pertain to the "occasion of revelation," strictly speaking, i.e., what the Prophet was doing when the verse was revealed.

The corpus of *asbāb al-nuzūl* associated with the Qur'anic inheritance verses manifests numerous internal variations that are difficult to reconcile with one another. These variations are best explained, in my opinion, by the assumption that the reports were put into circulation in order to serve as a supplementary form of exegesis, specifically: (1) to provide a religio-ethical rationalization for the introduction of the Qur'anic inheritance verses by setting them off against a *jāhilī* background; (2) to demonstrate the nature of Prophetic justice; (3) to explain certain mechanics of revelation (e.g., *ta'khīr al-bayān ʿan waqt al-khiṭāb*); (4) to establish a chronology of revelation in harmony with the requirements of the doctrine of abrogation; (5) to clarify certain obscure or ambiguous Qur'anic phrases (e.g., "females above two" in Q. 4:11); and (6) to provide a prophetic precedent for certain procedures of the Islamic law of inheritance. I suggest that accuracy was secondary, in the creation of the *asbāb al-nuzūl*, to the traditionists' concern with balance and harmony in Qur'anic interpretation. This corpus should therefore be used with extreme caution in any effort to reconstruct the formation of Islamic law.[62]

62. It may be appropriate, in this regard, to cite the following statement from the introduction to Wāḥidī's *Asbāb*, pp. 5–6:

> Those who desire the sciences of the Qur'an today are honest men and liars whom the forces of blame have been unable to repair. The matter has led us to become acquainted with the Beginners in the sciences of the Book in order to clarify the "occasions" on which it was revealed. This is because it is absolutely obligatory and of the utmost benefit to become acquainted with them [viz., the "occasions"] and to direct one's attention to them, due to the impossibility of knowing the meaning of a verse and the intention of its "way" without being acquainted with its story and the clarification of its revelation.
>
> It is not permitted to speak about the occasions of the revelation of the Book, except on the basis of oral transmission and direct contact with those who witnessed the Revelation, collected information about the "occasions," sought out knowledge of them, and exerted themselves in study.
>
> The Holy Law has threatened with Fire the ignorant who stumble in this knowledge. . . . And our pious forefathers acted with the utmost caution in speaking about the revelation of a verse . . .
>
> As for today, everyone invents things and creates lies and falsehoods, yielding to ignorance, oblivious to the warning to the person who is ignorant of the occasion of the verse's [revelation]. And this is what motivated me to dictate this book which collects the "occasions," so that students of this subject and those who discuss the revelation of the Qur'an will have recourse to it, and, as a result, will know the truth, have no need of embellishment and lying, and endeavor to commit it to memory after listening to it and studying it.

Summary

It will be remembered that, according to Joseph Schacht, Islamic law did not begin to develop until approximately one hundred years after the Prophet's death. But Schacht, in my opinion, unjustifiably extended the results of his research on jurisprudence to positive law and, more important, identified the origins of Islamic law with the emergence of the *ḥadīth* literature, while totally neglecting the Qur'anic legislation. I see no reason to assume that the Qur'anic legislation on marriage, divorce, and inheritance remained in a state of suspended animation for more than a century after the revelation of the Qur'an. Muslims married, divorced, and divided up estates on a daily basis, and it stands to reason, on *a priori* grounds, that they would have sought guidance on these matters in the Qur'anic legislation, and that this would have stimulated the development of Islamic law.

I have attempted to test this hypothesis by carrying out a systematic analysis of the Qur'anic inheritance laws. The results of my research suggest that Islamic law began to develop with the Qur'anic legislation, albeit not in the manner suggested by Islamic tradition. The very act of establishing the text of the Qur'an—the reading of words and the length, arrangement, and abrogation of verses—marked the first stage in the development of Islamic law. And once the text was established, the significance of the inheritance verses in the form they had taken necessitated further elucidation and elaboration. When discussing the formation of Islamic law, it is important to think in terms of a process that unfolded over the course of time, with different elements of the tradition developing at different speeds. I should now like to take the opportunity to summarize this process.

Tribal Customary Law and the Qur'anic Legislation

Any discussion of the tribal customary law of pre-Islamic Arabia ought to begin with an admission that there are few, if any, reliable sources that might shed light on this subject. Our knowledge of pre-Islamic Arabia is derived, for the most part, from Islamic sources that are inherently biased against the *jāhiliyya.* But to the extent that it is possible to "tease" certain elements of customary law out of historical sources, it can be said that the intergenerational transmission of property among the tribesmen of the Hijaz is more likely to have been governed by the principle of seniority than by that of direct descent.

This one clue provides an important key to understanding the relationship between tribal law and the Qur'anic legislation, which is perhaps best seen in terms of a transition from nomadism to sedentary life and from tribalism to individualism. As the Hijazi Arabs settled down in Mecca and Medina, the former a commercial town, the latter an agricultural oasis, they became involved in a system of socioeconomic relations that brought about certain changes in their worldview and life-style. The tribal system in which power and resources were controlled by groups of men gave way to a new system that not only left the individual free to make decisions about the ultimate devolution of his property, but also placed a much greater emphasis upon the rights of women to own and inherit property. The introduction of the Qur'anic inheritance laws should be seen, not as an attempt to modify or reform the tribal customary law of pre-Islamic Arabia, but as a call to abandon that law in favor of a new, more suitable, system of inheritance. The new system seems to have angered the tribal leaders by making the intergenerational transmission of property dependent upon the principle of direct descent from father to son, rather than on seniority; the resistance to these reforms on the part of the tribal leaders may be reflected in the closing words of Q. 4:11, addressed to Muhammad's opponents: "Your fathers and your sons, you know not which of them is closer to you in usefulness."

The Proto-Islamic Law of Inheritance

In part one of this study I attempted to reconstruct the system of inheritance introduced by Muhammad (the proto-Islamic law of inheritance) by working backwards from the accepted understanding of certain Qur'anic verses and prophetic *ḥadīth* to what I believe to have been their original significance. The proto-Islamic law of inheritance differs from the Islamic law of inheritance in two important respects. First, unlike Islamic law, which places severe restrictions upon testamentary dispositions, proto-Islamic law permits full power of testation: by means of a last will and testament, a person contemplating death could designate a testamentary heir and dispose of his property as he saw fit. Although the testator might designate a son, daughter, or other close relative as the testamentary heir, he was also free to designate an affinal relative such as a wife or daughter-in-law; in the latter case, however, relatives who would have inherited in the absence of the will would be awarded a small fractional share of the estate as compensation for the disherison (Q. 4:12b). The testator might, in addition to designating an heir, bequeath up to one-third of the estate (*al-waṣiyya fi'l-thulth*) to parents and/or other close relatives (Q. 2:180), as well as make provisions for the maintenance of his wife (Q. 2:240). A last will and testament, to be valid, had to be drawn up or dictated in the presence of two trustworthy witnesses (Q. 5:105–6). Tampering with the provisions of a will was discouraged (Q. 2:181), and disagreements over the provisions of a will were to be referred to a third party for settlement (Q. 2:182).

Secondly, whereas Islamic law imposes compulsory rules for the division of property, in proto-Islamic law the fixed rules for the division of property take effect only in the absence of a valid last will and testament. The general principles of the proto-Islamic law of intestacy may be summarized as follows: The right to inherit upon intestacy was limited to the blood relatives of the deceased (Q. 4:8); husbands and wives did not inherit from one another, except in the case of the unendowed spouse (Q. 4: 12a). Q. 4:11a, 4:11b, and 4:176 establish the order of priority according to which the different classes of heirs (e.g., children, parents, siblings) inherit, and illustrate the application of the rules of intestacy to a select number of cases. (These rules, incidentally, manifest none of the mathematical complexities of the Islamic law of inheritance.) A distinction can be drawn between primary heirs, who inherit between 50 and 100 percent of the estate, and secondary heirs, who inherit a maximum of one-third. This distinction accounts for the apparent contradiction between the Qur'anic statement, "a male is entitled to the share of two females" (Q. 4:11a and 4:176), on the one hand, and the award of equal shares of the estate to a father and mother (Q. 4: 11b) and a brother and sister (Q. 4:12b), on the other. When a male and female of the same class and degree of relationship to the deceased inherit as primary heirs, the male takes twice the share of a female; but when they inherit as secondary heirs, the male takes the same share as the female. Unlike children, who always inherit as primary heirs, parents and siblings may inherit either as primary or secondary heirs, depending on the circumstances.

Thus, unlike traditional Muslim scholars and western proponents of the superimposition theory who view the Qur'anic inheritance legislation as *ad hoc* reforms designed to supplement the tribal customary law of pre-Islamic Arabia, I maintain that the Qur'an introduced a complete system of inheritance containing provisions for both testate succession and intestacy that came to replace the tribal customary law of pre-Islamic Arabia.

The Formation of the Islamic Law of Inheritance

Subtle but far-reaching manipulations of the text of the Qur'an caused the proto-Islamic law of inheritance to be transformed into the "science of the shares." I have attempted to identify some of the historical causes of this transformation in the events of the first century A.H., i.e., a time when, according to most western scholars, Islamic law did not exist. The controversy over political succession, after the death of Muhammad, probably constituted the "first cause." The reference in Q. 4:12b to a mechanism for designating an heir would have been a source of embarrassment to Abū Bakr, the first caliph, who had not received a document of appointment from Muhammad. It would have been in the interest of Abū Bakr and his successors, ʿUmar and ʿUthmān, all of whom played a role in the collection of the Qur'an, to manipulate the interpretation of Q. 4:12b so as to remove the reference to the possibility of designating an heir. This was done by imposing a secondary reading upon the consonantal text of the Qur'an (the *yūrathu/imra'atun/yūṣā* complex) and redefining the word *kalāla*, originally "a female in-law," as "one who dies leaving neither parent nor child" or "all those except the parent and child." These two changes had the effect of eliminating the sole Qur'anic reference to the possibility of designating an heir, and of transforming a verse which awarded a share of the estate to disinherited siblings into a verse that came to be understood as awarding a share of the estate to siblings in general. The reinterpretation of Q. 4:12b, it should be noted, was effected without altering the consonantal text of the Qur'an in any way.

A number of secondary factors served to reinforce and give further impetus to the transition from proto-Islamic to Islamic law. The social, economic, and religious climate of the period of the conquests would have favored a system of inheritance imposing compulsory rules (perceived as being of divine origin) over one that left the individual free to determine whom his heirs would be and how much they would inherit. Compulsory rules that divide up property in an egalitarian manner would have promoted social cohesion at a time when Muslims were dying in large numbers either on the battlefield or as victims of the plague, and when large amounts of wealth and property were being channeled into a relatively small number of hands. And the identification of the Divinity as the source of these rules would have served to reinforce the emerging conception of Islamic law (*Sharīʿa*) as the working out, down to the smallest details, of God's plan for mankind.

These factors converged to cause a shift of emphasis from *heirs* to *shares*. Somehow—the increasing literalism of the period may have been a factor—the right to inherit came to be based upon the simple fact that the Qur'an awards a fractional share of the estate to a certain person. The increased emphasis upon shares of the estate—as opposed to classes of heirs—explains how the various components of the proto-Islamic law of inheritance, Q. 4:11a, 11b, 12a, 12b, and 176, were fused together to form a single unit that came to be known as the *āyat al-mīrāth* or inheritance verse. This process can be followed with relative ease.

One's understanding of Q. 4:11 varies depending upon the

angle from which the verse (see appendix A) is approached. A perspective that emphasizes *classes of heirs* causes the verse to appear as if composed of two sections: the first (Q. 4:11a), ending with the line, "Each one of his parents is entitled to one-sixth of what he leaves, if he has a child," treats cases in which the deceased is survived by children; the second (Q. 4:11b) opens with the line, "If he does not have a child, and his parents are his heirs," and treats cases in which the deceased leaves parents (and siblings), but no children. Each section or subverse thus deals with a different class of heirs, children and parents, respectively. But a perspective that emphasizes *shares* obscures the borderline between the first and second half of Q. 4:11, causing the verse to appear as a single unit that awards shares of the estate to the daughter(s), father, and mother, all of whom enjoy the same legal status as "sharers."

The shift of emphasis from heirs to shares was given further impetus by the reinterpretation of Q. 4:12a and 4:12b, respectively. The award in Q. 4:12a of a fractional share of the estate to an unendowed spouse, a provision that was originally intended to apply to an exceptional case, came to be understood as a norm. Similarly, the elimination in Q. 4:12b of the possibility of designating an heir transformed the share awarded to a disinherited sibling into a compulsory share awarded to any sibling. These two changes caused Q. 4:12a and 4:12b to appear as a single unit which awards shares of the estate to the husband, wife, brother, and/or sister, all of whom enjoy the same undifferentiated status as "sharers."

The final step in the formation of the inheritance verses involved a change in the relationship between Q. 4:12b and 4:176. Originally, Q. 4:12b awarded a share of the estate to disinherited siblings, whereas Q. 4:176 defined the rights of siblings upon intestacy. But the reinterpretation of Q. 4:12b had the effect of elevating the award to disinherited siblings to the level of a compulsory share, making the two verses appear as if they contradict one another: the former now awards a maximum of one-third of the estate to brothers and sisters who inherit on a basis of equality, and the latter distributes between 50 and 100 percent of the estate to brothers and sisters, a brother taking twice the share of a sister. The exegetes resolved the discrepancy by arguing that the variation in the size of the shares awarded in the two verses corresponds to a distinction between the type of sibling treated in each one. They explained that when God said "brother or sister" in Q. 4:12b, He meant "[uterine] brother or sister," while the same words in Q. 4:176 supposedly referred to a "[consanguine and/or germane] brother or sister." This arbitrary—but crucial—interpolation eliminated the apparent contradiction caused by the reinterpretation of Q. 4:12b and brought the two verses into a harmonious relation with one another.

Thus, by the time that the Muslim community began to work out the principles of the Islamic law of inheritance, a number of important decisions had already been made about the reading, length, and interpretation of the Qur'anic inheritance verses. As a result of these decisions, Q. 4:11, 4:12, and 4:176 came to be viewed as a single unit that awards fractional shares of the estate to the daughter(s), father, mother, husband, wife, [uterine] sibling(s), and [consanguine and/or germane] sister(s). The basic principle of the system worked out by the legists—what Coulson has referred to as the "golden rule of the Islamic law of inheritance"—is that the Qur'anic heirs take their allotted portions as the first charge upon the estate, and the male agnates then succeed to the residue.

The distinction between testate succession and intestacy was virtually eliminated during the first century A.H. The Muslim community, perhaps in an effort to promote social cohesion in a period of great turbulence, came to view the fractional shares mentioned in the inheritance verses as *compulsory* rules for the division of property, rather than as rules of intestacy. The shift to compulsory rules required that certain restrictions be placed upon the power of testation. Although the possibility of designating an heir—the primary function of a will—had already been eliminated by the reinterpretation of Q. 4:12b, the Qur'an still makes frequent reference to bequests. Q. 4:11–12, for example, award shares of the estate to the heirs "after any bequest he bequeaths," thereby indicating that testamentary dispositions remained licit. The relation between the compulsory and voluntary aspects of the new system, the "science of the shares," was established by two formal restrictions that were placed upon the freedom of testation. First, the prophetic dictum, "a bequest may not exceed one-third," which had originally served to strike a balance between the entitlement of the designated heir and the legatees, was adapted to the new conception of the nature of inheritance so that it came to be understood as striking a balance between the compulsory heirs (*ahl al-farā'iḍ* and *ʿaṣaba*), on the one hand, and legatees on the other.[1]

The second restriction came to eliminate an apparent overlap between the bequest verses, which encourage the testator to make provisions in his will for parents and wives, and the inheritance verses, which award shares of the estate to these same persons. If a parent or spouse were to receive a bequest of up to one-third of the estate in addition to the appropriate share specified in Q. 4:11–12, this would have the effect of changing the relative entitlement of the "sharers," that is to say, of altering the "limits of God." The legists apparently considered any such attempt to supplement the share of an individual heir as a transgression of the divine command, and they argued against such a possibility by invoking the phrase, "No bequest to an heir," which came into circulation as a general legal maxim towards the end of the first century A.H. and was put in the form of a prophetic dictum about one hundred years later. As such, it provided important doctrinal support for the contention that the inheritance verses had abrogated the bequest verses. Thus the abrogation of the bequest verses was not the result of any change in the divine will, but of changed perceptions of the meaning of the divine word in the years following the Prophet's death.

The final step in the formation of the Islamic law of inheritance involved the historicization or Islamicization of the process under consideration. By the time the *asbāb al-nuzūl* were put into circulation, proto-Islamic law had already been replaced by the "science of the shares," and it was the secondary understanding of the Qur'anic legislation for which the "occasions of the revelation" came to provide an appropriate narrative background. Clearly, these texts do not convey authentic historical events, nor do they accurately portray the formation of the Islamic law of inheritance.

1. See David S. Powers, "The Will of Saʿd b. Abī Waqqāṣ."

Appendix A
Translation of Qur'anic Inheritance Verses

The following translation of Qur'anic verses that are cited frequently in the book reflects the traditional Islamic interpretation of these verses.

Prescribed for you (m. pl.), when death approaches, if he leaves wealth, is a bequest for parents and relatives, according to what is approved by reason; an obligation upon those who fear. (2:180)

And those of you who die leaving wives, a bequest for their wives, provision for one year, without expulsion. But if they leave, you are not responsible for anything that they do of their own accord, within reason. God is powerful and knowing. (2:240)

To men a share of what parents and kindred leave, and to women a share of what parents and kindred leave, whether it be little or much, an apportioned share. (4:8)

God commands you concerning your children: a male is entitled to the share of two females. If they are females above two, then they are entitled to two-thirds of what he leaves. If there is one, then she is entitled to half. Each one of his parents is entitled to one-sixth of what he leaves, if he has a child. But if he does not have a child, and his parents are his heirs, then his mother is entitled to one-third. If he has brothers, then his mother is entitled to one-sixth, after any legacy he bequeaths, or debt. Your fathers and your sons, you know not which of them is closer to you in usefulness. A commandment from God. God is knowing, wise. (4:11)

You are entitled to half of what your wives leave, if they do not have a child. But if they have a child, then you are entitled to one-fourth of what they leave, after any legacy they bequeath, or debt. They are entitled to one-fourth of what you leave, if you do not have a child. But if you have a child, then they are entitled to one-eighth of what you leave, after any legacy you bequeath, or debt. If a man—or a woman—dies leaving neither parent nor child, and he [*sic*] has a [uterine] brother or sister, each one of them is entitled to one-sixth. If they are more than that, then they are partners with respect to one-third, after any legacy that is bequeathed, or debt, without injury. A commandment from God. God is knowing, forbearing. (4:12)

When they ask you for a decision, say: God decrees for you regarding the person who dies leaving neither parent nor child: If a man dies without a child, and he has a sister, then she is entitled to half of what he leaves. He is her heir if she does not have a child. If they (f.) are two, then they are entitled to two-thirds of what he leaves. If they are brothers and sisters, then a male is entitled to the share of two females. God makes clear for you [lest] you go astray. God is all-knowing. (4:176)

Appendix B
Qays b. Dharīḥ

The following story found in the *Kitāb al-aghānī* is presented here because it provides important support for my contention that the word *kalāla* referred, originally, to a female in-law. Note that the context here requires that *al-kalāla* signify a "daughter in-law."

Mention of Qays b. Dharīḥ, His Genealogy, and His Reports

He is, according to al-Kalbī, al-Qaḥdhamī and others: Qays b. Dharīḥ b. Sunna b. Ḥudhāfa b. Ṭarīf b. ʿUtwāra b. ʿĀmir b. Layth b. Bakr b. ʿAbd Manāt, who is ʿAlī b. Kināna b. Khuzayma b. Mudrika b. Ilyās b. Muḍar b. Nizār.

Abū Shurāʿa al-Qaysī mentioned that he is Qays b. Dharīḥ b. al-Ḥubāb b. Sunna, and the rest of the genealogy is identical [to the above] . . . .

Al-Qaḥdhamī mentioned that his mother is Bint Sunna b. al-Dhāhil b. ʿĀmir al-Khuzāʿī—and this is sound—and that he had a maternal uncle called ʿAmr b. Sunna, a poet . . . .

Al-Ḥasan b. ʿAlī—Muhammad b. Mūsā b. Ḥammād—Aḥmad b. al-Qāsim b. Yūsuf—Jaz' b. Qaṭan—Jassās b. Muhammad b. ʿAmr, one of the Banū al-Ḥārith b. Kaʿb—Muhammad b. Ubayy al-Sarī—Hishām b. al-Kalbī—several of the Kinānīs: Qays b. Dharīḥ was the foster-brother of al-Ḥusayn b. ʿAlī b. Abī Ṭālib, may God be pleased with the two of them, who was suckled by Umm Qays.

The story of Qays and Lubnā, his wife, was told to me by a group of our teachers in stories that are continuous and interrupted, and reports that are scattered and collected. I arranged all that [material] so that the telling would be in good order—except for isolated statements that are difficult to extract from the larger arrangement, hence I mentioned them separately.

Among those who related his story to us are: Aḥmad b. ʿAbd al-ʿAzīz al-Jawharī. He said: It was related to us by ʿUmar b. Shabba, and he did not transmit it to anyone else; and [by] Ibrāhīm b. Muhammad b. Ayyūb, on the authority of Ibn Qutayba; and [by] al-Ḥasan b. ʿAlī, on the authority of Muhammad b. Mūsā b. Ḥammād al-Barbarī, on the authority of Aḥmad b. al-Qāsim b. Yūsuf, on the authority of Jaz' b. Qaṭan, on the authority of Jassās b. Muhammad, on the authority of Muhammad b. Ubayy al-Sarī, on the authority of Hishām b. al-Kalbī—and his transmission is extremely reliable.

I also copied some things from his [viz., Qays's] reports, mentioned by al-Qaḥdhamī, on the authority of his informants, and [by] Khālid b. Kulthūm, on the authority of himself and those who transmit from him, and [by] Khālid b. Jamal.

And [I copied] a small amount related by al-Yūsufī, author of *al-Rasā'il,* on the authority of his father, on the authority of Aḥmad b. Ḥammād, on the authority of Jamīl, on the authority of Ibn Abī Jannāḥ al-Kaʿbī.

And I have related everything that is agreed upon in a continuous manner, while all matters upon which there is disagreement are attributed to their transmitters.

They all said: The camp site of his tribe was on the outskirts of Medina, and he and his father were from the town of Medina. But Khālid b. Kulthūm mentioned that the camp site was in Sarif . . . .

They said: Qays passed by the tents of the Banū Kaʿb b. Khuzāʿa, on account of some need, and he stopped in front of one of their tents, while the tribe was away, and the tent was the tent of Lubnā bint al-Ḥubāb, the Kaʿbiyya. He asked for water, and she gave him some, bringing it out to him. She was a tall woman, with blue-black eyes, a pleasant face, and a nice manner of speaking. When he saw her, she impressed him, and he drank the water. She said to him, "Will you dismount and refresh yourself among us?" He said, "Yes." And he dismounted. Her father came, and [Qays] turned to him and greeted him. Qays left, enamoured of Lubnā, and he began to recite poetry about her, until it was [widely] spread and transmitted. Then he came to her on another day, his passion for her having intensified, and he greeted her. She came out, returned his greeting, and showed him the honor due to a guest. He told her of his passion and love for her, and she did the same, at great length, and each one knew the other's heart.

He went to his father, informed him of his situation, and asked him to arrange the marriage. But his father refused, saying, "O my son, you must [marry] one of the daughters of your paternal uncle, because they have a greater claim to you." Dharīḥ was a wealthy man and he did not want his son to marry a strange woman. Qays left, grieved by his father's statement. He approached his mother and complained to her about the matter and asked her to intercede with his father. But he did not find any satisfaction from her. Then he approached al-Ḥusayn b. ʿAlī b. Abī Ṭālib and Ibn Abī ʿAtīq and complained to them of his problem and of his father's refusal [to arrange the marriage]. Al-Ḥusayn said to him, "I will act on your behalf." And he went with him to Abū Lubnā who, when he saw him, greeted him, hurried to him and said, "O [grand]son of the Apostle of God, what has brought you [here]? Verily, you need only have sent for me and I would have come to you." He said, "The matter about which I have come must be resolved by you, for I have come to you in order to ask the hand of your daughter, Lubnā, on behalf of Qays b. Dharīḥ." He said, "O [grand]son of the Apostle of God, we would not disobey you on any matter and we have no desire for the girl. However, we would prefer that Dharīḥ, his father, ask for her and that [the request] emanate from him. For we fear, if his father does not act himself in this, it will result in bringing shame and disgrace upon us.

So al-Ḥusayn, may God be pleased with him, came to Dharīḥ and his tribe, when they were assembled together, and they rose to honor him, speaking to him as the Khuzāʿīs had. Then he said to Dharīḥ, "I adjure you to seek the hand of Lubnā for your son Qays." He said, "I hear and obey your command." So the two of them went out, together with the prominent men of the tribe, until they came to Lubnā, and Dharīḥ asked her father to marry [Lubnā] to [Qays], and he did so, and she was brought to him afterwards. She lived with him for a while without anyone expressing disapproval.

[Now] Qays was respectful of his mother to the utmost, but Lubnā, and his devotion to her, diverted him from that, somewhat, and his mother became very angry and said, "That woman has distracted my son from honoring me." No sooner had she said that than Qays became very ill. When he recovered from his sickness, his mother said to his father, "I was afraid that Qays would die without leaving descendents, for children are denied to that woman. You are a man of wealth, so that [if Qays dies], your property will pass to the daughter in-law (*al-kalāla*). Therefore, marry him to another woman—perhaps God will provide him with children." And she urged him to do that.

But he gave Qays leave for a while until, when his tribe had assembled, he called to him and said, "O Qays, verily you became ill, and I was afraid for you, [since] you have no son and I have none besides you. This woman is barren, so marry one of the daughters of your paternal uncle—perhaps God will give you a son by whom your name and ours will be established." Qays said, "I will never marry anyone else." His father said to him, "But I have abundant wealth, so [at least] take a concubine." He said, "I would never cause her distress, by God." His father said, "Then I adjure you to divorce her." But he refused, saying, "Death, by God, would be easier for me than that. But I will ask you to choose one of three options." He said, "What are they?" [Qays] said, "You marry [another woman], so that God might provide you with another son besides me." He said, "There is no benefit for me in that." He said, "Then let me take my tent (*ahlī*) and leave you. [Then] do what you would have done [viz., with your property] had I died during my illness." He said, "Not that one." He said, "Then I will deposit Lubnā with you and I will leave you—perhaps I might be diverted from her. For, in truth, I could not bear to have her in my sight (*khiyāl*) after having renounced her." He said, "No, I want you to divorce her."

[Dharīḥ] swore that he would not take umbrage under the roof of a house until [Qays] divorced Lubnā. And he would go out and stand in the heat of the sun, and Qays would come and stand next to him, shading him with his cloak, and [Qays] would burn in the heat of the sun until the shade would return. Then he would leave him and go to Lubnā. He would embrace her and she would embrace him. He would cry and she would cry with him. And she would say to him, "O Qays, do not obey your father, for you will perish and cause me to perish." He would say, "I will never submit to anyone about you." It is said, "He held out in that manner for a year." Khālid b. Kulthūm said, "Ibn ʿĀ'isha said that he stood his ground for forty days and then divorced her." But that is not correct. (*Kitāb al-aghānī*, IX, 2300–04)

Glossary

āḥād—an isolated report; one related by only one or two Companions

ʿahd—succession covenant; testament

ahl al-ḥadīth—traditionists

ahl al-farāʾiḍ—"sharers," i.e., recipients of a Qur'anic share

aqrabūna (pl. of *aqrab*)—relations, relatives

ʿaṣabiyya—group feeling, tribal solidarity

asbāb al-nuzūl—circumstances or occasions of the revelation

asbāb mutaʿaddida—multiple occasions, i.e., for a single verse

ʿāṣib, pl. *ʿaṣaba*—male agnate

ʿawl—proportional reduction of the Qur'anic shares

āya—a verse of the Qur'an

āyat al-farḍ—an inheritance verse

āyat al-mīrāth—an inheritance verse

dalāla—indication, sign

dalīl—indicator

dayn—debt

faqīh, pl. *fuqahāʾ*—legist

fiqh—law

ḥadīth—a report of a saying or action of the Prophet Muhammad, or such reports collectively

ḥudūd allāh—the bounds or restrictions that God placed on man's freedom of action

ḥujja—authoritative source; competent authority

ḥukm—judgment; ruling; law

iḍmār—ellipsis

ijmāʿ—consensus

ʿilm al-farāʾiḍ—"science of the shares," the Islamic law of inheritance

imām—leader, authority

imraʾa—woman; wife

isnād—the chain of authorities upon which a report is based

jāhiliyya—pre-Islamic times, the "age of ignorance"

kalāla—(a) one who dies leaving neither parent nor child, or, all the heirs with the exception of parents and children.
(b) a bride, daughter-in-law, or sister-in-law

katif—shoulder blade

khabar—predicate

khilāfa—caliphate; succession

kitāb—a written document; the Qur'an

marfūʿ—a report traced back to Muhammad

matn—the text of a report

muḥkama—in force, i.e., not abrogated

munqaṭiʿ—an *isnād* in which the authority of the second generation (Followers) is missing

mutawātir—a report passed on by numerous Companions, which was generally known from early times, and to which objections have never been raised

naskh—suppression; replacement; abrogation

naskh al-ḥukm dūna al-tilāwa—suppression of the ruling without suppressing the recitation

qāḍī—legal specialist; judge

qirāʾa—recitation

qiyās—analogy

radd—return of surplus to Qur'anic heirs

raʾy—personal opinion

sabab, pl. *asbāb*—cause; occasion; circumstance

ṣadāq—bride-price

ṣadaqa—gift; charity

Sharīʿa—the revealed law of Islam

shawāhid (pl. of *shāhid*)—a quotation serving as textual evidence

sunna—custom or precedent, especially of Muhammad

sūra—a chapter of the Qur'an

Sūrat al-Nisā'—the fourth chapter of the Qur'an: "Women"

Sūrat al-Baqara—the second chapter of the Qur'an: "The Cow"

ta'khīr al-bayān ʿan waqt al-khiṭāb—to delay clarification of the meaning of a verse until a time subsequent to its revelation

takhṣīṣ—specification

taqdīr—a grammatical emendation

tarika—an estate

tartīb—an arrangement or sequence of words or verses

tawātur—widespread circulation of a report

tilāwa—public reading; recital

ʿUmariyyatān—two similar problems related to the Islamic law of inheritance, the solutions of which are attributed to the second caliph, ʿUmar

Umma—the Muslim community

ʿuṣba—a group of men belonging to the same tribe

uṣūl al-fiqh—the sources of law; jurisprudence

walā'—patronage

al-walā' li'l-kubr—patronage belongs to the eldest

waqf—a charitable endowment

wārith, pl. *waratha*—heir(s)

waritha min—to inherit from

warratha—to award an inheritance to someone

wasiyya, pl. *waṣāya*—a bequest, legacy

al-waṣiyya fi'l-thulth—a bequest may not exceed one-third of the estate

lā waṣiyya li-wārith—no bequest to an heir

yūrathu—to be inherited from

yūrithu—to designate someone as an heir

yūṣī—to bequeath

Bibliography

Primary Sources

ʿAbd al-Ghanī b. Ismāʿīl al-Nābulusī. *Taʿṭīr al-anām fī taʿbīr al-manām.* 2 vols. in 1. Cairo: Dār Iḥyā' al-Kutub al-ʿArabiyya, 1972.

ʿAbd al-Razzāq al-Ṣanʿānī. See al-Ṣanʿānī, ʿAbd al-Razzāq.

Abū Dā'ūd. See al-ʿAẓīmābādī, Muhammad Shams al-Ḥaqq.

Abū al-Faraj al-Iṣbahānī. *Kitāb al-Aghānī.* Edited by ʿAbd Allāh al-Alaylī et al. 23 vols. Beirut: Dār al-Thaqāfa, 1955–61. New edition, edited by Ibrāhīm al-Ibyārī. 22 vols. Cairo: Dār al-Shaʿb, 1388–/1969–.

Abū Ghānim al-Khurāsānī al-Ibāḍī. *Kitāb al-mudawwana al-kubrā.* Edited by Muhammad b. Yūsuf ʿAtfīsh. Beirut: Dār al-Yaqẓa al-ʿArabiyya, 1974.

Abū Nuʿaym Aḥmad b. ʿAbd Allāh al-Iṣbahānī. *Ḥilyat al-awliyā' wa-ṭabaqāt al-aṣfiyā'.* 10 vols. Cairo: 1351–57/1932–38. Reprinted Beirut: Dār al-Kitāb al-ʿArabī, 1967–68.

Ahlwardt, W., ed. *Der Dīwān des Regezdichters Rūba ben El-'Aggāg.* Berlin, 1903. Reprinted Baghdad, 1968.

———. *The Diwans of Six Ancient Arab Poets.* London, 1870. Reprinted Osnabrück: Biblio Verlag, 1972.

al-Alūsī, Abū al-Faḍl Shihāb al-Dīn Maḥmūd b. ʿAbd Allāh. *Rūḥ al-maʿānī fī tafsīr al-qur'ān al-ʿaẓīm wa'l-sabʿ al-mathānī.* Edited by Muhammad Zuhrī al-Najjār. 30 vols. Cairo, 1964–.

al-Anṣārī, Abū Zayd. *Kitāb al-nawādir fi'l-lugha.* Edited by S. Kh. al-Shartuni. Beirut, 1894.

al-ʿAqqād, ʿAbbās Maḥmūd. *ʿAbqarīyat ʿUmar.* Cairo: Dār al-Hilāl, 1971.

al-Azharī, Muḥammad b. Aḥmad. *Tahdhīb al-lugha.* 15 vols. Edited by ʿAbd al-Salām Muhammad Hārūn. Cairo: al-Dār al-Miṣriyya li'l-ta'līf wa'l-tarjama, 1384–87/1964–67.

al-ʿAẓīmābādī, Muhammad Shams al-Ḥaqq. *ʿAwn al-maʿbūd: sharh sunan Abī Dā'ūd*. Edited by ʿAbd al-Raḥmān Muhammad ʿUthmān. 14 vols. 2d ed. al-Madīna al-Munawwara: al-Maktaba al-Salafiyya, 1968–69.

al-Baghdādī. *Kitāb al-munammaq fī akhbār quraish*. Edited by Kh. A. Fariq. Hayderabad, 1384/1964.

al-Balādhurī, Aḥmad b. Yahyā. *Ansāb al-ashrāf*. Vol. IVb. Edited by M. Schloessinger. Jerusalem: The Magnes Press, 1938.

al-Baydāwī, ʿAbd Allāh b. ʿUmar. *Anwār al-tanzīl wa-asrār al-ta'wīl*. Edited by H. O. Fleischer. 2 vols. 1st ed., 1846–1848. Reprinted Osnabrück: Biblio Verlag, 1968.

al-Bayhaqī, Abū Bakr Aḥmad b. al-Husayn. *al-Sunan al-kubrā*. 10 vols. Hayderabad, A.H. 1344–57. Reprinted Beirut: Dār Ṣādir, 1968.

Bevan, A. A., ed. *Kitāb naqā'id Jarīr wa'l-Farazdak*. Leiden: E. J. Brill, 1905.

Bint al-Shāṭiʿ, [pseud]. *al-Iʿjāz al-bayānī li'l-qur'ān wa-masā'il Ibn al-Azraq*. Cairo: Dār al-Maʿārif, 1391/1971.

al-Bukhārī, Muhammad b. Ismāʿīl. *Kitāb al-ta'rīkh al-kabīr*. 4 vols. in 8. Hayderabad: Dā'irat al-Maʿārif al-ʿUthmāniyya, 1360–84/ 1941–64.

———. *Ṣaḥīḥ*. Edited by M. Ludolf Krehl and Th. W. Juynboll. 4 vols. Leiden: E. J. Brill, 1862–98.

Cheikho, L., ed. *Le Kitāb al-Ḥamāsa de Abū ʿUbādat al-Buḥturī*. Beirut, 1910. Reprinted Beirut: Dār al-Kitāb al-ʿArabī, 1967.

al-Dānī, Abū ʿAmr ʿUthmān b. Saʿīd. *Kitāb al-taysīr fi'l-qirā'āt al-sabʿ*. Edited by Otto Pretzl. Bibliotheca Islamica, 2. Istanbul, 1930. Reprinted Baghdad, 1964.

al-Dāwūdī, Muhammad b. ʿAlī. *Ṭabaqāt al-mufassirīn*. Edited by ʿAlī Muhammad ʿUmar. 2 vols. Cairo: Maktabat Wahba, 1392/1972.

al-Dhahabī, Muhammad b. Aḥmad. *al-ʿIbar fī khabar man ghabar*. Edited by Ṣalāḥ al-Dīn al-Munajjid and Fu'ād Sayyid. 4 vols. Kuwait: Dā'irat al-Maṭbuʿāt wa'l-Nashr, 1960.

———. *al-Kāshif fī maʿrifat man lahu riwāya fi'l-kutub al-sitta*. Edited by ʿIzzat ʿAlī ʿĪd ʿAṭiyya and Mūsā Muhammad ʿAlī al-Muwashshī. 3 vols. Cairo: Dār al-Kutub al-Ḥadītha, 1392/1972.

———. *Kitāb tadhkirat al-ḥuffāẓ*. 4th ed. 4 vols. Hayderabad: Majlis Dā'irat al-Maʿārif al-ʿUthmāniyya, 1388–/1968–.

———. *Mīzān al-iʿtidāl fī naqd al-rijāl*. Edited by ʿAlī Muhammad al-Bajāwī. 4 vols. Cairo: Dār Iḥyā' al-Kutub al-ʿArabiyya, 1382/1963.

———. *Talkhīṣ al-mustadrak*, on the margin of al-Ḥākim al-Nīsābūrī, *al-Mustadrak*. 4 vols. Riyad: Maktabat al-Naṣr al-Ḥadītha, 1968.

al-Fārisī, Abū ʿAlī al-Ḥasan b. Aḥmad. *al-Ḥujja fī ʿilal al-qirā'āt al-sabʿ*. Edited by ʿAlī al-Najdī Nāṣif, et al. Cairo: Dār al-Kātib al-ʿArabī, 1385/1965.

Freytag, G. W., ed. *Hamasae Carmina*. 2 vols. in 3. Bonn, 1828–51.

al-Ḥākim al-Nīsābūrī, Abū ʿAbd Allāh Muhammad. *al-Mustadrak ʿalā al-ṣaḥīḥayn fi'l-ḥadīth*. 4 vols. Riyad: Maktabat al-Naṣr al-Ḥadītha, 1968.

al-Ḥumaydī, ʿAbd Allāh b. al-Zubayr. *al-Musnad*. Edited by Ḥabīb al-Raḥmān al-Aʿẓamī. 2 vols. Karachi: Majlis ʿIlmī, 1382/1963.

Ibn ʿAbd al-Barr, Yūsuf b. ʿAbd Allāh. *al-Istīʿāb fī maʿrifat al-aṣḥāb*. Edited by ʿAlī Muhammad al-Bajāwī. 4 vols. Cairo: Maktabat Nahdat Miṣr, 196–.

Ibn Abī al-Ḥadīd, ʿAbd al-Ḥamīd b. Hibat Allāh. *Sharḥ nahj al-balāghah*. Edited by Muhammad Abū al-Faḍl Ibrāhīm. 20 vols. Cairo: ʿĪsā al-Bābī al-Ḥalabī, 1965–67.

Ibn Abī Shaybah, ʿAbd Allāh b. Muhammad. *Muṣannaf Ibn Abī Shaybah*. Edited by ʿAbd al-Khāliq Khān al-Afghānī. 5 vols. Hayderabad: Anṣārī Lāj, 1966–.

Ibn al-Anbārī, Abū al-Barakāt ʿAbd al-Raḥmān b. Muhammad. *al-Bayān fī gharīb iʿrāb al-qur'ān*. Edited by Ṭāhā ʿAbd al-Ḥamīd Ṭāhā. 2 vols. Cairo, 1969–70.

Ibn al-Anbārī, Muhammad b. al-Qāsim. *Kitāb Īḍāḥ al-waqf wa'l-ibtidā'*. Edited by Muḥyī al-Dīn ʿAbd al-Raḥmān Ramaḍān. 2 vols. Damascus: al-Maṭbaʿah al-Taʿāwuniyya, 1390/1971.

Ibn al-ʿArabī, Muhammad b. ʿAbd Allāh. *Aḥkām al-qur'ān*. Edited by ʿAlī Muhammad al-Bajāwī. 2d ed. 4 vols. Cairo: ʿĪsā al-Bābī al-Ḥalabī, 1387–88/1967–68.

Ibn ʿAṭiyya al-Andalusī. *al-Muḥarrar al-wajīz fī tafsīr al-kitāb al-ʿazīz*. Edited by Aḥmad Ṣādiq al-Mallāḥ. Cairo: al-Majlis al-Aʿlā li'l-Shu'ūn al-Islāmiyya. New edition, Fez: al-Majlis al-ʿIlmī, 1397–/1977–.

Ibn Ḥajar al-ʿAsqalānī, Aḥmad b. ʿAlī. *al-ʿIṣāba fī tamyīz al-ṣaḥāba*. Edited by Ṭāhā Muhammad al-Zaynī. 13 vols. Cairo: Maktabat al-Kulliyyāt al-Azhariyya, 1969–77. New edition, edited by ʿAlī Muhammad al-Bajāwī. 8 vols. Cairo: Dār Nahdat Miṣr, 1970–72.

———. *Tahdhīb al-tahdhīb*. 12 vols. Hayderabad: Dā'irat al-Maʿārif al-Niẓāmiyya, 1325–27/1907–09. Reprinted Beirut: Dār Ṣādir, 1968.

Ibn Ḥanbal, Aḥmad b. Muhammad. *Musnad al-Imām Aḥmad b. Ḥanbal*. 6 vols. Cairo, 1895. Reprinted Beirut: al-Maktab al-Islāmī li'l-Ṭabāʿa wa'l-Nashr, 1969. New edition, edited by Aḥmad Muhammad Shākir. 17 vols. Cairo: Dār al-Maʿārif, 1954–75.

Ibn Ḥazm, ʿAlī b. Aḥmad. *Fī maʿrifat al-nāsikh wa'l-mansūkh*. On the margin of al-Maḥallī, *Tafsīr*. Cairo: Dār al-Qalam, 1966.

———. *Ḥijjat al-wadāʿ*. Edited by Mamdūḥ Ḥaqqī. 2d ed. Beirut: Dār al-Yaqẓa al-ʿArabiyya, 1966.

———. *al-Iḥkām fī uṣūl al-aḥkām*. 2 vols. Cairo: Maṭbaʿat al-ʿĀṣimah, 1968.

———. *al-Muḥallā*. Edited by Zaydān Abū al-Makāram Ḥasan and Ḥasan Zaydān Ṭulbah. 12 vols. Cairo: Maktabat al-Jumhūriyya al-ʿArabiyya, 1967–71.

Ibn Ḥibbān, Muhammad. *Kitāb al-majrūḥīn min al-muḥaddithīn*. Edited by ʿAzīz al-Qādirī al-Naqshbandī. 2 vols. Hayderabad: al-Maṭbaʿa al-ʿAzīziyya, 1390–/1970–.

———. *Kitāb mashāhīr ʿulamā' al-amṣār*. Edited by Manfred Fleischhammer. Bibliotheca Islamica, 22. Cairo: Maṭbaʿat Lajnat al-Ta'līf wa'l-Tarjama wa'l-Nashr, 1379/1959.

———. *Kitāb al-thiqāt fī al-ṣaḥāba wa'l-tābiʿīn*. Edited by ʿAbd al-Khāliq al-Afghānī. Hayderabad: al-Majmaʿ al-ʿIlmī, 1388/1968.

Ibn Hishām, ʿAbd al-Malik. *Kitāb sīrat rasūl allāh*. Edited by F. Wüstenfeld. 2 vols. in 3. Göttingen: Dieterichsche Universitäts-Buchhandlung, 1858–60.

Ibn Jinnī, Abū al-Fatḥ ʿUthmān. *al-Muḥtasib fī wujūh shawādhdh al-qirā'āt wa'l-īḍāḥ ʿanhā*. Edited by ʿAlī al-Najdī Nāṣif et al. 2 vols. Cairo: Sharikat al-Iʿlānāt al-Sharqiyya, 1386–/1966–.

Ibn Juzayy, Muhammad b. Aḥmad. *Kitāb al-tashīl li-ʿulūm al-tanzīl*. Edited by Muhammad ʿAbd al-Munʿim al-Yūnusī and Ibrāhīm ʿAṭwah ʿAwaḍ. 4 vols. Cairo: Dār al-Kutub al-Ḥadītha, 1973–.

Ibn Kathīr, Abū al-Fidā' Ismāʿīl b. ʿUmar. *Tafsīr al-qur'ān al-ʿaẓīm*. 4 vols. Cairo: Dār al-Kutub, 1970.

Ibn Khālawayh, Ḥusayn b. Aḥmad. *al-Ḥujja fi'l-qirā'āt al-sabʿ*. Edited by ʿAbd al-ʿĀl Sālim Makram. Beirut: Dār al-Shurūq, 1971.

———. *Mukhtaṣar fī shawādhdh al-qur'ān*. Edited by G. Bergsträsser. Bibliotheca Islamica, 7. Leipzig, 1934. Reprinted Baghdad: Maktabat al-Muthannā, 1968.

Ibn Khaldūn. *The Muqaddimah: An Introduction to History*. Translated by Franz Rosenthal. Bollingen Series XLIII. 3 vols. 2d ed. Princeton: Princeton University Press, 1967.

Ibn Māja, Abū ʿAbd Allāh Muhammad b. Yazīd. *Sunan*. Edited by Muhammad Fu'ād ʿAbd al-Bāqī. 2 vols. Cairo: ʿĪsā al-Bābī al-Ḥalabī, 1972.

Ibn Manẓūr, Muhammad b. Mukarram. *Lisān al-ʿarab*. 15 vols. Beirut: Dār Ṣādir, 1955–56.

Ibn Mujāhid, Aḥmad b. Mūsā. *Kitāb al-sabʿa fi'l-qirā'āt*. Edited by Shawkī Ḍayf. Cairo: Dār al-Maʿārif, 1972.

Ibn Qayyim al-Jawziyya. *Sharḥ sunan Abī Dā'ūd*. Edited by ʿAbd al-Raḥmān Muhammad ʿUthmān. 2d ed. 14 vols. al-Madīna al-Munawwara: al-Maktaba al-Salafiyya, 1388–89/1968–69.

Ibn Qudāmah, Muwaffaq al-Dīn ʿAbd Allāh b. Aḥmad. *al-Mughnī*. Edited by Muhammad Khalīl Har'as. 10 vols. Cairo: Maṭbaʿat al-Imām, 1964.

Ibn Qutayba, ʿAbd Allāh b. Muslim. *al-Shiʿr waʾl-shuʿarāʾ*. Edited by A. M. Shakir. Cairo: Dār al-Maʿārif, 1387/1967.

———. *Taʾwīl mukhtalif al-ḥadīth*. Edited by Muhammad Zuhrī al-Najjār. Cairo: Maktabat al-Kulliyāt al-Azhariyya, 1386/1966. Translated by Gérard Lecomte as *Le Traité des Divergences du Ḥadīṯ d'Ibn Qutayba*. Damascus: Institut Français, 1962.

———. *Taʾwīl mushkil al-qurʾān*. Edited by Aḥmad Ṣaqr. Cairo: Dār al-Turāth, 1393/1973.

Ibn Rushd al-Qurṭubī, Muhammad b. Aḥmad. *Bidāyat al-mujtahid wa-nihāyat al-muqtaṣid*. 2 vols. Cairo: Maktabat al-Kulliyyāt al-Azhariyya, 1386–89/1966–69.

Ibn Saʿd, Muhammad. *al-Ṭabaqāt al-kubrā*. 9 vols. Beirut: Dār Ṣādir, 1957–68.

Ibn Salāmah, Abū al-Qāsim Hibat Allāh. *al-Nāsikh waʾl-mansūkh*. Cairo, 1379/1960.

Ibn Shuʿbah, Saʿīd b. Manṣūr. *Kitāb al-sunan*. Edited by Ḥabīb al-Raḥmān al-Aʿẓamī. Vol. 3. Dabhil: Majlis ʿIlmī, 1967–.

Ibn al-Sikkīt. *Iṣlāḥ al-manṭiq*. Edited by Aḥmad Muhammad Shākir and ʿAbd al-Salām Muhammad Hārūn. 3d ed. Cairo: Dār al-Maʿārif, 1970.

Ibn Taymiyyah, ʿAbd al-Salām b. ʿAbd Allāh. *al-Muntaqā min aḥādīth al-aḥkām*. Cairo: al-Maṭbaʿa al-Salafiyya, 196–.

Ibn al-Turkomanī, ʿAlī b. ʿUthmān. *al-Jawhar al-naqī*. On the margin of Bayhaqī, *al-Sunan al-kubrā*. 10 vols. Hayderabad, A.H. 1344–57. Reprinted Beirut: Dār Ṣādir, 1968.

al-Jaṣṣāṣ Aḥmad b. ʿAlī. *Kitāb aḥkām al-qurʾān*. 3 vols. in 2. Istanbul: Maṭbaʿat al-Awqāf al-Islāmiyya, 1335–38/1917–20.

Jeffery, Arthur, comp. *Two Muqaddimas to the Qur'anic Sciences*. Cairo: Maktabat al-Khānijī, 1972.

al-Khaṭīb al-Tibrīzī, Muhammad b. ʿAbd Allāh. *Mishkāt al-Maṣābīḥ*. Edited by Muhammad Nāṣir al-Dīn al-Albānī. 3 vols. Damascus: al-Maktab al-Islāmī liʾl-Ṭabāʿa waʾl-Nashr, 1381–82/1961–62.

Khaṭṭāb, Maḥmūd Shīt. *ʿUmar b. al-Khaṭṭāb: al-fārūq al-qāʾid*. 2d ed. Beirut: Dār Maktabat al-Ḥayāt, 1385/1966.

al-Khazrajī, Aḥmad b. ʿAbd Allāh. *Khulāṣat tadhhīb tahdhīb al-kamāl fī asmāʾ al-rijāl*. Edited by Maḥmūd ʿAbd al-Wahhāb Fāyid. 3 vols. Cairo: 1301/1883. Reprinted Cairo: Maktabat al-Qāhira, 1971–.

Krenkow, F., ed. *Ḥamāsat Ibn al-Shajarī*. Hayderabad, 1354.

Lyall, Sir Charles, ed. and tr. *The Diwans of ʿAbīd ibn al-Abras, of Asad, and ʿĀmir ibn al-Ṭufail, of ʿĀmir ibn Saʿsaʿah*. Gibb Memorial Series, vol. 21. London: Luzac and Leiden: E. J. Brill, 1917.

MacCartney, C. H. H., ed. *The Dīwān of Ghailān ibn ʿUqbah, known as Dhu'r-Rumma*. Cambridge: Cambridge University Press, 1919.

al-Maḥallī, Jalāl al-Dīn Muhammad b. Aḥmad, and al-Suyūṭī, Jalāl al-Dīn ʿAbd al-Raḥmān b. Abī Bakr. *Tafsīr al-qur'ān al-karīm*, Cairo: Dār al-Qalam, 1966.

Malaṭī, Muhammad b. Aḥmad. *Kitāb al-tanbīh wa'l-radd ʿalā ahl al-ahwā' wa'l-bidaʿ*. Bibliotheca Islamica, 9. Istanbul: Maṭbaʿat al-Dawla, 1936.

Mālik b. Anas. *al-Muwaṭṭa'*. Edited by Muhammad Fu'ād ʿAbd al-Bāqī. 2 vols. Cairo: Dār Iḥyā' al-Kutub al-ʿArabiyya, 1951.

al-Maqrīzī, Aḥmad b. ʿAlī. *Maʿrifat mā yajibu li-āl al-bayt al-nabawī*. Edited by Muhammad Aḥmad ʿĀshūr. 2d ed. Cairo: Dār al-Iʿtiṣām, 1393/1973.

al-Marzūqī, Abū ʿAlī. *Sharḥ dīwān al-ḥamāsa*. Edited by Aḥmad Amīn and ʿAbd al-Salām Hārūn. Cairo: Lajnat al-Ta'līf wa'l-Tarjama, 1371/1952.

Muḥaysin, Muhammad Sālim. *al-Irshādāt al-jaliyya fi'l-qirā'āt al-sabʿ*. Cairo: Maktabat al-Kulliyyāt al-Azhariyya, 1389/1969.

———. *al-Muhadhdhab fi'l-qirā'āt al-ʿashr*. Cairo: Maktabat al-Kulliyyāt al-Azhariyya, 1969–.

Muqātil b. Sulaymān. *Kitāb tafsīr al-khams mi'āt āya min al-qur'ān*. Edited by Isaiah Goldfeld. Shfaram: al-Mashriq Press, 1980.

Muslim b. al-Ḥajjāj al-Qushayrī. *Ṣaḥīḥ*. Edited by Muhammad Fu'ād ʿAbd al-Bāqī. 5 vols. Cairo: Dār Iḥyā' al-Kutub al-ʿArabiyya, 1375/1955.

al-Muttaqī al-Hindī, ʿAlī b. ʿAbd al-Malik. *Kanz al-ʿummāl fī sunan al-aqwāl wa'l-afʿāl*. Edited by Muhammad ʿAbd al-Muʿīd Khān. 2d ed. 22 vols. Hayderabad: Dā'irat al-Maʿārif al-ʿUthmāniyya, 1364–95/1945–75.

al-Nadīm, Abū al-Faraj. *al-Fihrist*. Edited and translated by Bayard Dodge as *The Fihrist of al-Nadīm: A Tenth-Century Survey of Muslim Culture*. 2 vols. Records of Civilization: Sources and Studies, no. LXXXIII. New York: Columbia University Press, 1970.

al-Naḥḥās, Abū Jaʿfar Aḥmad b. Muhammad. *Kitāb al-nāsikh wa'l-mansūkh fi'l-qur'ān al-karīm*. Cairo: al-Maktaba al-ʿĀlamiyya, 1357/1938.

al-Nasafī, Abū al-Barakāt ʿAbd Allāh. *Tafsīr al-Nasafī*. 4 vols. Beirut: Dār al-Kitāb al-ʿArabī, 1967.

al-Nasā'ī, Aḥmad b. Shuʿayb. *Sunan*. 8 vols. Cairo: Muṣṭafā al-Bābī al-Ḥalabī, 1383–84/1964–65.

al-Nīsābūrī, Niẓām al-Dīn al-Ḥasan b. Muhammad. *Gharā'ib al-qur'ān wa-raghā'ib al-furqān*. Edited by Ibrāhīm ʿAṭwah ʿAwaḍ. 30 vols. in 10. Cairo: Muṣṭafā al-Bābī al-Ḥalabī, 1962–70.

al-Qāḍī, ʿAbd al-Fattāḥ. *Sharḥ al-naẓm al-jāmiʿ li-qirā'āt al-imām Nāfiʿ*. 2d ed. Tanta: al-Maktaba al-Islāmiyya al-Tijāriyya, 1961.

al-Qarāfī, Aḥmad b. Idrīs. *al-Dhakhīrah.* Cairo: Maṭbaᶜat Kulliyyāt al-Sharīᶜa, 1381/1961.

al-Qasṭallānī, Aḥmad b. Muhammad. *Irshād al-sārī li-sharḥ ṣaḥīḥ al-Bukhārī.* 10 vols. Bulaq, 1886–88. Reprinted Beirut: Dār Ṣādir, 1971.

———. *Laṭā'if al-ishārāt li-funūn al-qirā'āt.* Edited by ᶜĀmir al-Sayyid ᶜUthmān and ᶜAbd al-Ṣābūr Shāhīn. Cairo: Lajnat Iḥyā' al-Turāth al-Islāmī, 1972–.

al-Qurṭubī, Abū ᶜAbd Allāh Muhammad b. Aḥmad. *al-Jāmiᶜ li-aḥkām al-qur'ān.* 20 vols. Cairo: Dār al-Kātib al-ᶜArabī, 1387/1967.

al-Rāghib al-Iṣfahānī, Abū al-Qāsim al-Ḥusayn b. Muhammad. *al-Mufradāt fī gharīb al-qur'ān.* Edited by Muhammad Aḥmad Khalaf Allāh. 2 vols. Cairo: al-Maṭbaᶜa al-Fanniyya al-Ḥadītha, 1970.

al-Rāzī, Fakhr al-Dīn. *al-Tafsīr al-kabīr.* Edited by Muhammad Muḥyī al-Dīn ᶜAbdulḥamīd. 32 vols. Cairo: al-Maṭbaᶜa al-Bahiyya, 1934–62.

Riḍā, Rashīd. *Tafsīr al-qur'ān al-karīm,* known as *Tafsīr al-manār.* 12 vols. Cairo, A.H. 1346–66.

al-Ṣafadī, Khalīl b. Aybak. *al-Wāfī bi'l-wafayāt.* Edited by H. Ritter et al. Bibliotheca Islamica, 6. Wiesbaden: Franz Steiner, 1962–.

Ṣafwat, Aḥmad Zakī. *Jamharat rasā'il al-ᶜarab fī ᶜuṣūr al-ᶜarabiyya al-zāhira.* 4 vols. Cairo: Muṣṭafā al-Bābī al-Ḥalabī, 1937–38.

al-Ṣanᶜānī, ᶜAbd al-Razzāq b. Ḥammām. *al-Muṣannaf.* Edited by Ḥabīb al-Raḥmān al-Aᶜẓamī. 11 vols. Karachi: Majlis ᶜIlmī, 1390–92/1970–72.

al-Sāwī al-Mālikī, Aḥmad b. Muhammad. *Bulghat al-sālik li-aqrab al-masālik ilā madhhab al-imām Mālik.* 3 vols. Cairo: ᶜĪsā al-Bābī al-Ḥalabī, 1978.

al-Shāfiᶜī, Muhammad b. Idrīs. *al-Umm.* Edited by Muhammad Zuhrī al-Najjār. 8 vols. Cairo: Maktabat al-Kulliyyāt al-Azhariyya, 1961.

———. *al-Risāla.* Edited by Muhammad Sayyid Kaylānī. Cairo: Muṣṭafā al-Bābī al-Ḥalabī, 1388/1969. Translated by Majid Khadduri as *Islamic Jurisprudence: Shāfiᶜī's Risāla.* Baltimore: Johns Hopkins Press, 1961.

al-Shawkānī, Muhammad b. ᶜAlī. *Nayl al-awṭār.* 2d ed. 8 vols. in 4. Cairo: Muṣṭafā al-Bābī al-Ḥalabī, 1952.

Shiblī, Maḥmūd. *Ḥayāt ᶜUmar.* Cairo: Maktabat al-Qāhira, 1388/1968.

Sufyān b. Saᶜīd al-Thawrī. *Tafsīr al-qur'ān al-karīm.* Edited by Imtiyāz ᶜAlī ᶜArshī. Raza Library Publication Series, 13. Rampur, 1965.

al-Suyūṭī, Jalāl al-Dīn ᶜAbd al-Raḥmān. *Bughyat al-wuᶜāh fī ṭabaqāt al-lughawiyyīn wa'l-nuḥāt.* Edited by Muhammad Abū al-Faḍl Ibrāhīm. 2 vols. Cairo: Maṭbaᶜat ᶜĪsā al-Bābī al-Ḥalabī, 1964–65.

———. *al-Itqān fī ᶜulūm al-qur'ān.* Edited by Mowlawies Basheerood-Deen. Calcutta: Asiatic Society of Bengal, 1853–54.

———. *al-La'ālī al-maṣnū'ah fi'l-aḥādīth al-mawḍū'a.* 2 vols. in 1. Cairo: al-Maktaba al-Tijāniyya al-Kubrā, 196–.

———. *Lubāb al-nuqūl fī asbāb al-nuzūl.* On the margin of al-Maḥallī, *Tafsīr.* Cairo: Dār al-Qalam, 1966.

———. *Mu'tarak al-aqrān fī i'jāz al-qur'ān.* Edited by 'Alī Muhammad al-Bajāwī. 3 vols. Cairo: Dār al-Fikr al-'Arabī, 1969–.

al-Ṭabarī, Abū Ja'far Muhammad. *Jāmi' al-bayān 'an ta'wīl āy al-qur'ān.* 3d ed. 30 vols. in 12. Cairo: Muṣṭafā al-Bābī al-Ḥalabī, 1954–68.

———. *Ta'rīkh al-rusul wa'l-mulūk.* Edited by Muhammad Abū al-Faḍl Ibrāhīm. 2d ed. 10 vols. Cairo: Dār al-Ma'ārif, 1960–69.

al-Ṭabarsī, Abū al-Faḍl b. al-Ḥasan. *Majma' al-bayān li-'ulūm al-qur'ān.* 12 vols. Cairo: Dār al-Taqrīb Bayna al-Madhāhib al-Islāmiyya, 1958–.

al-Ṭabāṭabā'ī, Muhammad Ḥusayn. *al-Mīzān fī tafsīr al-qur'ān.* 5 vols. Beirut: al-Maṭba'a al-Tijāriyya, 1970–.

al-Tirmidhī, Abū 'Īsā Muhammad b. 'Īsā. *Sunan al-Tirmidhī.* Edited by 'Abd al-Wahhāb 'Abd al-Laṭīf and 'Abd al-Raḥmān Muhammad 'Uthmān. 5 vols. Cairo: al-Maktaba al-Salafiyya, 1965–67.

Ṭulaymāt, 'Abd al-Qādir Aḥmad. *Sa'd b. Abī Waqqāṣ.* Cairo: Dār al-Qalam, 1961.

al-Ṭūsī, Muhammad b. al-Ḥasan. *al-Nihāya fī mujarrad al-fiqh wa'l-fatāwā.* Beirut: Dār al-Kitāb al-'Arabī, 1390/1970.

al-Wāḥidī, 'Alī b. Aḥmad. *Asbāb nuzūl al-qur'ān.* Edited by Aḥmad Ṣaqr. Cairo: Dār al-Kitāb al-Jadīd, 1389/1969.

al-Wāqidī, Muhammad b. 'Umar. *Kitāb al-maghāzī.* Edited by Marsden Jones. 3 vols. London: Oxford University Press, 1966.

Ya'qūb b. Shaybah. *Musnad 'Umar b. al-Khaṭṭāb.* Edited by Sāmi Ḥaddād. Beirut, 1359/1940.

al-Ya'qūbī, Aḥmad b. Abī Ya'qūb. *Ta'rīkh al-Ya'qūbī.* Edited by Muhammad Ṣādiq. 3 vols. Najaf: al-Maktaba al-Haydariyya, 1384/1964.

al-Zamakhsharī, Abū al-Qāsim Maḥmūd b. 'Umar. *al-Kashshāf 'an haqā'iq ghawāmiḍ al-tanzīl.* 4 vols. Beirut: Dār al-Kitāb al-'Arabī, 1947.

Secondary Sources

Abbott, Nabia. *Studies in Arabic Literary Papyri.* 3 vols. Oriental Institute Publications, vols. 75–77. Chicago: University of Chicago Press, 1957–72.

Adams, Charles J. "Islamic Religious Tradition." In *The Study of the Middle East: Research and Scholarship in the Humanities and Social Sciences,* edited by L. Binder. New York: John Wiley & Sons, 1976.

Adontz, Nicholas. *Armenia in the Period of Justinian: The Political Conditions Based on the Naxarar System.* Translated by Nina Garsoïan. Lisbon, 1970.

Ali, Maulana Muhammad. *Early Caliphate.* 2d ed. Lahore: Ahmadiyya Anjuman-i-Ishaʿat-i-Islam, 1947.

el-Ali, Saleh A. "Muslim Estates in the Hidjaz in the First Century A.H." *Journal of the Economic and Social History of the Orient* 2 (1959): 247–61.

Anderson, J. N. D. "Recent Developments in *Sharīʿa* Law, IX: The Waqf System." *The Muslim World* 42 (1952): 257–76.

———. *Islamic Law in the Modern World.* New York: New York University Press, 1959.

Anees, Munawar Ahmad and Athar, ʿĀlia Nasreen, eds. *Ḥadīth and Sīra Literature in Western Languages: A Bibliographic Study.* n.p., 1980.

Anwar ul-Haqq. *Abrogation in the Koran.* Lucknow: Methodist Publishing House, 1925.

Aptowitzer, V. "The Controversy over the Syro-Roman Code." *Jewish Quarterly Review,* New Series 2 (1911–12): 55–74.

Arkoun, Muhammad. "Comment lire le Coran?" In *Le Coran.* French translation by Kazimirski. Garnier-Flammarion, 1970.

———. *Essais sur la pensée islamique.* Vol. 1. Paris: G.-P. Maisonneuve et Larose, 1973.

———. "Lecture de la Fâtiḥa." In *Mélanges d'islamologie,* 1, edited by Pierre Salmon. Leiden: E. J. Brill, 1974.

———. "Manifestations of Arab Thought in Western Islam." *Diogenes* 93 (1976): 105–33.

———. "Le problème de l'authenticité divine du Coran." In *Recherches d'islamologie: recueil d'articles offerts à Georges C. Anawati et Louis Gardet par leurs collègues et amis.* Bibliothèque philosophique de Louvain, 26. Louvain: Peeters, 1977.

———. *Lectures du Coran.* Paris: G.-P. Maisonneuve et Larose, 1982.

Arnaldez, Roger. *Grammaire et théologie chez Ibn Ḥazm de Cordoue: Essai sur la structure et les conditions de la pensée musulmane.* Paris: Librairie Philosophique J. Vrin, 1956.

Asad, Talal. *The Kababish Arabs: Power, Authority, and Consent in a Nomadic Tribe.* New York: Praeger, 1970.

Aswad, Barbara. *Property Control and Social Strategies in Settlers in a Middle Eastern Plain.* Ann Arbor: University of Michigan, 1971.

Azami, Mohammad Mustafa. *Studies in Early Ḥadīth Literature: With a Critical Edition of Some Early Texts.* Indianapolis: American Trust Publications, 1978.

Baer, Gabriel. *Population and Society in the Arab East.* Translated from Hebrew by Hannah Szoke. London: Routledge & K. Paul, 1964.

Baljon, J. M. S. *Modern Muslim Koran Interpretation (1880–1960).* Leiden: E. J. Brill, 1961.

Barth, Fredrik. *Nomads of South-Persia: The Basseri Tribe of the Khamseh Confederacy.* The Little, Brown series in anthropology. Boston: Little, Brown, 1961.

Beck, Lois, and Keddie, Nikkie, eds. *Women in the Muslim World.* Cambridge: Harvard University Press, 1978.

Beeston, A. F. L. "Notes on South Arabian Lexicography, XII." *Le Muséon* 94 (1981): 55–74.

Bell, Richard. *Introduction to the Qur'an.* Edinburgh: Edinburgh University Press, 1953.

Ben-Barak, Zafira. "Inheritance by Daughters in the Ancient Near East." *Journal of Semitic Studies* 25 (1980): 22–33.

Berger, Morroe. *The Arab World Today.* New York: Anchor Books, 1964.

Bergsträsser, G. "Die Koranlesung des Hasan von Basra." *Islamica* 2 (1926): 11–57.

Bialoblocki, Samuel. *Materialien zum islamischen und jüdischen Eherecht.* Giesen: Alfred Töpelmann, 1928.

Bijlefeld, William A. "Some Recent Contributions to Qur'anic Studies: Selected Publications in English, French, and German: 1964–1973." *The Muslim World* 64 (1974): 79–102, 172–79, 259–74.

Birkeland, Harris. *Old Muslim Opposition Against Interpretation of the Koran.* Avhandlinger utgitt av Det Norske Videnskaps-Akademi i Oslo ii. Hist.-Filos. Klasse, No. 1. Oslo: I Kommisjon Hos Jacob Dybwad, 1955.

Blachère, Régis. "L'allocution de Mahomet lors du Pèlerinage d'Adieu." In *Mélanges Louis Massignon.* Vol. 1. Damascus: Institut Français de Damas, 1956–.

———. *Introduction au Coran.* Paris: G.-P. Maisonneuve, 1959.

Boulos, M. M. F. *La succession en droit musulman: Son origine et son évolution.* Paris: Jouve, 1925.

Bousquet, G.-H. and Peltier, F. *Les successions agnatiques mitigées: Etude comparée du régime successoral en droit germanique et en droit musulman.* L'Institut d'Etudes Orientales de la Faculté des Lettres d'Alger, 1. Paris: Librairie Orientaliste Paul Geuthner, 1935.

Bravmann, M. M. *The Spiritual Background of Early Islam: Studies in Ancient Arab Concepts.* Leiden: E. J. Brill, 1972.

———. *Studies in Semitic Philology.* Leiden: E. J. Brill, 1977.

Brugman, J. "The Islamic Law of Inheritance." In *Essays on Oriental Laws of Succession,* edited by M. David et al. Leiden: E. J. Brill, 1969.

Bruns, Karl G., ed. and tr. *Syrisch-römisches Rechtsbuch aus dem fünften Jahrhundert.* Leipzig, 1880. Reprinted Aalen: Scientia, 1961.

Brunschvig, Robert. *Etudes d'islamologie.* 2 vols. Paris: G.-P. Maisonneuve et Larose, 1976.

Buckland, W. W. *A Text-book of Roman Law from Augustus to Justinian.* 3d ed. Edited and revised by Peter Stein. Cambridge: Cambridge University Press, 1963.

Burling, Robbins. *The Passage of Power.* New York: Academic Press, 1974.

Burton, John. "Those are the High-Flying Cranes." *Journal of Semitic Studies* 15 (1970): 246–65.

———. "The Meaning of *Iḥṣān.*" *Journal of Semitic Studies* 19 (1974): 47–76.

———. *The Collection of the Quran.* Cambridge: Cambridge University Press, 1977.

Caetani, Leone. *Annali dell'Islam.* Vol. 5. Milan: Ulrico Hoepli, 1912.

Chejne, Anwar G. *Succession to the Rule in Islam: With Special Reference to the Early ʿAbbasid Period.* Lahore: Sh. Muhammad Ashraf, 1960.

———. *Ibn Hazm.* Chicago: Kazi Publications, 1982.

Chelhod, Joseph. *Le droit dans la société bédouine: recherches ethnologiques sur l'orf ou droit coutoumier des Bédouins.* Paris: M. Rivière, 1971.

Cherbonneau, E. and Sautraya, E. *Droit musulman: Du statut personnel et des successions.* 2 vols. Paris: Maisonneuve, 1873–74.

Chirri, Mohammad Jawad. *The Brother of the Prophet Mohammad (The Imam Ali): An Extensive Research of the Shiʿite Islamic School of Thought.* Detroit: The Islamic Center, 1979.

Chouemi, Moustapha. *Le verbe dans le Coran: racines et formes.* Etudes arabes et islamiques, ser. 3. Etudes et documents, 6. Paris: Librairie C. Klincksieck, 1966.

Cilardo, Agostino, "Un antico documento di diritto ereditario musulmano." *Annali* 42 (1982): 103–26.

The Civil Law. Edited and translated by S. P. Scott. 17 vols. Cincinnati: The Central Trust Company, 1932.

Cohen, D. *Dictionnaire des racines sémitiques ou attestées dans les langues sémitiques.* Paris: Mouton, 1970.

Cohen, Haim H. "Secularization of Divine Law." In *Scripta Hierosolymitana* 16 (1966). Reprinted in *Jewish Law in Ancient and Modern Israel.* New York: Ktav, 1971.

Cole, Donald Powell. *Nomads of the Nomads: The Āl Murrah Bedouin of the Empty Quarter.* Chicago: Aldine, 1975.

Comaroff, J. L., ed. *The Meaning of Marriage Payments.* London: Academic Press, 1980.

Conrad, Lawrence I. "Arabic Plague Chronologies and Treatises: Social and Historical Factors in the Formation of a Literary Genre." *Studia Islamica* 54 (1981): 51–93.

Cook, Michael. *Early Muslim Dogma: A Source-Critical Study.* Cambridge: Cambridge University Press, 1981.

Coulson, Noel J. *A History of Islamic Law.* Islamic Surveys, 2. Edinburgh: Edinburgh University Press, 1964.

———. "Correspondence." *Middle Eastern Studies* 3 (1967): 195–203.

———. *Conflicts and Tensions in Islamic Jurisprudence.* Publications of the Center for Middle Eastern Studies, 5. Chicago: University of Chicago Press, 1969.

———. *Succession in the Muslim Family.* Cambridge: Cambridge University Press, 1971.

Crone, Patricia. *Slaves on Horses: The Evolution of the Islamic Polity.* Cambridge: Cambridge University Press, 1980.

Crone, Patricia, and Cook, Michael. *Hagarism: The Making of the Islamic World.* Cambridge: Cambridge University Press, 1977.

Cuisenier, Jean. *Economie et parenté: leurs affinités de structure dans le domaine turc et dans le domaine arabe.* Paris: Mouton, 1975.

Cuisenier, Jean, and Miquel, A. "Les termes de parenté arabes: analyse sémantique et analyse componentielle." *L'Homme* 5 (1965): 15–79.

Dalman, Gustaf H., ed. *Aramäisch-neuhebräisches Handwörterbuch zu Targum, Talmud und Midrasch.* Göttingen, 1938. Reprinted Hildesheim: G. Olms, 1967.

Daube, David. "The Preponderance of Intestacy at Rome." *Tulane Law Review* 39 (1965): 253–62.

Denffer, Ahmad von. *Literature on Hadith in European Languages: A Bibliography.* London: The Islamic Foundation, 1981.

Djaït, Hichem. "Les Yamanites à Kufa au Ier Siècle de l'Hégire." *Journal of the Economic and Social History of the Orient* 19 (1976): 148–81.

Donner, Fred McGraw. *The Early Islamic Conquests.* Princeton: Princeton University Press, 1981.

Eickleman, Dale F. "Islamic Education and Its Social Reproduction." *Comparative Studies in Society and History* 20 (1978): 485–516.

Eliash, J. "'The Shīʿite Qur'ān', A Reconsideration of Goldziher's Interpretation." *Arabica* 16 (1969): 15–25.

Encyclopedia of Islam. 1st ed. Edited by M. T. Houtsma et al. 4 vols. and *Supplement.* Leiden: E. J. Brill, 1913–36. 2d ed. Edited by H. A. R. Gibb et al. Leiden: E. J. Brill, 1954–.

Esposito, John L. *Women in Muslim Family Law.* Syracuse: Syracuse University Press, 1982.

Faris, Nabih Amin. "*Khalifa* or *Khaliqa*: A Variant Reading of Surah 2:28." *The Moslem World* 24 (1934): 183–86.

Fitzgerald, S. Vesey, "The Alleged Debt of Islamic to Roman Law." *Law Quarterly Review* 67 (1951): 81–102.

Forte, David. "Islamic Law: The Impact of Joseph Schacht." *Loyola of*

Los Angeles International and Comparative Law Annual 1 (1978): 1–36.

Fraenkel, Siegmund. *Die aramäischen Fremdwörter im Arabischen.* Leiden, 1886. Reprinted Hildesheim: G. Olms, 1962.

Fyzee, Asaf A. A. *Outlines of Muhammadan Law.* 4th ed. Delhi: Oxford University Press, 1974.

Gandz, S. "The Algebra of Inheritance: A Rehabilitation of al-Khuwārizmī." *Osiris* 5 (1938): 319–91.

Garthwaite, G. R. "Two Persian Wills of Hajj ʿAli Quli Khan Sardar Asʿad." *Journal of the American Oriental Society* 95 (1975): 645–51.

Gelb, Ignace et al., eds. *The Assyrian Dictionary.* Chicago: Oriental Institute, 1956–.

Goitein, S. D. *Studies in Islamic History and Institutions.* Leiden: E. J. Brill, 1966.

Goldfeld, Isaiah. "The *Tafsīr* of ʿAbdallāh b. ʿAbbās." *Der Islam* 58 (1981): 125–35.

Goldziher, Ignaz. *Die Ẓâhiriten: Ihr Lehrsystem und ihre Geschichte.* Leipzig, 1884. Translated and edited by Wolfgang Behn as *The Ẓāhiris: Their Doctrine and their History.* Leiden: E. J. Brill, 1971.

———. *Muhammedanische Studien.* 2 vols. Halle, 1889–90. Translated and edited by S. M. Stern as *Muslim Studies.* Chicago: Aldine-Atherton, 1971.

———. *Die Richtungen der islamischen Koranauslegung.* De Goeje-Stiftung, 6. Leiden: E. J. Brill, 1952.

Goody, Jack. *Succession to High Office.* Cambridge Papers in Social Anthropology, 4. Cambridge: Cambridge University Press, 1966.

Goody, Jack, and Tambiah, S. J. *Bridewealth and Dowry.* Cambridge Papers in Social Anthropology, 7. Cambridge: Cambridge University Press, 1973.

Goto, Akira. "An Aspect of Arab Society of the Early Seventh Century—Non-related People in the Male Line Descendent's Groups." *Orient* 12 (1976): 75–88.

Gottleib, Isaac. "Succession in Elephantine and Jewish Law." *Journal of Semitic Studies* 26 (1981): 193–204.

Graham, William A. *Divine Word and Prophetic Word in Early Islam.* Religion and Society, 7. The Hague: Mouton, 1977.

Grohmann, Adolf. *Arabic Papyri in the Egyptian Library.* 2 vols. Cairo: Egyptian Library Press, 1934.

———. "The Problem of Dating Early Qur'ans." *Der Islam* 33 (1958): 213–31.

Guillaume, Alfred. *The Traditions of Islam: An Introduction to the Study of the Hadith Literature.* Oxford, 1924. Reprinted Beirut: Khayats, 1966.

———, trans. *The Life of Muhammad: A Translation of Iṣḥāq's "Sīrat Rasūl Allāh."* London: Oxford University Press, 1955.

Gutas, Dimitri. "Classical Arabic Wisdom Literature: Nature and Scope." *Journal of the American Oriental Society* 101 (1981): 49–86.

Haarman, Ulrich. "Religioses Recht und Grammatik im Klassischen Islam." In *Zeitschrift der deutschen morgenländischen Gesellschaft. Supplement II. XVIII Deutscher Orientalistentag.* Wiesbaden: Franz Steiner, 1974.

Hahn, Ernest. "Sir Sayyid Ahmad Khān's 'The Controversy over Abrogation (in the Qur'ān)': An Annotated Translation." *The Muslim World* 64 (1974): 124–33.

Hammond, William Gardiner. *An Introduction to Sandar's Institutes of Justinian.* Chicago: Callaghan and Co., 1876.

Haque, Ziaul. *Landlord and Peasant in Early Islam: A Study of the Legal Doctrine of "Muzāraʿa" or Sharecropping.* Islamabad: Islamic Research Institute, 1977.

Hasan, Ahmad. "The Theory of *Naskh.*" *Islamic Studies* 4 (1965): 181–200.

———. *The Early Development of Islamic Jurisprudence.* Pakistan: Islamic Research Institute, 1970.

Hassam, Abdel-Rahman. "Le droit musulman et le droit romain." *Archives d'histoire du droit oriental* 4 (1949): 301–17.

Hawting, G. R. "The Significance of the Slogan *Lā Ḥukm Illā Lillāh* and the References to the *Ḥudūd* in the Traditions about the *Fitna* and the Murder of ʿUthmān." *Bulletin of the School of Oriental and African Studies* 41 (1978): 452–63.

Hinds, Martin. "Kufan Political Alignments and Their Background in the Mid-Seventh Century A.D." *International Journal of Middle East Studies* 2 (1971): 346–67.

Hodgson, Marshall G. S. *The Venture of Islam: Conscience and History in a World Civilization.* 3 vols. Chicago: University of Chicago Press, 1974.

Horovitz, J. "Alter und Ursprung des *Isnād.*" *Der Islam* 8 (1917–18): 39–47.

Horst, Heribert von. "Zur Überlieferung im Korankommentar aṭ-Ṭabarīs." *Zeitschrift der deutschen morgenländischen Gesellschaft* 103 (1953): 290–307.

Howard, I. K. A. "*Mutʿa* Marriage Reconsidered in the Context of the Formal Procedures for Islamic Marriage." *Journal of Semitic Studies* 20 (1975): 82–92.

———. "The Development of *adhān* and *iqāma.*" *Journal of Semitic Studies* 26 (1981): 219–28.

The Institutes of Justinian: Texts, Translation and Commentary. Translated by J. A. C. Thomas. Cape Town: Juta & Co., 1975.

Jastrow, Marcus. *A Dictionary of the Targumim, The Talmud Babli and Yerushalmi, and the Midrashic Literature.* 2 vols. London, 1903. Reprinted New York: Pardes, 1950.

Jeffery, Arthur. "The Qur'anic Readings of Zaid b. ʿAlī." *Revista degli Studi Orientali* 16 (1936): 249–89.

———, ed. *Materials for the History of the Text of the Qur'ān: The Old Codices.* Leiden: E. J. Brill, 1937.

———. *The Foreign Vocabulary of the Qur'an.* Baroda: Oriental Institute, 1938. Reprinted Lahore: Al-Biruni, 1977.

———. *The Qur'ān as Scripture.* New York: Russel F. Moore Co., 1952.

Jennings, Ronald. "Women in Early Seventeenth Century Ottoman Judicial Records: The Sharia Court of Anatolian Kayseri." *Journal of the Economic and Social History of the Orient* 18 (1975): 53–114.

Jolowicz, H. F. *Historical Introduction to the Study of Roman Law.* 2d ed. Cambridge: Cambridge University Press, 1965.

Jomier, J. *Le commentaire coranique du manâr: Tendances modernes de l'exégèse coranique en Egypte. Islam d'hier et d'aujourd'hui,* vol. 11. Paris: G.-P. Maisonneuve, 1954.

———. "Qui a commenté l'ensemble des Sourates al-ʿAnkabūt à Yāsīn (29–36) dans *'Le Tafsīr al-Kabīr'* de l'Imām Fakhr al-Dīn al-Rāzī?". *International Journal of Middle East Studies* 11 (1980): 467–85.

Jones, Sir William, trans. *Al-Sirājiyyah or The Mahommedan Law of Inheritance.* Calcutta, 1792. Reprinted with notes and appendix by Almaric Rumsey. Lahore: The Premier Book House, 1956.

Juynboll, G. H. A. "The Date of the Great *Fitna.*" *Arabica* 20 (1973): 142–59.

———. "The Position of Qur'an Recitation in Early Islam." *Journal of Semitic Studies* 19 (1974): 240–51.

———, ed. *Studies on the First Century of Islamic Society.* Papers on Islamic History, 5. Carbondale and Edwardsville: Southern Illinois University Press, 1982.

———. *Muslim Tradition: Studies in Chronology, Provenance and Authorship of Early Hadith.* Cambridge: Cambridge University Press, 1983.

Kahle, Paul. "The Qur'ān and the ʿArabīya." In *Ignace Goldziher Memorial Volume,* pt. 1, edited by S. Lowinger and S. Somogyi. Budapest, 1948.

Kholeif, Fathalla. *A Study of Fakhr al-Dīn al-Rāzī and His Controversies in Transoxiana.* Beirut: Dar al-Machreq, 1966.

Kister, M. J. *Studies in Jahiliyya and Early Islam.* London: Variorum Reprints, 1980.

Kohlberg, Etan. "Some Notes on the Imāmite Attitude to the Qur'ān." In *Islamic Philosophy and the Classical Tradition: Essays presented by his friends and pupils to Richard Walzer on his seventieth birthday*, edited by S. M. Stern et al. Oriental Studies, 5. Columbia: University of South Carolina Press, 1972.

———. "An Unusual Shīʿī *Isnād*." *Israel Oriental Studies* 5 (1975): 142–50.

———. "Some Zaydī Views on the Companions of the Prophet." *Bulletin of the School of Oriental and African Studies* 39 (1976): 91–98.

Kopf, Lothar. "Religious Influences on Medieval Arabic Philology." *Studia Islamica* 5 (1956): 33–59.

———. "The Treatment of Foreign Words in Medieval Arabic Lexicography." In *Studies in Islamic History and Civilization*, edited by U. Heyd. Scripta Hierosolymitana, 9. Jerusalem: The Magnes Press, 1961.

———. *Studies in Arabic and Hebrew Lexicography*, edited by M. H. Goshen-Gottstein. Jerusalem: The Magnes Press, 1976.

Kraus, Paul. "The 'Controversies' of Fakhr al-Dīn Rāzī." *Islamic Culture* 12 (1938): 131–53.

Kressel, Gideon. "Bride-Price, Reconsidered" (Hebrew). *Hamizrah Hehadash* 26 (1976): 203–31.

Lammens, Henri. *Fāṭima et les filles de Mahomet: Notes critiques pour l'étude de la 'Sīra'*. Rome: Pontificium Institutum Biblicum, 1912.

Lane, Edward W. *An Arabic-English Lexicon*. 8 parts. London and Edinburgh: Williams and Norgate, 1863–93.

Layish, Aharon. *Women and Islamic Law in a non-Muslim State: a study based on decisions of the Shariʿa courts in Israel*. New York: John Wiley and Sons, Halsted Press, 1975.

———. "Women and Succession in the Druze Family in Israel." *Asian and African Studies* 11 (1976): 101–19.

———. *Marriage, Divorce, and Succession in the Druze Family*. Social, Economic and Political Studies of the Middle East, 31. Leiden: E. J. Brill, 1982.

———. "The Mālikī Family *Waqf* According to Wills and *Waqfiyyāt*." *Bulletin of the School of Oriental and African Studies* 46 (1983): 1–32.

Lazarus-Yafeh, Hava. "ʿUmar b. al-Khaṭṭāb—Paul of Islam?" (Hebrew). In *Studies in Geniza and Sephardi Heritage*. Jerusalem, 1981. Reprinted, in English, in her *Some Religious Aspects of Islam: A collection of articles*. Studies in the History of Religions, 42. Leiden: E. J. Brill, 1981.

Lech, Klaus. *Geschichte des islamischen Kultus*. Vol. 1: *Das ramaḍān Fasten*. Wiesbaden: Otto Harrassowitz, 1979.

Leemhuis, F. *The D and H Stems in Koranic Arabic.* Netherlands Institute of Archaeology and Arabic Studies in Cairo, 2. Leiden: E. J. Brill, 1977.

———. "Qur'anic *siggīl* and Aramaic *sgyl.*" *Journal of Semitic Studies* 27 (1982): 47–56.

Leslau, Wolf. *Ethiopic and South Arabic Contributions to the Hebrew Lexicon.* University of California Publications in Semitic Philology, vol. 20. Berkeley: University of California, 1958.

Lewin, Bernhard. *A Vocabulary of Hudailian Poems.* Göteborg, 1978.

Lichtenstadter, Ilse. "A Note on the *gharānīq* and Related Qur'anic Problems." *Israel Oriental Studies* 5 (1975): 54–61.

———. *Introduction to Classical Arabic Literature.* New York: Schocken Books, 1976.

Madelung, Wilfred. "Shiʿi Attitudes Towards Women as Reflected in Fiqh." In *Society and Sexes in Medieval Islam,* edited by Afaf Lutfi al-Sayyid-Marsot. Giorgio Levi Della Vida Conferences, 6. Malibu: Undena, 1979.

Magnin, M. J. G. "Innovations juridiques: régime successoral et testaments." *Revue IBLA* 22 (1959): 349–54.

Maher, Vanessa. "Divorce and Property in the Middle Atlas of Morocco." *Man* 9 (1974): 103–22.

———. *Women and Property in Morocco: Their changing relation to the process of social stratification in the Middle Atlas.* Cambridge Studies in Social Anthropology, 10. Cambridge: Cambridge University Press, 1974.

Mahmassani, S. *Falsafat al-tashrīʿ fi al-islām.* Translated by Farhat Ziadeh as *The Philosophy of Jurisprudence in Islam.* Leiden: E. J. Brill, 1961.

Maine, Sir Henry. *Ancient Law.* New York: Scribner, 1864. Reprinted London: Oxford University Press, 1931.

Marçais, W. *Des parents et alliés successibles en droit musulman.* Thesis. Rennes, 1898.

Merchant, Muhammad V. *A Book of Quranic Laws.* Lahore: Sh. Muhammad Ashraf, 1947. Reprinted 1960.

Miquel, André. "Les successions dans le *Kitāb al-ifṣāḥ* du vizir Ibn Hubayra (m. 560/1165)." *Revue des Etudes Islamiques* 36 (1968): 133–53.

Milad, Salwa ʿAli Ibrahim. "Registres Judiciaires du Tribunal de la *Ṣāliḥiyya Nağmiyya.*" *Annales Islamologiques* 13 (1974): 161–243.

Mohsen, Safia K. "Aspects of the Legal Status of Women Among Awlad ʿAli." In *Peoples and Cultures of the Middle East,* 1, edited by Louise Sweet. Garden City: Natural History Press, 1970.

Muir, Sir William. *The Life of Mahomet.* London: Smith Elder, 1861.

———. *The Caliphate: Its Rise, Decline and Fall.* London, 1898. Reprinted Beirut: Khayats, 1963.

Mundy, Martha. "Women's Inheritance of Land in Highland Yemen." *Arabian Studies* 5 (1979): 161–88.

Nallino, Carlo A. *Raccolta di Scritti Editi E Inediti.* Vol. 4. Rome: Istituto per l'Oriente, 1942.

Nicholas, Barry. *An Introduction to Roman Law.* Clarendon Law Series. Oxford: The Clarendon Press, 1962. Reprinted 1975.

Nöldeke, Theodor. *Geschichte des Qorāns.* 3 vols. in 1. Edited by F. Schwally. Leipzig, 1909. Reprinted Hildesheim: G. Olms, 1961.

Noth, Albrecht. *Quellenkritische Studien zu Themen, Formen und Tendenzen früislamischer Geschichtsüberlieferung. Teil 1: Themen und Formen.* Bonner Orientalistiche Studien, 25. Bonn: Selbstverlag des Orientalischen Seminars, 1973.

Nuʿmānī, ʿAllāma Shiblī. *Omar the Great.* 2 vols. Lahore: Sh. Muhammad Ashraf, 1961–62.

O'Shaughnessy, Thomas. *Muhammad's Thoughts on Death: A Thematic Study of the Qur'anic Data.* Leiden: E. J. Brill, 1969.

Paradise, Jonathan. "A Daughter and Her Father's Property at Nuzi." *Journal of Cuneiform Studies* 32 (1980): 189–207.

Paret, Rudi, ed. *Der Koran.* Darmstadt: Wissenschaftliche Buchgesellschaft, 1975.

Peristiany, Jean G., ed. *Mediterranean Family Structures.* Cambridge Studies in Social Anthropology, 13. Cambridge: Cambridge University Press, 1976.

Pestman, P. W. *Marriage and Matrimonial Property in Ancient Egypt: A Contribution to Establishing the Legal Position of Women.* Papyrologica Lugduno-Batava, 9. Leiden: E. J. Brill, 1961.

———. "The Law of Succession in Ancient Egypt." In *Essays on Oriental Laws of Succession.* Leiden: E. J. Brill, 1969.

Peterson, Erling L. *ʿAlī and Muʿāwiya in Early Arabic Tradition.* Copenhagen: Munksgaard, 1964.

Pretzl, Otto. "Die Wissenschaft der Koranlesung (*ʿIlm al-Qirā'a*): ihre literarischen Quellen und ihre aussprachegrundlagen (*uṣūl*)." *Islamica* 6 (1934): 1–47.

Porten, Bezalel, and Szubin, H. Z. "Exchange of Inherited Property at Elephantine (Cowley I)." *Journal of the American Oriental Society* 102 (1982): 651–54.

Powers, David S. "The Will of Saʿd b. Abī Waqqāṣ: A Reassessment." *Studia Islamica* 58 (1983): 33–53.

Pritchard, J. B., ed. *The Ancient Near East: An Anthology of Texts and Pictures.* Princeton: Princeton University Press, 1958.

Puin, Gerd-Rüdiger. *Der Dīwān von ʿUmar ibn al-Ḫaṭṭāb: ein Beitrag* zur frühislamischen Verwaltungsgeschichte. Bonn: Rheinischen Friedrich-Wilhelms-Universität, 1970.

Rahbar, D. "Relation of Shiʿa Theology to the Qur'an." *The Moslem World* 51 (1961): 92–98; 52 (1962): 17–21, 124–28.

Raddatz, Hans-Peter. "Frühislamisches Erbrecht nach dem *Kitāb al-Farā'iḍ* des Sufyān aṯ-Ṯaurī." *Welt des Islams* 13 (1971): 26–78.

Rahman, Fazlur. *Islamic Methodology in History.* Karachi: Central Institute of Islamic Research, 1965.

Rippin, Andrew. "Qur'an 21: 95: 'A Ban is Upon Any Town.'" *Journal of Semitic Studies* 24 (1979): 43–55.

———. "Qur'an 7.40: 'Until the Camel Passes Through the Eye of the Needle.'" *Arabica* 27 (1980): 107–13.

———. "The Quranic *Asbāb al-Nuzūl* Material: An Analysis of its Use and Development in Exegesis." Ph.D. thesis, McGill, 1981.

———. "The present status of *tafsīr* studies." *The Muslim World* 72 (1982): 224–38.

———. "Al-Zuhrī, *Naskh al-Qur'ān* and the problem of early *tafsīr* texts." *Bulletin of the School of Oriental and African Studies* 47 (1984): 22–43.

———. "The exegetical genre *asbāb al-nuzūl*: a bibliographical and terminological survey." *Bulletin of the School of Oriental and African Studies* 48 (1985): 1–15.

Roberts, Robert. *The Social Laws of the Qoran.* London, 1925. Reprinted London: Curzon Press, 1971.

Robson, James. "Ibn Iṣḥāq's Use of *Isnād.*" *Bulletin of the John Rylands Library* 38 (1955–56): 449–65.

———. "Tradition, the Second Foundation of Islam." *The Muslim World* 41 (1951): 22–33.

———. "Tradition: Investigation and Classification." *The Muslim World* 41 (1951): 98–112.

Rodinson, Maxime. *Islam et le capitalisme.* Paris, 1966. Translated by Brian Pierce as *Islam and Capitalism.* New York: Pantheon, 1973.

———. *Mohammed.* Translated by Anne Carter. New York: Vintage Books, 1974.

Roussier, J. "Dispositions nouvelles dans le statut successoral en droit tunisien." *Studia Islamica* 12 (1960): 131–44.

Royster, James. "The Study of Muhammad: A Survey of Approaches from the Perspective of the History and Phenomenology of Religion." *The Muslim World* 62 (1972): 49–70.

Rubin, Uri. "Prophets and Progenitors in the Early Shīʿa Tradition." *Jerusalem Studies in Arabic and Islam* 1 (1979): 41–65.

Salim, Shakir Mustafa. *Marsh Dwellers of the Euphrates Delta.* Monographs on Social Anthropology, 23. London: University of London, Athlone Press, 1962.

Sayed, Redwan. *Die Revolte des Ibn al-Ašʿaṯ und die Koranleser.* Islamkundliche Untersuchungen, 45. Freiburg: Klaus Schwarz Verlag, 1977.

Schacht, Joseph. "A Revaluation of Islamic Tradition." *Journal of the Royal Asiatic Society* 49 (1949): 143–54.

———. "Foreign Elements in Ancient Islamic Law." *Journal of Comparative Legislation* 32 (1950): 9–16.

———. *The Origins of Muhammadan Jurisprudence.* Oxford: The Clarendon Press, 1950.

———. "The Law." In *Unity and Variety in Muslim Civilization,* edited by G. von Grunebaum. Chicago: University of Chicago Press, 1955.

———. *An Introduction to Islamic Law.* Oxford: The Clarendon Press, 1964.

———. "Modernism and Traditionalism in a History of Islamic law." *Middle Eastern Studies* 1 (1965): 388–400.

———. "Law and Justice." In *The Cambridge History of Islam.* Vol. II. Cambridge: Cambridge University Press, 1970.

Selb, Walter. *Zur Bedeutung des syrisch-römischen Rechtsbuchs.* Beiträge zur Papyrusforschung und Antiken Rechtsgeschichte, 49. Munich: C. H. Beck'sche Verlagsbuchhandlung, 1964.

Selms, Adriaan van. "*Siǧǧīn* and *siǧǧīl* in the Qur'an." *Welt Des Orients* 9 (1977): 99–103.

Sezgin, Fuat. *Geschichte des arabischen Schrifttums.* Vol. 1. Leiden: E. J. Brill, 1967.

Shahid, Irfan. *The Martyrs of Najran: New Documents.* Brussels, Société des Bollandistes, Bd. Saint-Michel, 24, 1971.

Shorter Encyclopedia of Islam. Edited by Gibb and Kramers. Ithaca: Cornell University Press, 1953.

Siddiqi, Muhammad Z. *Ḥadīth Literature: Its Origin, Development, Special Features and Criticism.* Calcutta: Calcutta University, 1961.

Skaist, Aaron, "Inheritance Laws and their Social Background." *Journal of the American Oriental Society* 95 (1975): 242–48.

Smith [Margoliouth], J. Payne, ed. *A Compendious Syriac Dictionary.* Oxford: The Clarendon Press, 1903.

Smith, William Robertson. *Kinship and Marriage in Early Arabia.* Cambridge: Cambridge University Press, 1885. Reprinted London: A. and C. Black, 1903.

Speight, R. M. "The *Musnad* of al-Ṭayālisī: A Study of *Ḥadīth* as Oral Literature." Dissertation, The Hartford Seminary Foundation, 1970.

———. "The Will of Saʿd b. a. Waqqāṣ: The Growth of a Tradition." *Der Islam* 50 (1973): 248–67.

Stetter, Eckart. *Topoi und Schemata im Ḥadīth.* Tübingen: University of Tübingen, 1965.

Stirling, Paul. *Turkish Village.* London: Weidenfeld and Nicholson, 1965.

Strauss, Leo. *Persecution and the Art of Writing.* Glencoe, Illinois: The Free Press, 1952. Reprinted Westport, Conn.: Greenwood Press, 1973.

Sweetman, J. W. *Islam and Christian Theology.* 2 vols. London: Butterworth Press, 1947.

Szlechter, Emile. "Le Statut Juridique de la Veuve dans la Mésopotamie Ancienne." *Zeitschrift der deutschen morgenländischen Gesellschaft. Supplement II. XVIII Deutscher Orientalistentag.* Wiesbaden: Franz Steiner, 1974.

Tabataba'i, Muhammad Husayn. *Shiʿite Islam.* Translated by Seyyed Hossein Nasr. Albany: State University of New York Press, 1975.

Taubenschlag, Raphael. *The Law of Greco-Roman Egypt in the Light of the Papyri.* New York: Herald Square Press, 1944.

———. *Opera Minora.* 2 vols. Warsaw: Panstwowe Wydawnictwo Naukowe, 1959.

Tyan, Emile. *Institutions du droit public musulman.* 2 vols. Paris: Recueil Sirey, 1954–56.

Valensi, Lucette. *Fellahs tunisiens: l'économie rurale et la vie des compagnes aux 18e et 19e siècles.* Paris: Mouton, 1977.

Van Ess, Josef. "The Beginnings of Islamic Theology." In *The Cultural Context of Medieval Learning,* edited by J. E. Murdoch and E. D. Sylla. Boston Studies in the Philosophy of Science, 26. Boston: D. Reidel Publishing Co., 1975.

———. *Zwischen Ḥadīṯ und Theologie: Studien zum Entstehen prädestinatianischer Überlieferung.* Studien zur Sprache, Geschichte und Kultur des islamischen Orients, 7. Berlin: Walter de Gruyter, 1975.

Vesey-Fitzgerald, S. "Nature and Sources of the Shari'a." In *Law in the Middle East.* Edited by M. Khadduri and H. Liebesny. Washington: Middle East Institute, 1955.

Volterra, E. "Introduction à l'histoire du droit romain dans ses rapports avec l'Orient." *Archives d'histoire du droit oriental* 4 (1949): 117–60.

Wagtendonk, K. *Fasting in the Qur'an.* Leiden: E. J. Brill, 1968.

Wansbrough, John. *Quranic Studies: Sources and Methods of Scriptural Interpretation.* London Oriental Series, vol. 31. Oxford: Oxford University Press, 1977.

———. *The Sectarian Milieu: Content and Composition of Islamic Salvation History.* London Oriental Series, vol. 34. Oxford: Oxford University Press, 1978.

Watson, Alan. *The Law of Succession in the Later Roman Empire.* Oxford: The Clarendon Press, 1971.

Watt, W. M. *Muhammad at Mecca.* Oxford: Clarendon Press, 1953.

———. *Muhammad at Medina.* Oxford: Clarendon Press, 1956.

———, ed. *Bell's Introduction to the Qur'an.* Islamic Surveys, 8. Edinburgh: Edinburgh University Press, 1970.

———. *The Formative Period of Islamic Thought.* Edinburgh: Edinburgh University Press, 1973.

Weber, Max. *Wirtschaft und Gesellschaft.* 2d ed., 1925. Edited by M. Rheinstein and translated by E. Shils as *Max Weber on Law in Economy and Society.* New York: Simon & Schuster, 1954.

Wegner, Judith Romney. "Islamic and Talmudic Jurisprudence: The Four Roots of Islamic Law and Their Talmudic Counterparts." *The American Journal of Legal History* 26 (1982): 25–71.

———. "The Status of Women in Jewish and Islamic Marriage and Divorce Law." *Harvard Women's Law Journal* 5 (1982): 1–33.

Welch, Alford T., ed. *Studies in Qur'ān and Tafsīr.* In *Journal of the American Academy of Religion* 47 : 4s (1979): 620–758.

Wellhausen, J. *Das arabische reich und sein Sturz.* 1927. Translated by Margaret G. Weir as *The Arab Kingdom and its Fall.* Beirut: Khayats, 1963.

Wendell, Charles. "The Pre-Islamic Period of *Sīrat al-Nabī.*" *The Muslim World* 62 (1972): 12–41.

Wensinck, A. J. *A Handbook of Early Muhammadan Tradition.* Leiden: E. J. Brill, 1927.

———. *Concordance et indices de la tradition musulmane.* 7 vols. Leiden: E. J. Brill, 1936–69.

Widengren, G. *Muhammad, the Apostle of God and his Ascension.* Uppsala Universitets arsskrift 1955, 1. Uppsala: Lundequista bokhandeln, 1955.

Wörterbuch der klassischen arabischen Sprache. Wiesbaden: O. Harrassowitz, 1957–.

Wright. W. *A Grammar of the Arabic Language.* 3d ed., revised by W. Robertson Smith and M. J. De Goeje. London, 1896–98. Reprinted Cambridge: Cambridge University Press, 1977.

Index

Designer: Betty Gee
Compositor: G&S Typesetters, Inc.
Text: 11/13 Trump Medieval
Display: Trump Medieval
Printer: Thomson-Shore, Inc.
Binder: John H. Dekker & Sons